Governing China in the 21st Century

Series Editors
Zhimin Chen
School of International Relations and Public Affairs
Fudan University
Shanghai, China

Yijia Jing
Institute for Global Public Policy & School of International
Relations and Public Affairs
Fudan University
Shanghai, China

Since 1978, China's political and social systems have transformed significantly to accommodate the world's largest population and second largest economy. These changes have grown more complex and challenging as China deals with modernization, globalization, and informatization. The unique path of sociopolitical development of China hardly fits within any existing frame of reference. The number of scientific explorations of China's political and social development, as well as contributions to international literature from Chinese scholars living and researching in Mainland China, has been growing fast. This series publishes research by Chinese and international scholars on China's politics, diplomacy, public affairs, and social and economic issues for the international academic community.

More information about this series at
http://www.palgrave.com/gp/series/15023

Jose A. Puppim de Oliveira · Yijia Jing
Editors

International Development Assistance and the BRICS

palgrave
macmillan

Editors
Jose A. Puppim de Oliveira
Department of Public Management
Fundação Getulio Vargas
São Paulo, Brazil

Yijia Jing
Institute for Global Public Policy &
School of International Relations
and Public Affairs
Fudan University
Shanghai, China

ISSN 2524-3586   ISSN 2524-3594   (electronic)
Governing China in the 21st Century
ISBN 978-981-32-9643-5   ISBN 978-981-32-9644-2   (eBook)
https://doi.org/10.1007/978-981-32-9644-2

This Palgrave Macmillan imprint is published by the registered company Springer Nature
Singapore Pte Ltd.
The registered company address is: 152 Beach Road, #21-01/04 Gateway East, Singapore
189721, Singapore

Acknowledgements

This book resulted from two symposia organized to discuss the development and governance in the BRICS with a perspective of public affairs and we would like to thank all the participants and supporting organizations that made these meetings possible. The Second International Symposium on Development and Governance in the BRICS happened in Fudan University, Shanghai, China, on 24 and 25 September 2017 and had the theme "International Development Aid in the BRICS," bringing together several experts in international development. The Third International Symposium on Development and Governance in the BRICS "Governance and Policy Capacity in the BRICS and Latin America: New Development Models?" was held in Sao Paulo between 04 and 06 December 2018. The symposium debated the different models of development the BRICS has the potential to bring about. It was funded by the São Paulo Research Foundation (FAPESP) grant number 2018/12817-5 and the Coordination for the Improvement of Higher Education Personnel (CAPES) by the call 09/2018 of the Program to Support Events in Brazil (PAEP). The meetings had the support from several organizations particularly Fundação Getulio Vargas (FGV EAESP and FGV EBAPE) and Fudan University (the School of International Relations and Public Affairs, the Dr. Seaker Chan Center for Comparative Political Development Studies, and the Institute for Global Public Policy).

CONTENTS

Part II   BRICS and Development Banks

NOTES ON CONTRIBUTORS

Patrick Bond is Distinguished Professor of Political Economy at the University of the Witwatersrand, Johannesburg. He also taught at the University of KwaZulu-Natal where he directed the Centre for Civil Society (2004–2016). His books include the co-edited *BRICS* (2015) as well as *Elite Transition* (2014), *Politics of Climate Justice* (2012), *Talk Left Walk Right* (2006), *Looting Africa* (2006) and *Against Global Apartheid* (2003). He drafted policies in the South African presidency under Nelson Mandela (1994 and 1996). His doctorate at Johns Hopkins (1993) was supervised by David Harvey, and he also studied at the Wharton School of Finance and Swarthmore College.

Caio Borges is a Ph.D. student at the University of Sao Paulo's Law School and lawyer/coordinator with the Development and Socio-Environmental Rights Program at Conectas Human Rights, Brazil. Master's in Law and Development from the Getulio Vargas Foundation School of Law (FGV-SP).

Yijia Jing is a Changjiang Scholar in Public Management, Dean of the Institute for Global Public Policy, and Chair Professor of Public Management at the School of International Relations and Public Affairs, Fudan University. He got his B.A./M.A. in Economics from Peking University, M.A. in Sociology from University of Maryland College Park, and Ph.D. in Public Policy from the Ohio State University. He conducts research on privatization, governance, and collaborative service delivery. He is editor-in-chief of *Fudan Public Administration Review* and co-editor of *International Public Management Journal*. He is the founding co-editor of the Palgrave book series, Governing China in the twenty-first century.

Shigehisa Kasahara a resident researcher at the International Institute of Social Studies (ISS), The Netherlands, is a former staff member, an economist, of the UNCTAD secretariat (1986–2013). He was mostly in the area of research and publication. He has been a lecturer at various universities, most recently a lecturer/supervisor for B.A. graduation theses at Leiden University (2018), and has maintained close working relations with UNCAD as a consultant. He is expecting the Public Defense of his Ph.D. research in the near future.

Rostam J. Neuwirth is Professor of Law and Coordinator of the Master Program in International Business Law at the Faculty of Law of University of Macau (China). He received law degrees from the European University Institute in Florence (Ph.D.), McGill University in Montreal (LL.M.) and the Karl-Franzens University of Graz (Mag. iur.). Before joining Macau University, he taught at the Hidayatullah National Law University (HNLU) in Raipur and the National University of Juridical Sciences (NUJS) in Kolkata (India) and worked in the International Law Bureau of the Austrian Federal Ministry for Foreign Affairs. He is the co-editor of the book *The BRICS-Lawyers' Guide to Global Cooperation* (CUP, 2017) and author of *Law in the Time of Oxymora* (Routledge, 2018).

Rogerio F. Pinto a Brazilian national is an international consultant in Public Management and Institutional Development with extended experience in international development as staff of the World Bank, the Inter-American Development Bank and the Organization of American States. He has worked around the world in different capacities (mostly in Africa and Latin America). Retired from the World Bank, he taught at the Brazilian School of Public and Business Management of the Getulio Vargas Foundation (FGV) in Brazil. He has delivered consulting and teaching assignments with governments, NGOs, universities, and international organizations in different countries.

Jose A. Puppim de Oliveira is a faculty member at Fundação Getulio Vargas (FGV/EAESP and FGV/EBAPE), Brazil. He also teaches at the Fudan University (Shanghai). His research interests concentrate in patterns of governance, institution building and policy implementation at different levels, looking at how global and national institutions are interlinked to local governance and action. He holds a Ph.D. in Planning from the Massachusetts Institute of Technology (MIT).

Alexandr Svetlicinii LL.M. (CEU), MRes (EUI), Ph.D. (EUI) is an Assistant Professor at the University of Macau, Faculty of Law.

Lisa Thompson does research on the political economy of development at the University of the Western Cape. She directs the Centre for Citizenship and Democracy at the School of Government. Relevant publications include Social Movements in the South (with Chris Tapscott) and Beyond Aid? International Development Cooperation: Re-colonising Africa? (forthcoming 2019).

Laura Trajber Waisbich is an associate researcher at the South-South Cooperation Research and Policy Centre (Articulação SUL) and the Brazilian Centre for Analysis and Planning (CEBRAP), Brazil. She is currently a Ph.D. student at the University of Cambridge (UK).

List of Figures

List of Tables

CHAPTER 1

The BRICS and International Development Assistance: Between the Old and the New

Jose A. Puppim de Oliveira and Yijia Jing

INTRODUCTION

The group of countries that includes Brazil, Russia, India, China, and South Africa, or BRICS, has become a major player on the international stage. In 2018, the five BRICS had a combined nominal Gross Domestic Product (GDP) of USD 20.1 trillion, about 24% of the world's GDP (IMF 2019a), and a combined GDP (PPP) of around USD 44.1 trillion or approximately 33% of world's GDP PPP (IMF 2019b). The BRICS had an estimated

J. A. Puppim de Oliveira (✉)
FGV EAESP, Fundação Getulio
Vargas (FGV), São Paulo, Brazil
e-mail: jose.puppim@fgv.br

FGV EBAPE, Fundação Getulio Vargas (FGV), Rio de Janeiro, Brazil

J. A. Puppim de Oliveira · Y. Jing
Institute for Global Public Policy & School of International Relations and Public Affairs, Fudan University, Shanghai, China
e-mail: jingyj@fudan.edu.cn

© The Author(s) 2020
J. A. Puppim de Oliveira and Y. Jing (eds.), *International Development Assistance and the BRICS*, Governing China in the 21st Century,
https://doi.org/10.1007/978-981-32-9644-2_1

1

2018 population of 3.1 billion or approximately 42% of the world's population (based on UNDESA 2019) (see Tables 1.1, 1.2, and 1.3). Thus, what happens in the BRICS countries has a huge influence on the world's economic, political, social, and environmental affairs.

Over the last decade, the loose BRICS coalition has evolved to become a formal partnership on both economic and political fronts. The first formal meeting of the then-four BRIC countries took place in 2006 during the United Nations General Assembly. This was followed in 2009 by the first

Table 1.1   BRICS population

Country	Population (2018 estimates in 1000 inhabitants)	World ranking
Brazil	209,469	5
Russia	145,734	9
India	1,352,642	2
China	1,427,648	1
South Africa	57,793	25
Total	3,193,286	
World	7,631,091	
Total BRICS/world	41.8%	

Source UNDESA (2019)

Table 1.2   GDP by country

Country	GDP 2018 (IMF) nominal (millions of USD)	World ranking GDP nominal	GDP PPP 2018 (IMF) (millions of USD)	World ranking GDP PPP
China	13,407,398	2	25,270,066	1
India	2,716,746	7	10,505,288	3
Brazil	2,072,201	8	3,365,343	8
Russia	1,630,659	11	4,213,403	6
South Africa	368,135	33	789,423	29
Total	20,195.139		44,143,523	
World	84,740,322		135,178,320	
Total BRICS/world	23.8%		32.7%	

Source IMF (2019a)

Table 1.3 GDP per capita by country

Country	GDP per capita nominal (USD)	Ranking IMF	GDP per capita PPP (USD)	Ranking GDP per capita PPP
China	9608	67	18,110	73
India	2036	142	7874	119
Brazil	8968	73	16,154	80
Russia	11,327	60	29,267	49
South Africa	6377	86	13,675	89
Total (weighted BRICS)	6379		14,075	
World	11,355		16,779	
Total BRICS/world	56%		84%	

Source IMF (2019b)

summit of BRICS' heads of state in Russia, an event which has been convened annually ever since. In November 2019, the eleventh BRICS summit is in Brasilia, Brazil.

The alliance of BRICS countries reflects their growing influence worldwide, and the proportional decline of the weight of the developed countries in the world economy. The GDP PPP of the advanced economies (OECD countries with high income) had their proportion of the world's GDP dropped from 64% to 40% between 1990 and 2018. Emerging economies now comprise of three-fifths of the world's economy (IMF 2019a), though their per capita income still lags behind those of the rich countries (Table 1.3). In the last three decades, BRICS partners have significantly increased their political, financial, and economic influence worldwide. Some have become important aid donors to developing states and significant investors in both emerging and developed economies. China, in particular, is now one of the leading investors worldwide. In the last Forum on China-Africa Cooperation (FOCAC) in 2018, President Xi Jinping announced a total investment of USD 60 billion in Africa in grants, loans, and direct investments. The BRICS created the New Development Bank (NDB) headquartered in Shanghai and China played a leading role in the establishment of the Asian Infrastructure Investment Bank (AIIB) based in Beijing. China has strategically structured its IDA and other investments in the Belt and Road Initiative (BRI). India has consolidated its approach to international development using its own strategy, with a mix of investments, grants, and technical cooperation (Chaturvedi and Mulakala 2016). There is hope that the BRICS' investments may assist in transforming the international aid landscape to become more pluralistic and equitable. The BRICS states have also expressed interest in using aid to transfer some of their successful experiences to emerging economies and to exert soft power in stimulating their growth. In pursuit of this objective, BRICS' agencies and officials are paying considerably more attention to the effectiveness of aid and investment in other countries. On the other hand, while many countries recognize the importance of BRICS in the international aid landscape, concerns have also been expressed about the negative impact of BRICS' aid on the recipient countries, such as an increase in (unpayable) debt.

However, research on the potential impacts of the flow of international development aid to, from, and between BRICS countries has been limited. Adding complexity to this process, some BRICS states are both recipients of aid and simultaneously donors and confront the dual task of governing the inflows and outflows of aid. The BRICS have increasing, but limited, experience in aid governance, development management, and measurement of the effectiveness of IDA. Therefore, this book aims to explore the varied dimensions of international development aid in the BRICS, particularly the models of development and development assistance disseminated by the BRICS and the joint development organizations (NDB and AIIB). In this chapter, we analyze their theoretical and practical implications for public administration and development.

The Emergence of the BRICS in the IDA Landscape

The emergence of the BRICS as a strong player in the landscape of IDA[1] came with many expectations of changes in the way IDA was performed, where the multilateral organizations and Development Assistance Committee (DAC)[2] countries had a leading major role in defining and providing development aid. The BRICS IDA follows different procedures and even definition of international aid based on their own interpretations and past experiences with inflows and outflows of IDA.

The relevance of BRICS in the international IDA arena also came along with other changes in the landscape of flows of resources to less developed countries that have some impact on their development in the last decades (Mawdsley 2012; Gu et al. 2016), coined as New Development Assistance—NDA (Jing et al. 2019). Besides the BRICS, other emerging countries, such as Turkey and Gulf states, have increased their efforts in international development and investments in developing countries (OECD

2017). ODA from non-DAC countries amounted more than USD 63 billion in 2014. ODA from Saudi Arabia and United Arab Emirates reached more than 1% of their GDPs in 2016 (OECD 2019). Private donors have also augmented their roles in international development, particularly some large foundations and NGOs, such as the Gates Foundation, which has invested heavily in research and programs in the health sector with focus on diseases that affect poor countries. Moreover, the flow of foreign direct investment (FDI) has played a significant part of the financial flow to developing countries in the last decades with an increasing role of the organizations based in the BRICS and other emerging economies as investors. Finally, there are other flows of financial and technical resources coming with globalization, i.e., the movement of people, information, and resources across countries, such as the international remittances sent by people who emigrated. The World Bank estimates the personal remittances of around 0.7% of the world's GDP. In some countries, remittances play a key role in development as they reach a significant amount of the country's GDP (nominal), such as Haiti (32%), Tajikistan (31%), Nepal (27%), The Gambia (15%), Philippines (10%), and El Salvador (20%) (World Bank 2019).

The BRICS' relevance in the IDA landscape was welcomed with optimism by some scholars and practitioners in the development field and with skepticism by others. The optimists hoped the BRICS could change the way development assistance is provided and even bringing in new development models to challenge the "Washington Consensus" neoliberal model propagated by the traditional multilateral banks. On the other hand, the critics mention that the BRICS model faces the same problems as those of the traditional donors. BRICS IDA is just a change in the countries that give the IDA, or even worse, arguing that, as compared to DAC countries, loans from the BRICS go without much transparency and analysis whether the country really needs and how best the money is used.

The BRICS brought their own experience as recipients of IDA, as all BRICS are still recipients of IDA from DAC countries and multilateral organizations. Having the experience of receiving assistance could help them to identify the main problems of the traditional way of delivering IDA by DAC countries with a perspective from the recipient. Their initial discourse was that IDA had too many conditionalities and had little room for recipient countries to steer the development processes in their own ways. The existence of little degree of conditionalities in the bilateral IDA and loans given to developing countries is common among the

IDA coming from the BRICS, at least in the discourse. China particularly is known to offer financial support without much restriction in terms of conditionalities with the argument that China does not want to interfere in countries' internal affairs (Mthembu 2018). There is also the trend of the BRICS, as in some other donors, including some traditional donors, to combine grants, technical cooperation, loans, and investments all together (Jing et al. 2019), which can bring synergies, but can also create problems of ownership and transparency. Critics argue that the lack of conditionality, transparency, and scrutiny in the loans can lead to several problems in the borrowing countries, such as corruption, misused resources, or "debt traps," where countries would borrow more than what they can afford. This would benefit the lending country to have a political leverage to acquire benefits from the borrowing countries that cannot pay back. For example, Sri Lanka could not afford the payment of the debts with China for building infrastructure and had to give the concession of the Hambantota port to Chinese companies. The new Malaysian government in 2018 gave up some infrastructure projects financed by China with the argument that the country could not afford the costs (Malhi 2018).

The BRICS also had the familiarity in the South–South Cooperation that in principle is claimed to be more equalitarian in terms of negotiating the terms of development assistance and sharing development experience (Cheru 2016). Brazil has been a keen advocate of South–South development assistance, which Brazilian organizations call Technical Cooperation among Developing Countries (TCDC). The country has an international cooperation agency, the Brazilian Agency for Cooperation (or Agência Brasileira de Cooperação—ABC). There are many experiences of Brazil's TCDC in Africa with agricultural development. For example, Brazil engaged with Mozambique in a TCDC for the development of the ethanol chain in Mozambique. The ABC had less a role of a typical international development agency and more as coordinator of the involvement of several organizations in the TCDC, such as other ministries (e.g., Ministry of Agriculture), the private sector, international entities, and NGOs.

As the BRICS countries developed their relations as a formal block, some of the experiences that each country had in its own bilateral cooperation started to shape the discourse and practice of IDA of the BRICS as a block, including the NDB. Issues such as lack of conditionalities for loans are constant in the discourse of the BRICS. The NDB also adopted no conditionality as part of its lending policy. It also innovates in lending in local currency and in speed that the loans are approved, which are some of the issues aid recipients tend to struggle with. The speed of the loan disbursement, just a few months, is related to the lack of conditionality, besides the updated technology and procedures used in the bank, according to the NDB management. The NDB also avoids engagement in "policy dialogue," which facilitates the speed of the approval of the projects and loans. Thus, little by little, the BRICS are defining their own style of multilateral IDA.

This Book

The chapters in this book discuss how the IDA in the BRICS has evolved in the last decade. They are divided into two groups, Part I and Part II. Part I is about models of development and development assistance in the BRICS. Part II is about development banks led by the BRICS.

In Part I, the three chapters discuss the changes in the models of development and which model of development the BRICS disseminate as well as the practices of its development assistance. Neuwirth (2019) argues that the concept of development assistance, as we know it, has been challenged in several fronts and may disappear in the future. The end of the distinction between developing and developed countries in the terminology used by the World Bank is one indication that the division between the former "rich" countries and developing countries is blurred. The emergence of the BRICS as more active development aid donors may have influenced the changes in the aid vocabulary, as a first sign of how BRICS can reshape IDA. He suggests that the BRICS have the potential to help in the establishment of a more equitable global legal order that advances the interests of less developed nations. On a different perspective, in the next chapter, Thompson (2019) analyzes the development paradigm promoted by the BRICS within the "Beyond Aid" debate linked to the idea of South–South Cooperation. In her analysis, she concludes that the BRICS official development assistance discourse and practice are embedded in the current framework of North–South domination, similar to those of the traditional Northern-dominated DAC donors and multilateral organizations. The BRICS model of development tends to replicate patterns of economic dependency seen in the practice of some traditional donors and may reinforce, instead of alleviating, the problems of inequality and social exploitation in developing countries. In the last chapter of this part, Rogerio Pinto (2019) examines the relatively extended experience of Brazil in development assistance. Brazil, maybe the BRICS country with the longest experience in IDA, has concentrated the management of aid through the ABC, a development agency linked to the Ministry of Foreign Affairs (Collins 1985). Brazil has been a leading country in the promotion of South–South Cooperation and prefers to call IDA as TCDC. Nevertheless, even though Brazil has a long history of inflow and outflow of development assistance, there are many areas for improvement, particularly in understanding the effectiveness of its practice in order to improve it.

The four chapters in Part II focus their analyses on the practice of IDA of the multilateral organizations led by BRICS countries, particularly NDB and the AIIB, both headquartered in China, which has had a leading role in both organizations. Kasahara (2019) analyzes the two banks. Both were created as part of a frustration of the BRICS with their limited role in the governance of the traditional multilateral development banks, such as the World Bank and the Asian Development Bank (ADB). Even though the economic power of the BRICS grew dramatically in the last three decades, the share of the BRICS in those multilateral organizations has not reflected their economic and political importance. The chapter compares the NDB and AIIB in several dimensions, including purposes, membership, governance structure, and capital. Even though the BRICS play an important role in the governance and management, they are quite different. The IIAB is more similar to the established multilateral banks with a large membership and traditional financing procedures. The NDB has a limited membership (only BRICS) and tries to differentiate itself from the traditional donors in the lending procedures, even though the financing projects and development models are similar. In the next chapter, Svetlicinii (2019) scrutinizes the approaches used by the NDB to articulate the concept of sustainable development, reflected in the UN's Sustainable Development Goals (SDGs), in its banking practices of development assistance. He concludes that the NDB is still struggling to clarify its meaning of sustainable development in practice and differentiate it from the traditional donors. The international discourses and practices of sustainable development are still shaped by the Western countries and Bretton Woods organizations. In the following chapter, Waisbich and Borges (2019) corroborate Svetlicinii's analysis that the NDB, and the BRICS themselves, still struggles between the "old" and the "new" ideas and practice of development assistance. The NDB has the inspiration of South–South Cooperation of the past experiences of the BRICS as donors, where it has roots. However, the NDB has to follow many of the international banking and IDA standards, which are mostly developed and set by the Western countries, in order to get good reputation, and consequently credit ratings, to facilitate its operations. On the other hand, there is a steady move in the traditional donors to change its IDA practices to respond to the BRICS's contest. Finally, the last chapter by Bond (2019) brings how the ambitious efforts from the BRICS with the NDB for changing the IDA landscape have had a series of challenges to create a new model of development concept and practice. The more radical new ideas of development processes from the beginning of the establishment of the bank, particularly those influenced by the leftist Workers' Party in Brazil, have watered down to an older approach of the dependency theories. The author examines how the NDB has had limitations to handle some of the challenges of the twenty-first century such as corruption and climate change. The changes in government, particularly in Brazil, may shape, again, the future of NDB in its search for a "BRICS sustainable development model."

Between the New and the Old

The BRICS have long complained about the small role they have in the traditional multilateral organizations, such as the World Bank, IMF, and ADB (Jing et al. 2019). As new multilateral organizations are built, with the BRICS leading them, there are opportunities to innovate in IDA by developing alternative assistance models to those already in existence in order to challenge the "old" paradigms of development as well as the way to provide IDA and promote development. However, the alternative development model promoted by the BRICS is not well defined, except that the BRICS want the countries themselves to define their development objectives. In practice, there are not many clear differences in the models from those led by the Western countries that have dominated the IDA landscape in the last decades, which is based on economic growth fueled by infrastructure and large investments. The BRICS discourses on sustainable development, based on the SDGs, are still in line with the Western-led organizations (Svetlicinii 2019).

On the other hand, the BRICS have spurred changes in the traditional donors (Gulrajani and Faure 2019). The emergence of the BRICS as powerful actors in the IDA landscape has catalyzed reforms in the way traditional donors provide IDA, at least in the discourse. There is a recognition that the vocabulary of IDA has become more complex (Lauria and Fumagalli 2019) and the old terms do not fit in the new reality where the power between developed and developing countries is more balanced. The dichotomy between developing and developed countries is disappearing as in the documents of the World Bank (Neuwirth 2019).

In terms of delivering international assistance, the BRICS have striven between the DAC guidelines and its own style. The BRICS have made several innovations in delivering IDA and, through the NDB, they are creating their own style of delivering international assistance. Inexistence of conditionalities, at least explicitly, lending in local currency, and focus on infrastructure and green projects are the bet of the NDB to deliver assistance more effectively and efficiently. These go in line with the demands from the aid recipients, though currently the NDB only lends to BRICS countries. The other BRICS (or China) led bank, the IIAB, follows a more traditional approach to disbursing loans, where some conditionality exists (Serrano Oswald 2019). The more disperse share in the governance of the IIAB, particularly the significant shares of European countries, makes innovations more difficult as those create risks and are not well accepted by the international community of investors, from where the development banks leverage their funding portfolio, which are still bound to the traditional rules of investments.

Thus, the BRICS IDA struggles between the old and new. There is a consistent discourse about different IDA and new development models and ways the BRICS support them, but putting this in practice has shown that changes are not always easy. We have seen limited changes in the development models, mainly through some innovations in development assistance in the NDB, but with little understanding of the impacts of those innovations. This book is an attempt to analyze the approaches the BRICS have to IDA as a block and identify potential opportunities to advance the development agenda in a new way. Hopefully, in the near future, we will be able to evaluate the outcomes of the BRICS' way of IDA. Nevertheless, the own existence of the BRICS as an alternative to the traditional donors is already an opportunity to create something new, and reform the old, which can certainly bring benefits to the countries that receive IDA.

Acknowledgements Jose A. Puppim de Oliveira thanks the support of FAPESP grant number 2018/12817-5 and CAPES grant number 88881.191451/2018-01 for funding *The Third International Symposium on Development and Governance in the BRICS in São Paulo between 04 and 06 of December 2018.* Yijia Jing acknowledges the support from the National Research Foundation of Korea Grant NRF-2014S1A3A2044898.

NOTES

1. We use the term IDA that includes a broad range of mechanisms to provide assistance from one country or organization (e.g., multilateral banks or NGOs) to another aiming at achieving development objectives. IDA can include grants, concessional loans, technical cooperation, private investments, and training.
2. DAC countries are countries that are members of the Development Assistance Committee of the Organisation for Economic Co-operation and Development (OECD). DAC is the forum of the mostly developed countries to monitor and discuss development aid, including Official Development Assistance (ODA) and other forms of international development assistance. ODA is defined by OECD as "government aid that promotes and specifically targets the economic development and welfare of developing countries" (OECD 2019).

REFERENCES

Chaturvedi, Sachin, and Anthea Mulakala, eds. 2016. *India's Approach to International Cooperation*. London: Routledge.

Cheru, Fantu. 2016. "Emerging Southern Powers and New Forms of South–South Cooperation: Ethiopia's Strategic Engagement with China and India." *Third World Quarterly* 37 (4): 592–610.

Collins, Paul. 1985. "Brazil in Africa: Perspectives on the Growth and Prospects of Economic Cooperation Between Developing Countries." *Development Policy Review (ODI)* No.1.

Gu, Jing, Alex Shankland, and Anuradha Chenoy, eds. 2016. *The BRICS in International Development*. New York: Springer.

Gulrajani, Nilima, and Raphaelle Faure. 2019. "Northern Donors in Transition and the Future of Development Cooperation: What Does the Data from Brazil, India, China and South Africa Reveal?" *Public Administration and Development* (in press). https://doi.org/10.1002/pad.1861.

IMF-International Monetary Fund. 2019a. *World Economic Outlook Database*. Washington, DC: International Monetary Fund.

IMF-International Monetary Fund. 2019b. *Report for Selected Country Groups and Subjects (PPP valuation of country GDP)*. Washington, DC: International Monetary Fund.

Jing, Yijia, Alvaro Méndez, and Yu Zheng, eds. 2019. *New Development Assistance: Emerging Economies and the New Landscape of Development Assistance*. London: Palgrave Macmillan.

Lauria, Valeria, and Corrado Fumagalli. 2019. "BRICS, the Southern Model, and the Evolving Landscape of Development Assistance: Toward a New Taxonomy."

Public Administration and Development (in press). https://doi.org/10.1002/pad.1851.

Malhi, Amrita. 2018. "Race, Debt and Sovereignty—The 'China Factor' in Malaysia's GE14." *The Round Table* 107 (6): 717–28.

Mawdsley, Doctor Emma. 2012. *From Recipients to Donors: The Emerging Powers and the Changing Development Landscape.* London: Zed Books.

Mthembu, Philani. 2018. "An Overview of China and India's Development Cooperation in Africa." In *China and India's Development Cooperation in Africa,* edited by Philani Mthembu, 29–53. Cham: Palgrave Macmillan.

Organisation for Economic Co-operation and Development (OECD). 2017. "Development Finance of Countries Beyond the DAC." *Development Co-operation Report 2017: Data for Development.* Accessed on April 10, 2019. https://www.oecd.org/dac/stats/non-dac-reporting.htm.

Organisation for Economic Co-operation and Development (OECD). 2019. "What Is ODA? Brochure." Accessed on May 10, 2019. www.oecd.org/dac/financing-sustainable-development/development-finance-standards/What-is-ODA.pdf.

Serrano Oswald, Omar Ramon. 2019. "The New Architects: Brazil, China, and Innovation in Multilateral Development Lending." *Public Administration and Development* (in press). https://doi.org/10.1002/pad.1837.

United Nations, Department of Economic and Social Affairs (UNDESA), Population Division. 2019. *World Population Prospects 2019.* Accessed on April 10, 2019. https://population.un.org/wpp/Download/Standard/Population/.

World Bank. 2019. "Personal Remittances, Received (% of GDP)." Accessed on April 19, 2019. https://data.worldbank.org/indicator/BX.TRF.PWKR.DT.GD.ZS?locations=KG.

PART I

BRICS, Development Models and Development Assistance

CHAPTER 2

The End of "Development Assistance" and the BRICS

Rostam J. Neuwirth

INTRODUCTION

The best way of predicting it [the future] is to create it!

(Neuwirth 2017b, 23)

In the past, the prevailing question about the BRICS countries' cooperation as a regional bloc was their actual role and potential contribution to the governance of global affairs at large. In the meantime, and especially since the 9th BRICS Summit in Xiamen (China) held in September 2017, it can be asserted that the BRICS have consolidated their cooperation "beyond the demandeur style associated with earlier challenges of the global South via the campaign for a New International Economic Order" (Cooper 2016, ix). Yet a central issue related to their actual role remains the search for an adequate BRICS governance mode (Tapscott et al. 2017). In this respect, however, it is the role of law in global governance that is

R. J. Neuwirth (✉)
University of Macau, Taipa, Macau, China
e-mail: rjn@um.edu.mo

© The Author(s) 2020
J. A. Puppim de Oliveira and Y. Jing (eds.), *International Development Assistance and the BRICS*, Governing China in the 21st Century,
https://doi.org/10.1007/978-981-32-9644-2_2

15

often forgotten amid concerns of a political and economic nature. The governance of both economic and political affairs requires a sound legal framework, as law can only function adequately in the right economic and political settings supported by a sound and future-oriented philosophical and scientific paradigm. Other important issues relate to the question of the precise legal qualification of the BRICS countries' mode of cooperation and the search for novel modes of governance not based on their diversity but derived from the difference that the BRICS can make (Neuwirth 2017b, 20). Overall, the evaluation of the *raison d'être* of the BRICS countries as a recently formed so-called cooperation and dialogue platform continues to polarize. In less than a decade, their contribution to the global governance went from being assessed as "laying the bricks of a new global legal order" (Kornegay and Bohler-Muller 2013) to "remaining tentative at best and problematic at worst" (Pant 2013, 105). Moreover, the decision of Britain to exit from the EU (i.e., "Brexit") was used to suggest a possible exit of Brazil from the BRICS (i.e., "Braxit") (Simha 2016). These rapidly changing fluctuations not only underscore the importance of law in providing stability and continuity but also the significance of a coherent, inclusive and sustainable development policy.

It is again for some of the media to announce an end or "doomsday" of the BRICS forum of cooperation, whereas scholars may beg to differ in their more constructive assessment (Shahrokhi et al. 2017, 11). In this regard, the critical commentators seem to overlook that the BRICS countries together account for more than 40% of the world's population and almost 30% of its landmass (BRICS 2012, xiii, 1). This means that the BRICS countries, spread over four different continents, are here to stay, and thus their cooperation is, at best, highly useful and beneficial for everyone and, at worst, does not change much at all. A steadily growing body of research tends to reflect the actual and potential benefits derived from BRICS cooperation as well as the unlimited scope for their cooperation in different (legal) fields (Neuwirth et al. 2017; Stuenkel 2015; De Coning et al. 2015; Kornegay and Bohler-Muller 2013). Yet for future BRICS cooperation to succeed, it will require a constructive and constructivist approach that sees the glass as half full instead of half empty. It is an approach that may be circumscribed by the statement that "the best way of predicting the future of the BRICS cooperation is to create it" (Neuwirth 2017b, 23).

Yet for a constructive approach to succeed, it is necessary to start from the best available premises and to also consider some success stories indicating the correctness of the choice. For this reason, the present article will take the "end of development assistance", inaugurated and expressed by the change in terminology by the World Bank in its 2016 World Indicators, as a factor directly or indirectly contributable to the BRICS countries. It will also use it as a starting point for a constructivist approach to the future organization of such coherent, inclusive and sustainable development policy.

To this end, the article first briefly discusses the beginning of the "end of development assistance" to illustrate how a linear mode of thinking about time has repeatedly frustrated the expectations raised by political announcements or plans for a brighter world without widespread poverty and various inequalities. This kind of thinking is reflected in various changes in language, notably in those from development assistance (or aid) to development cooperation. In order to gain insights about how the abandonment of the "developing-developed country dichotomy" must be interpreted, the following section revisits some of the most notorious "end of ..." stories as a critique of a widely prevalent "*Endzeitdenken*", i.e., a mode of thinking influenced by the end of time or a so-called eschatological expectation. This historical review is undertaken with the purpose of paving the way for the BRICS to change the path of global development along the lines discussed in the final section. There the life-death dichotomy serves as an example of an outdated mode of thinking that may impede an adequate interpretation of the meaning of "sustainable development" as well as many similar oxymoronic concepts that dominate the present global discourses in science, technology and policymaking. In concluding, the article aims to show how thinking differently, especially about one of life's most fundamental enigmas, namely death, by, for instance, referring to it instead as "life-after-life", can help to alter perceptions and make a difference in the way we think, act and organize life.

The Beginning of the "End of Development Assistance"

A story has no beginning or end: arbitrarily one chooses that moment of experience from which to look back or from which, to look ahead.

(Greene 1974, 1)

To recap the present state of the world, it was in 2015 that the General Assembly of the United Nations adopted the resolution on the 2030 Agenda for Sustainable Development. Also known as the Sustainable Development Goals (SDGs), the central purpose of the 2030 Agenda was explained as follows:

> This Agenda is a plan of action for people, planet and prosperity. It also seeks to strengthen universal peace in larger freedom. We recognize that eradicating poverty in all its forms and dimensions, including extreme poverty, is the greatest global challenge and an indispensable requirement for sustainable development. (United Nations General Assembly 2015, 2)

To briefly recall, the SDGs replaced the Millennium Development Goals (MDGs) formulated in 2000, mainly as a result of their failure to achieve the goals laid out therein (Sachs 2012, 2206). Or more emphatically, the MDGs produced the awareness that "inequalities persist and that progress has been uneven" (United Nations 2015, 3). Chronologically going back in history confirms that, at every moment, inequality and distributive injustice often caused by conflicts and manifest in poverty and related human sufferings have always coexisted with efforts to combat them. Taking the example of the post-World War II order, it was US President Harry Truman who in 1949 in his inaugural address announced his concept of a "fair deal", with which he inaugurated the present "development age". More specifically, he said in point four that more than half the people of the world are living "in conditions approaching misery", their food being inadequate, as victims of disease and with their economic life being "primitive and stagnant", while, at the same time, stating that "for the first time in history, humanity possesses the knowledge and skill to relieve the suffering of these people" (Rist 2008, 71). This "development age" from the period of post-World War II until now also meant the creation of greater inequalities and many more failures in the efforts to tackle the problems related to poverty.

Moreover, we saw greater divides introduced into the humanity inhabiting this single celestial body called "Earth" as the gradual introduction of the "developing-developed country" dichotomy shows, as flawed as it may always have been in conceptual, factual and philosophical terms (Neuwirth 2010; De Beukelaer 2014; Neuwirth 2017a). Similarly, the same approach also ranked different peoples and countries based on dubious and inconsistent criteria in a first, second or third world, which progressively turned the dream of improvement into a nightmare (Escobar 1995, 4).

In other words, the change from development to post-development thinking (Rist 2008; Ziai 2007) was not quickly and sufficiently followed by related terminological shifts from first development aid (or development assistance) to development cooperation and then to "development policy". Given the delay in terminological change, the conditions found in 1949 at the time of Truman's speech, in 2000 at the time of the adoption of the MDGs and again in 2015 at the adoption of the SDGs, were still similar to the point of their identification. It seems that the global community was back to square one, despite (or paradoxically because of) unprecedented advances in science and technology. These conditions resemble the Lampedusa paradox, where changes are made to maintain the status quo. The result was perhaps best summarized by the words used by James N. Rosenau in 1995, when he described the imminent global governance challenges as "hope embedded in despair" (Rosenau 1995, 13). Consequently, one may realistically ask what can make us believe that this time, just after the adoption of the SDGs, affairs will be different from numerous other moments in history. Or even, why should the BRICS make a difference at all? Yet not knowing the future, it is still best to try to predict the future by creating it or, at least, to fail while at least trying to succeed.

At the least, there are some signs for hope at both the global level and the BRICS level. First globally, it is because the World Bank, an offspring of the Bretton Woods system conceived in 1944, has recently announced the following with regard to the use of the terminology of the developed-developing country dichotomy:

> Motivated by the universal agenda of the Sustainable Development Goals, this edition of *World Development Indicators* also introduces a change in the way that global and regional aggregates are presented in tables and figures. Unless otherwise noted, *there is no longer a distinction between developing countries* (defined in previous editions as low- and middle-income countries) *and developed countries* (defined in previous editions as high-income countries). (World Bank 2016, iii)

Similarly, the SDGs have also noted that they are universal goals and targets "which involve the entire world, developed and developing countries alike" (United Nations General Assembly 2015, 3).

Second, when it comes to the BRICS, the hope may be sought in various official BRICS documents, such as the one from 2015 using the motto "Welfare for everyone, development for all" (BRICS 2015) and the Delhi

Declaration 2012, which states that "We stand ready to work with others, developed and developing countries together". More practically, other signs of hope related to the BRICS potentially making a tangible difference may be vested in the newly established so-called BRICS Bank or New Development Bank (NDB) (Khanna 2014). The hope vested in the BRICS in this article, however, is sought in the deeper layers of human beings and current trends, the outlines of which will be presented next.

"The End of ..." Stories Revisited

Life, or will, thereby returns to its own original, its most elemental and natural mode of being. It returns to itself, where the beginning is the end and the end is the beginning [...].

(Nishitani 1990, 98)

It is another strange paradox that humans generally tend to place a great deal of hope in the future. The same problem was described by Jeremy Rifkin as the "entropy paradox", which highlights the strange fact that in our perception, the history of the universe appears to be shifting from a perfect state toward decay and chaos, while our notion of history follows the opposite course, that is to say, it is seemingly shifting from a state of chaos to a progressively more ordered world (Rifkin 1985, 57). Thus, this human trait appears strange given that, at the end of a distant future, future's only seeming certainty is "the end". In German, this feeling is described by the notion of *Endzeitdenken*, i.e., a mode of thinking influenced by the end of time or a so-called eschatological expectation. In other words, it can also be understood as a linear thinking about phenomena being terminal, if only in terms of their conceptual delimitation between two apparently mutually exclusive or antagonistic concepts. This kind of thinking also gradually invaded scientific thought and surfaces in numerous publications using a "the end of ..." terminology, which can easily be verified by a catalogue search in any library. It is interesting to note that some of the more recent examples include publications calling for an "end of the third world" (Harris 1986), which has also been related to the "end of the cold war" (Kalinovsky and Radchenko 2011). Equally, the "end of development" itself was announced (Parfitt 2002). Other well-known titles include "the end of history" (Fukuyama 1992), "the end of geography" (Greig 2002; Betlehem 2014) or "the end of war" (Chappell and de Becker

2010). Even though it may just have begun with the twenty-first century, even the "end of the Asian century" has already been announced (Auslin 2017). Finally, one may ask, is it only a matter of time until "the end of BRICS" will also be predicted in a published book? The fact is that it has already been mentioned as a possibility in view of recent economic and political problems in some of the BRICS countries (Chenoy et al. 2016, 207).

However, possibly, it is less a matter of time but rather "the end of time" itself that announces itself based on revolutionary discoveries from the world of physics (Barbour 1999). Nonetheless, there are strong reasons also provided by other scientific fields that may support the argument of time (or at least our dominant mode of perception of time) coming to an end. For instance, numerous observers have noted a drastic acceleration in our perception of time or memory (Nora 1989, 15; Gleick 2000, 6). A similar trend has also been found to dominate the current epoch of the Anthropocene, which means that "human activities are significantly influencing Earth's environment", many of which have been found to be accelerating (Ehlers and Krafft 2006, 5). Called the "Great Acceleration of the Anthropocene", the beginning of which was dated to 1945, the "human enterprise" is said to have "suddenly accelerated" in many ways, ranging from population growth to oil consumption or the increasing interconnectedness of cultures (Steffen et al. 2007, 617). Equally, strong trends of technological convergence in economics also testify to this trend (Lee and Olson 2010). These trends in technology and industry are also mirrored in language at large; this can be seen in the changes in language as observed by linguistics—manifest in both an increasing amount of neologisms and a special category of so-called essentially oxymoronic concepts (Neuwirth 2013, 2018).

Generally, when applying an *Endzeit* thinking, most of the time, it is forgotten that the announcement of the eventual end of something will not end existence but instead immediately means the beginning of something new or "the return of history and the end of dreams" (Kagan 2008). In this respect, it may thus be a shortcoming particularly of a specific branch of Western scientific thought or an educational system favoring a linear mode of thinking based on exclusive logic applied to an understanding of time that seems to overemphasize the end without duly considering the possibility that it means a beginning of something new (or possibly just the repetition of the existing in perhaps a circular loop). This tendency is becoming more problematic in view of the ongoing trend of an acceleration of the perception of changes in time (and correlated accelerations in the means of transport), as it means that time itself seems to disappear. With all cycles becoming shorter, such as those for changes in fashion, product cycles, or cycles of financial crises, etc., we face serious challenges regarding an efficient and sustainable mode of planning or development in general, as well as the rule of law in general and the expectations toward legal predictability and certainty in particular. In all related regulatory questions, it seems then that we miss one important link in the striving for scientific discovery, which is sound knowledge about "the end" and, most likely, what happens "after 'the end' finally ended".

Ironically or tragically, in the current scientific paradigm, we invest so much time, energy and money on different aspects allegedly aiming at improving human life for all, when, in fact, we do not even know about the most fundamental aspect of life itself, namely its apparent opposite, i.e., the greatest human illusory enigma that we call "death" (Benoît 1973, 154). This irony manifests itself in the paradox that we invest more in artificial intelligence than in improving human intelligence, given that we seem to be only aware of approximately 10% of our cognitive or brain abilities (OECD 2007, 113–14). Similarly, we seem to prefer to search for livable habitats elsewhere in the universe instead of making coordinated and serious efforts to save the one we inhabit right now. In health policy too, we not only fail to coordinate conventional, traditional and alternative medicines (Neuwirth and Svetlicinii 2015) and integrate them with mental health but, most of all, completely neglect the necessity to focus scientific research holistically on the quality of life, including the "life after life" (Moody 1976). Sadly, many questions about life after life, as death can also be called, are sadly relegated to pseudoscientific or paranormal phenomena or to a world belonging to religion (separated from science altogether).

Consequently, this scientific failure also affects the principal understanding of development as well. It may also be responsible for the repeated failures in history to achieve the goals we set for "development aid" or, better, "development cooperation" as we currently call it. We not only apply a linguistically flawed opposition between the terms developing and the developed countries but also inconsistent logic. Most of all, we are pretty ignorant about the most fundamental question of all, i.e., the nature of life including the life after life (not seen in binary terms as mutually exclusive, incompatible and antagonistic concepts). Overall, the world is experiencing a global scientific crisis of faith in the sense of continuing to split unitary phenomena in half, dividing them into numerous pairs of dichotomies, such as developing or developed countries, or life and death.

In the question about the deficiencies of dichotomies in general and the (flawed) distinction in "developing and developed countries" in particular, it is not always clear what terminology should replace them. Moreover, it may be uncertain what the change in terminology means for the concrete policies and implementing measures that follow them. For instance, it may be alleged that abandoning the distinction will have a negative effect on those countries currently using the developing country status, particularly in international trade. It may also be abused by developed countries to reduce their commitments in development assistance. In response, however, it must be clear that the mere abandonment of the terminology and related rights or privileges (such as preferential treatment in international trade law) cannot be a stand-alone measure seen in isolation from other rights and policies. The reason for this is that the discrimination related to the dichotomy has not only been applied to economic factors, such as Gross Domestic Product (GDP). Instead, it has also spread and affected other areas, including a weak or total lack of representation in international institutions.

Therefore, the abandonment of the terminology alone is not sufficient. It is a first step, which must be followed by novel and more inclusive concepts, as well as a coherent set of flanking measures aimed at the better integration of the countries in question into "a more just, equitable, fair, democratic and representative international political and economic order" to use a phrase in the 2017 Xiamen BRICS summit Declaration. It is in this crisis of faith that the BRICS are called to make a difference. They are in a good position to make a difference, because of their own distinct historical, economic, political and cultural memory, as well as their present state and rate of development. Generally, their ability to make a difference is not because the people in the BRICS are generally speaking "distinct". Paradoxically, it is rather the unique distinctiveness of each individual that makes everyone the same. However, inhabiting a planet of a spherical shape, no human appears to ever react the same way (as it is impossible to be at the same place in time and space, which is why no one ever has the identical source of sensory information on which subsequent decisions are being based). This means that the hope in the BRICS cooperation is vested in specific historical, cultural and philosophical reasons, and their current dynamism in the geopolitical context, such as increasing levels of glocalization, the dawn of the Asian century, or an unprecedented pace and volume of scientific progress. In sum, the BRICS, like any other country, city and person on this planet, need to regard themselves as a *pars pro toto*, i.e., a part of the whole in the process of shaping human destiny. The overall success in this endeavor will depend on the degree to which the BRICS can use their potential strength in this regard and formulate it into a more inclusive—possibly even oxymoronic—global and sustainable development policy, the contours of which shall be outlined in the following section.

The BRICS and "Development" After Development Assistance

Indeed, without death there would hardly have been any philosophizing.
(Schopenhauer 1958, 463)

The hope associated with the BRICS countries in the field of development policy is rooted notably in their various economic, political and developmental achievements made over the past few decades (Gu et al. 2016, 5–7). Among the tangible results in global development is the gradual recognition of the absurdity of the development terminology, including notions such as "development aid" and the "developing-developed country dichotomy". This derives from the insight that development has always started from self-help, as an internal process or one created from within and not from outside by coercion (Beisser 1970, 77) or what could also be critically connoted as "coercive charity". The present is, therefore, an opportune moment to call for an "end of development assistance" (as we have known it). This is because in a rapidly changing environment, characterized by a strong diversity of global actors and the increasing complexity of global issues, new cognitive modes are urgently needed. The reason for this is that numerous oxymoronic concepts, such as the one of sustainable development itself (Sachs 1999, 38; Njiro 2002; Redclift 2005), call for novel approaches to how we understand life as a whole. Given that we are currently adapting our understanding to the possibility that the sole certainty in life is change, we increasingly focus on processes rather than specific objectives. This explains why we all want to be living in "(constantly) developing countries" and why, in being "developed", there is no certainty that the same level of well-being can be maintained in the future.

This is precisely the conceptual challenge derived from the concept of sustainable development and many more oxymora dominating our current governance discourses (Neuwirth 2018). It means to accept that opposites expressed in antagonistic concepts do not simply mutually exclude each other but may instead complement each other and provide a means for reaching a higher level of understanding. For many of the so-called "trade and ... " issues, such as "trade and environment", this means that introducing green products does not mean a zero-sum game at the cost of economic growth. Instead, awareness is rising that investment in green technologies provides the means for economic growth sustained over a longer period that also has beneficial effects on the environment. The same thinking can be applied to all other "trade and ... pairs", such as the one of "trade and development", as well as the apparent dilemmas expressed in dichotomies. So why not also apply it to one of the most fundamental human dichotomies: the one of life versus death. In this respect, the BRICS countries' particular history, and notably their cultural, spiritual and religious backgrounds, can provide the starting point for the hope that—even though some concepts from the past international development cooperation are being repeated in the related documents formulated by the BRICS—the BRICS will make a difference.

At first sight, when it comes to the life-death dichotomy, two BRICS countries, China and India, seem to share a similar stance based on their historical ties rooted in Buddhism, which has also affected trade and diplomacy (Sen 2003, 7). Conceiving life not as ending with death but as a stage in a longer, possibly eternal process has wider repercussions for how we feel and organize the present (Flannelly et al. 2012). Moreover, it is closely tied to our understanding of evolution and the evolution of cognition, as well as dualistic thinking (e.g., the mind-body dichotomy) (Bering 2006). At a closer look, not only the other BRICS countries' populations but everyone on the planet also has a similar view on the matter. It has been reported that often majorities of people in the so-called West believe in a life after life (Flannelly et al. 2012, 651–52). This hardly comes as a surprise given that the world's major religions, Judaism, Christianity, Islam and Hinduism as well as Buddhism, essentially concur in this matter (Obayashi 1992; Koslowski 2002). However, as Arthur Schopenhauer stated, different religions share their attempts to console us concerning death or to provide an antidote but diverge in the degree to which they attain this end (Schopenhauer 1958, 463). It has also been argued that, paradoxically, religion is both the cause of and the relief from human anxiety (Homans 1941; Leming 1980, 347). Thus again, we encounter a paradox or essential problem rooted in a dualistic mode of thinking based on binary logic. It is thus the same problem that relates to the enigma hidden in the oxymoronic concept of "sustainable development" that challenges a binary logic or solely dualist mode of thinking. Whence the need for more paradoxical thinking, which was outlined in the following statement about the future of education:

> The educated person of the next century will be required to adapt to constant change and apply the basic skills of language, mathematics, and problem solving in a variety of situations that cannot be predicted today. (Eliason 1996, 341)

In this regard, the studies in cultural geography of a geography of thought give rise to hope, given that it was found that Eastern people are more open to "a search for the 'Middle Way' between opposing propositions" (Nisbett 2003, 293) than their Western counterparts, who tend to see paradox as "as a condition based in conflict" (Kalamaras 1994, 6). Yet it would amount to a serious mistake to think that these findings are rooted strictly in geography or even in genetics. These preferences have no fixed geography, as geography itself is not fixed (considering the tectonic shifts) but they reflect years of educational and cultural traditions that have crystallized into habits or innate modes of thinking that are difficult but not impossible to change (Segal 2008, 101). The same observations also explain why it is so hard to abandon the developing-developed country dichotomy, as flawed as it may be linguistically, philosophically or logically. In short, these brief observations may help to strengthen not only the hope in the BRICS countries, which account for almost half of the world's population, but also their responsibility in recalling humanity's traditional and alternative thoughts and philosophies, and to merge them with novel and original scientific ideas and research about the destiny of humanity. This has already been shown in the field of medicine, where the renaissance of Chinese or Eastern traditional medicines has provided a great opportunity for countries elsewhere to re-discover their own traditional medicines to complement the advances in a globalized pharmaceutical industry (Neuwirth and Svetlicinii 2015, 341, 353).

To briefly summarize the significance of these observations for the formulation and implementation of a global sustainable development policy for the future, it is necessary for the BRICS cooperation and dialogue forum to first continue, and where possible, step up their cooperation in every possible field. Second, the BRICS countries must remain open to the entire world and other countries or regional blocs, as well as the global community as a whole, given that "BRIC(K)S are for building bridges not walls" (Neuwirth 2017b, 21). Third, their rich and diverse cultural heritages from ancient times provide a strong basis for cooperation in innovative research not only in the fields of technology but also in those of the social sciences and the arts and humanities. It may also help to focus on those areas where, at present, no global consensus can be reached. Overall, there shall be no initial boundaries as to what is scientific or possible but only a strong interest in trying to discover new aspects about humans' fundamental traits and needs as strongly reflected in the life-death dichotomy. In this regard, the notion of "sustainable development" is not to be interpreted as a novel buzzword of international development cooperation that merely replaces the previous ones of "development aid or assistance" but a true reminder of the power of new ideas bringing new possibilities.

Conclusion

Those who believe that life consists in change because change implies movement, should remember that there must be an underlying thread of unity or the change, being unmeaning, will cause conflict and clash.

(Tagore 2007, 707)

In the beginning, the present discussion picked up on the continuing skepticism about the ability of the "BRICS cooperation and dialogue forum" to deliver a notable contribution to the governance of global affairs. In addition to obvious factual statistical reasons related to their size in land and people for their cooperation to continue, it builds on their diversity and many differences, which helps to explain the reasons why the BRICS can make a difference in global governance in general and in the context of an emerging global sustainable development policy in particular. It argued that the BRICS countries have already delivered noticeable and tangible results in this area, such as through their contribution to a change of mind by the World Bank in abandoning the "developing-developed country dichotomy" or the creation of the NDB or so-called BRICS Bank. These significant terminological and institutional changes may be taken as the beginning of the "end of development assistance" as we have known it.

This end of development assistance, as other "end of stories" have revealed, however, is only temporal in an age of an acceleration of change toward a continuous space-time continuum as supported by discoveries in physics regarding time, technological trends of convergence, as well as linguistic trends rooted in the rise of the rhetorical figures called "essentially oxymoronic concepts" (Neuwirth 2013). One of the most prominent representatives is the one of "sustainable development" itself. These trends underscore the importance of philosophy as the underlying thread of thoughts that constantly affects the decisions we make and the actions we take. This is also important for law, as "pure law", i.e., law as a merely theoretical exercise, has been deemed to be an oxymoron, as "law always needs a context within which it is to be considered".[1] This also goes for development, which is not merely about rates of economic growth measured by the GDP. It also enables people to freely make a choice in accordance with their capabilities and even dreams (Sen 2000). This means that it is necessary to find novel ways to render global development both inclusive and sustainable, connoting that it will benefit everyone and have a lasting effect.

Consequently, as an example of the importance of linguistic changes as both the harbinger and the cause of change in action, the life-death dichotomy was chosen to exemplify the shortcomings of development thinking in terms of dualistic modes of thinking and binary logic as infamously reflected in the developing-developed country distinction. Thus, in trying to cast light on the time after development, it was shown that the belief in "life-after-life" as a continuum rather than a possibly illusory terminal state called "death" is not only strong in the ancient philosophies of the BRICS countries but equally in the world religions and in wide sections of the entire world's population. The BRICS were said to be "for building bridges, not walls", and this refers most of all to the building of cognitive bridges closing the gaps left between the two opposite poles created by binary thinking and its expression in numerous dichotomies. In other words, it is necessary for the BRICS to continue their cooperation in the broadest sense possible and to push the boundaries even beyond their apparent limits: limits set more by our own imagination rather than by physical laws. Some time ago, the Indian poet Rabindranath Tagore wrote about the history of science being like going "through a maze of mistakes" (Tagore 1914, 48). The same can be applied to the history of development but the importance, as he remarked in the following, is not to remember the history for its innumerable mistakes but instead, for the "progressive ascertainment of truth" (Tagore 1914, 48). In this regard, the end of the use of the terms "development assistance" and "developed as opposed to developing countries" can be seen as the precondition for the inauguration of the beginning of a more sustainable continuum of a more equitable global legal order.

Acknowledgements The author would like to thank the organizers of the International Symposium on Development and Governance in the BRICS held at Fudan University in Shanghai (CHINA) in 2017 for providing the impetus for the writing of this article. The author gratefully acknowledges the financial support provided by the University of Macau [MYRG2015-00222-FLL and MYRG2016-00116-FLL] underlying the research that went into the writing of this article.

NOTE

1. Ontario Superior Court of Justice, *Silveira v. Ontario (Minister of Transportation)* [2011], O.J. No. 3157 at 22.

REFERENCES

Auslin, Michael R. 2017. *The End of the Asian Century: War, Stagnation, and the Risks to the World's Most Dynamic Region*. New Haven: Yale University Press.

Barbour, Julian. 1999. *The End of Time: The Next Revolution in Physics*. Oxford: Oxford University Press.

Beisser, Arnold. 1970. "A Paradoxical Theory of Change." In *Gestalt Therapy Now: Theory, Techniques, Applications*, edited by Joen Fagan and Irma L. Shepherd, 70–80. Palo Alto: Science and Behavior Books.

Benoît, Hubert. 1973. *Let Go: Theory and Practice of Detachment According to Zen*. New York: Weiser.

Bering, Jesse M. 2006. "The Folk Psychology of Souls." *Behavioral and Brain Sciences* 29: 453–98.

Bethlehem, Daniel. 2014. "The End of Geography: The Changing Nature of the International System and the Challenge to International Law." *The European Journal of International Law* 25 (1): 9–24.

BRICS. 2012. *The BRICS Report: A Study of Brazil, Russia, India, China, and South Africa with Special Focus on Synergies and Complementarities*. Oxford: Oxford University Press.

BRICS. 2015. *Strategy for BRICS Economic Partnership*. Ufa: Russia.

Chappell, Paul K., and Gavin de Becker. 2010. *The End of War: How Waging Peace Can Save Humanity, Our Planet, and Our Future*. Westport: Easton Studio Press.

Chenoy, Anuradha, Marina Larionova, Richard Manning, and Jennifer Constantine. 2016. "Looking Across BRICS: An Emerging International Development Agenda?" In *The BRICS in International Development*, edited by Jing Gu, Alex Shankland, and Anuradha Chenoy, 207–42. London: Palgrave Macmillan.

Cooper, Andrew F. 2016. *The BRICS: A Very Short Introduction*. New York: Oxford University Press.

De Beukelaer, Christiaan. 2014. "Creative Industries in 'Developing' Countries: Questioning Country Classifications in the UNCTAD Creative Economy Reports." *Cultural Trends* 23 (4): 232–51.

De Coning, Cedric, Thomas Mandrup, and Liselotte Odgaard, eds. 2015. *The BRICS and Coexistence: An Alternative Vision of World Order*. London: Routledge.

Ehlers, Eckart, and Thomas Krafft. 2006. "Managing Global Change: Earth System Science in the Anthropocene." In *Earth System Science in the Anthropocene*, edited by Eckart Ehlers and Thomas Krafft, 5–12. Berlin: Springer.

Eliason, James L. 1996. "Using Paradoxes to Teach Critical Thinking in Science." *Journal of College Science Teaching* 25 (5): 341–45.

Escobar, Arturo. 1995. *Encountering Development: The Making and Unmaking of the Third World*. Princeton: Princeton University Press.

Flannelly, Kevin J., Christopher G. Ellison, Kathleen Galek, and Nava R. Silton. 2012. "Belief in Life-After-Death, Beliefs About the World, and Psychiatric Symptoms." *Journal of Religion & Health* 51 (3): 651–62.

Fukuyama, Francis. 1992. *The End of History and the Last Man*. New York: Avon Books.

Gleick, James. 2000. *Faster: The Acceleration of Just About Everything*. New York: Vintage Books.

Greene, Graham. 1974. *The End of the Affair*. London: Heinemann.

Greig, J. Michael. 2002. "The End of Geography?: Globalization, Communications, and Culture in the International System." *The Journal of Conflict Resolution* 46 (2): 225–43.

Gu, Jing, Richard Carey, Alex Shankland, and Anuradha Chenoy. 2016. "Introduction: International Development, South-South Cooperation and the Rising Powers." In *The BRICS in International Development*, edited by Jing Gu, Alex Shankland, and Anuradha Chenoy, 1–24. London: Palgrave Macmillan.

Harris, Nigel. 1986. *The End of the Third World: Newly Industrializing Countries and the Decline of an Ideology*. London: I.B. Tauris.

Homans, George C. 1941. "Anxiety and Ritual: The Theories of Malinowski and Radcliffe-Brown." *American Anthropologist* 43 (2): 164–72.

Kagan, Robert. 2008. *The Return of History and the End of Dreams*. New York: Alfred A. Knopf.

Kalamaras, George. 1994. *Reclaiming the Tacit Dimension: Symbolic Form in the Rhetoric of Silence*. Albany: State University of New York Press.

Kalinovsky, Artemy M., and Sergey Radchenko, eds. 2011. *The End of the Cold War and the Third World: New Perspectives on Regional Conflict*. London: Routledge.

Khanna, Parag. 2014. "New BRICS Bank a Building Block of Alternative World Order." *New Perspectives Quarterly* 31 (4): 46–48.

Kornegay, Francis A., and Narnia Bohler-Muller, eds. 2013. *Laying the BRICS of a New Global Order: From Yekaterinburg 2009 to Ethekwini 2013*. Pretoria: Africa Institute of South Africa.

Koslowski, Peter, ed. 2002. *Progress, Apocalypse, and Completion of History and Life After Death of the Human Person in the World Religions*. Dordrecht: Springer.

Lee, Sang M., and David L. Olson. 2010. *Convergenomics: Strategic Innovation in the Convergence Era*. Farnham: Gower.

Leming, Michael R. 1980. "Religion and Death: A Test of Homans' Thesis." *Omega* 10 (4): 347–64.

Moody, Raymond A., Jr. 1976. *Life After Life: The Investigation of a Phenomenon—Survival of Bodily Death*. New York: Bantam Books.

Neuwirth, Rostam J. 2010. "A Constitutional Tribute to Global Governance: Overcoming the Chimera of the Developing-Developed Country Dichotomy." European University Institute (EUI) Working Paper LAW 2010/20.

Neuwirth, Rostam J. 2013. "Essentially Oxymoronic Concepts." *Global Journal of Comparative Law* 2 (2): 147–66.

Neuwirth, Rostam J. 2017a. "Global Law and Sustainable Development: Change and the 'Developing-Developed Country' Terminology." *European Journal of Development Research* 29 (4): 911–25.

Neuwirth, Rostam J. 2017b. "The Enantiosis of BRICS: BRICS La[w]yers and the Difference That They Can Make." In *The BRICS-Lawyers Guide to Global Cooperation*, edited by Rostam J. Neuwirth, Alexandr Svetlicinii, and Denis De Castro Halis, 8–30. Cambridge: Cambridge University Press.

Neuwirth, Rostam J. 2018. *Law in the Time of Oxymora: A Synaesthesia of Language, Logic and Law*. New York: Routledge.

Neuwirth, Rostam J., and Alexandr Svetlicinii. 2015. "Law as a Social Medicine: Enhancing International Inter-Regime Regulatory Coopetition as a Means for the Establishment of a Global Health Governance Framework." *Journal of Legal Medicine* 36 (3–4): 330–66.

Neuwirth, Rostam J., Alexandr Svetlicinii, and Denis De Castro Halis, eds. 2017. *The BRICS-Lawyers Guide to Global Cooperation*. Cambridge: Cambridge University Press.

Nisbett, Richard E. 2003. *The Geography of Thought: How Asians and Westerners Think Differently... and Why*. New York: Free Press.

Nishitani, Keiji. 1990. *The Self-Overcoming of Nihilism*. Albany: State University of New York.

Njiro, Esther. 2002. "Introduction: Sustainable Development an Oxymoron?" *Agenda* 52: 3–7.

Nora, Paul. 1989. "Between Memory and History: Les lieux de mémoire." *Representations* 26: 7–24.

Obayashi, Hiroshi. 1992. *Death and Afterlife: Perspectives of World Religions*. New York: Praeger.

OECD. 2007. *Understanding the Brain: The Birth of a Learning Science*. Paris: OECD.

Pant, Harsh V. 2013. "The BRICS Fallacy." *The Washington Quarterly* 36 (3): 91–105.

Parfitt, Trevor. 2002. *The End of Development?: Modernity, Post-modernity and Development*. Sterling: Pluto Press.

Redclift, Michael. 2005. "Sustainable Development (1987–2005): An Oxymoron Comes of Age." *Sustainable Development* 13: 212–27.

Rifkin, Jeremy. 1985. *Entropy: A New World View*. London: Paladin.

Rist, Gilbert. 2008. *The History of Development: From Western Origins to Global Faith*. London: ZED Books.

Rosenau, James N. 1995. "Governance in the 21st Century." *Global Governance* 1(1): 13–43.

Sachs, Wolfgang. 1999. "Sustainable Development and the Crisis of Nature: On the Political Anatomy of an Oxymoron." In *Living with Nature: Environmental Politics as Cultural Discourse*, edited by Frank Fischer and Maarten A. Hajer, 23–41. Oxford: Oxford University Press.

Sachs, Jeffrey D. 2012. "From Millennium Development Goals to Sustainable Development Goals." *Lancet* 379: 2206–11.

Schopenhauer, Arthur. 1958. *The World in Will and Representation*. Vol. 2. New York: Dover.

Segal, Gabriel. 2008. "Poverty of Stimulus Arguments Concerning Language and Folk Psychology." In *The Innate Mind: Foundations and the Future*, edited by Peter Carruthers, Stephen Laurence, and Stephen Stich, vol. 3, 90–105. Oxford: Oxford University Press.

Sen, Amartya. 2000. *Development as Freedom*. New York: Alfred A. Knopf.

Sen, Tansen. 2003. *Buddhism, Diplomacy, and Trade: The Realignment of Sino-Indian Relations, 600–1400*. Honolulu: Association for Asian Studies.

Shahrokhi, Manuchehr, Huifang Cheng, Krishnan Dandapani, Antonio Figueiredo, Ali M. Parhizgari, and Yochanan Shachmurove. 2017. "The Evolution and Future of the BRICS: Unbundling Politics from Economics." *Global Finance Journal* 32: 1–15.

Simha, Rakesh Krishnan. 2016. "BRICS Should Prepare for 'Braxit': A Brazilian Exit." *Russia Beyond*, July 4. https://in.rbth.com/blogs/stranger_than_fiction/2016/07/04/brics-should-prepare-for-braxit-a-brazilian-exit_608637.

Steffen, Will, Paul J. Crutzen, and John R. McNeill. 2007. "The Anthropocene: Are Humans Now Overwhelming the Great Forces of Nature?" *Ambio* 16 (5): 614–21.

Stuenkel, Oliver. 2015. *The BRICS and the Future of Global Order*. Lanham: Lexington Books.

Tagore, Rabindranath. 1914. *Sādhanā: The Realisation of Life*. New York: Macmillan.

Tagore, Rabindranath. 2007. *The English Writings of Rabindranath Tagore: Essays*. Vol. 4. New Delhi: Atlantic.

Tapscott, Christopher, Jose A. Puppim de Oliveira, Yijia Jing, Alexey G. Barabashev, and Navdeep Mathur. 2017. "Introduction: BRICS in Search of Governance Models." *Chinese Political Science Review* 2 (1): 1–6.

United Nations. 2015. *The Millennium Development Goals Report 2015*. New York: United Nations.

United Nations General Assembly. 2015. "Transforming Our World: The 2030 Agenda for Sustainable Development." A/RES/70/1, October 21.

World Bank. 2016. *World Development Indicators 2016*. Washington, DC: World Bank.

Ziai, Aram, ed. 2007. *Exploring Post-development: Theory and Practice, Problems and Perspectives*. New York: Routledge.

CHAPTER 3

Locating BRICS Development Strategies in Global Development Policy Narratives

Lisa Thompson

INTRODUCTION

A consistent feature of BRICS over the last five years is that official narratives focus pragmatically and instrumentally on BRICS South–South collaboration (SSC). CEO of the BRICS Think Tank in South Africa, Sarah Mosoetsa locates this perspective well in a quote made prior to the 2018 BRICS Academic Forum and Johannesburg Summit,

> … the five member states making up BRICS seek to bring about a radical reinterpretation of the current narrative regarding the political economy, the second golden decade of BRICS co-operation and solidarity. In driving these objectives, the *BRICS Academic Review* will examine new narratives and policy alternatives being mooted in South Africa. These are many and varied… the theme for South Africa's tenure of the BRICS presidency is *Inclusive Development Through a Socially Responsive Economy*. The time is

L. Thompson (✉)
University of Western Cape, Cape Town, South Africa
e-mail: lthompson@uwc.ac.za

© The Author(s) 2020
J. A. Puppim de Oliveira and Y. Jing (eds.), *International Development Assistance and the BRICS*, Governing China in the 21st Century,
https://doi.org/10.1007/978-981-32-9644-2_3

ripe for new ideas; join us ... as we map out an ever more promising future for BRICS. (Mosoetsa 2018, 2)

The BRICS diplomatic romance on inclusive, collective development is also in a sense pivotal to the official FOCAC narrative. The 2018 FOCAC Declaration calls for a '...community of human destiny' which is characterized by a "safe common prosperity, open and inclusive, clean and beautiful world, built on a new type of mutual respect, fairness, justice, cooperation and win-win (that) safeguard(s) and promote(s) world peace and development" (FOCAC 2018).

Yet, the policy narrative does not focus on development alternatives for the Global South that forefront the main economic problem the BRICS face: poverty and extreme inequality (Thompson and de Wet 2017; Bond 2018a). In this sense, the BRICS development trajectory remains firmly within the liberal economic frame of the 2001 conceptualization by Jim O'Neill of Goldman-Sachs, who coined the acronym 'BRIC' to describe the four fastest-growing emerging economies at the turn of the twenty-first century.

BRICS as a bloc, inclusive of South Africa as of 2010, remains all about growth and geostrategic rivalries, cast arbitrarily, and in the fuzziest of ideological framings, as a dichotomy of the North and South in developmental terms. While the bloc's inability to deal with socioeconomic inequalities is recognized by academics and policy-makers who support BRICS, the empirically unsubstantiated argument that BRICS poses a development alternative is reinforced in the African context. The South African Presidency, followed by the FOCAC Summit in Beijing in September, reinforced the view of the 'newness' of SSC. President Ramaphosa stated in Beijing, that '... FOCAC refutes the view that a new colonialism is taking hold in Africa as our detractors would have us believe' (Dooley 2018).

At South African BRICS Think Tank level, this argument is well illustrated by Magida who states,

> ...BRICS is largely understood as a force with the capability to discipline the global political order – mainly the inequitable distribution of economic and political power at international level that favours the Western powers. This relic of western imperialism remains visible in the constitution of multilateral organisations like the United Nations, the International Monetary Fund (IMF) and the World Bank, and in international trade arrangements. Simply put, Western nations ... continue to dominate the world order, leaving a trail

of despicable injustices in their wake. Their riches – the wealth and welfare of their populations – come at the expense of the people of the developing world. The BRICS formation has largely shaped up as an effort to rectify these persisting geopolitical injustices. (Magida 2018, 8)

This optimism could be justified in terms of the size and influence of the BRICS in the global political economy. Together economically, BRICS offer a bloc-based geostrategic alternative to Northern dominance, taking into account the standard measure of the size and potential influence of the economies of BRICS+ and Africa (Gu and Kitano 2018). In an ideal world, BRICS inclusive development policies could positively influence the lives of the vast majority of those living in relative deprivation or poverty in the BRICS and the regions they dominate. Yet to date, this potential is largely unrealized. BRICS states tend to shore up Northern political and economic interests more often than providing solidaristic and counter-hegemonic policy stances (Thakur 2014; Bond 2018a, b). This chapter attempts to unpack the policy content of the BRICS state-led narrative on International Development Assistance and Cooperation (IDA and IDC) and SSC. The chapter is set against the background of prevailing development narratives as they manifest in public discourse. Drawing on examples of development policy impact, the analysis further examines both the conceptions and the practices of IDC and SSC.

The chapter illustrates that the 'Beyond Aid' debate may provide further legitimacy for BRICS authoritarian regimes and therefore, paradoxically, provide further grist to the neoliberal economists of the North to argue that BRICS alternative development policy debates are backward, 'anti-developmental' and 'anti-democratic.' While challenges to the official constructions of BRICS development are embedded in the struggles within BRICS states for inclusion and sustainable livelihoods, these struggles may become the subject of further state-based repression (Mohanty 2018; Ayers 2018; Bond 2018b). Given the authoritarian nature of all but one of the BRICS states, its official narrative of inclusive development may be used as a rationale for further authoritarian national policies, 'threatened' by 'insubordinate,' radical groups. This is already happening in India with the house arrests of the derogatively labeled Urban Naxal movement, where leaders have been vilified for their 'marxist-maoist' activism. The presidency of ultra-right-wing populist Jair Bolsonaro of Brazil from 2019, the year that Brazil takes Presidency of BRICS, is further reason for concern. Bolsonaro has threatened to crush the environmental movement and the left, especially left-wing grassroots activists and interfering International Non-Governmental Organizations (INGOS). For example, during an Amazon pre-presidential motorcade rally, Bolsonaro stated '… (t)his cowardly business of international NGOs like WWF and so many others from England sticking their noses into Brazil is going to end! This tomfoolery stops right here!'. Thus, old world geostrategic military security travesties of the states in BRICS may be justified and endorsed by the BRICS as exercises of 'sovereignty' (Lipton 2017).

At the same time, BRICS have taken the economic liberal moral high ground in global economic institutions, calling for a collective free trade global strategy. In policy terms, this would enforce what the North has stood for on global platforms such as the WTO at a time when the United States and the EU are retreating from economic free trade commitments (Bond 2018a, b). Ironically, China through FOCAC is leading the support for free trade, '… (f)acing the current grim situation, (we) firmly advocate multilateralism, oppose all forms of unilateralism and protectionism, and support the multilateral trade system with the WTO as the core…' (FOCAC 2018, point 12). The following section examines the contradictions of the BRICS bloc and China's leading role in the IDA discourse in relation to contemporary public discourse on development.

NORTH–SOUTH DEVELOPMENT POLICY DEBATES

Earlier international development and global political economy debates polarized the policy debate into socialist/Marxist/dependency developmental strategies versus (neo)liberal economic development (Ayers 2018). During the Cold War, geostrategic alliances were also formed as a result of these state policy allegiances, whether in fact they had resonance in reality or not. This polarity remained a feature of the post-World War II era.

The Cold War thaw, marked in November 9, 1991 by the fall of the Berlin Wall, paved the way for the subsequent 'there is no alternative' (TINA) North–South development triumphalist phase for organizations like the IMF and World Bank. The intervening decades have seen a variety of different approaches to development policy; however, these are centered mostly in terms of getting the liberal capitalist development model 'right,' through the correct mix of public policy instruments and incentives that will lead to economic growth. Northern lending and multilateral institutions (IMF, World Bank, WTO) have played the defining role in determining the definitions and rules of development (Mohanty 2018; Ayers 2018; Bond

2018a, b). In some, but not all instances, for example India, Brazil, and latterly South Africa, this period resulted in greater attention to democratizing development. This concept and the policy framings that have arisen from its absorption into developmental public policy are ostensibly orientated toward greater procedural and redistributive justice (Mohanty 2018; Gomes and Esteves 2018). The TINA phase also ushered in a new policy rhetoric of 'good governance' linked to OECD/DAC aid disbursement to developing states in the South struggling with a range of economic crises and structural economic distortions (Thompson and Tapscott 2010).

During this same period, many of the emerging economies in South-East Asia, including China, grew at rapid rates and in co-dependency with the United States in particular (Zhang 2017; Bello 2006; Lesufi and Thompson 2019). Ironically, this growth and economic interdependency were not underpinned by democratic state practices. The mix of economic policies leading to rapid industrialization and manufacturing diversification arose largely the result of a combination of both the economic and geostrategic significance of certain states to the United States and in relation to alleviating over-accumulation problems with the US economy (the Asian Tigers were prime examples, as is China) (Bello 2006; Brautigam and Tang 2012; Zhang 2017; Lesufi and Thompson 2019).

In BRICS and through FOCAC, the development debate is increasingly arbitrarily constructed multilaterally. North and South have been redefined by the geostrategic labels 'global North and South' on global multilateral platforms. The labels have been invented to indicate new forms of southern solidarity as a result of Northern patterns of hegemonic dominance that prevail through 'the old boys' clubs,' such as the UN Security Council (Magida 2018). BRICS is not consistently solidaristic on key aspects of inequity and redress in multilateral economic platforms; a key example is the recent redistribution of votes within the IMF: China's voting power increased by a massive 37%, Brazil's rose 23%, India's by a modest 11%, and Russia's vote by 8%. Africa as a continent and in terms of geostrategic state power, lost hugely: Nigeria lost a massive 41% of its voting power, Libya also lost 39%, Morocco's vote fell 27%, Gabon's by 26%, Algeria by 26%, Namibia by 26% and South Africa, the gateway to Africa, lost 21% (Bond 2018b; Magida 2018).

BRICS as the Global South: What Is Not New to the IDA Narrative

The debates about reconstituting the Northern security and the Northern economic old boys club will go on: the UN Security Council and IMF influence remain critical to old-style hegemony. Within these debates, the notion of 'global' South–South cooperation and solidarity is deceiving, as in multilateral spaces of engagement, and global governance, the bloc is sometimes collaborative, but just as often conflictual (Weiss and Abdenur 2014; Thakur 2014; Alden and Schoeman 2015; Bond 2015; Lipton 2017). Yet, the bloc at state level has created an official development discourse that firmly defends the myth of a development alternative. Central to the discussion of alternative South–South cooperation is the New Development Bank (NDB). Buenaventura and Lucey illustrate this optimism,

> The African Regional Center (ARC) of the NDB, launched in August 2017, heralds cautious optimism for the African continent. From the NDB's initial proclamations, it appears that there is a real opportunity for this new source of financing to provide resources for sustainable infrastructure that will first benefit South Africa, and then the continent at large, in a people-centered way. (Buenaventura and Lucey 2018, 17)

The NDB narrative of a financial alternative promotes the image of BRICS as leaders of the global South, supporting global good governance (defined as support for sovereignty and free trade) and no strings attached IDA. The new image of development, popularized by the media close to governments in the BRICS states, complicates the discussions of development. As Alvares reminded us in 1992, 'knowledge is power, but power is also knowledge' (1992, 230). The new SSC blurs the analytical distinction between the North in the South and vice versa. BRICS as the 'global South' but also 'emerging powers' have the highest inequality levels in the world, yet to be addressed at the policy level, and many citizens, particularly peri-urban and rural areas, live below the poverty line (Bond 2018a; Magida 2018). At the same time, the facts and figures on North—South trade, investment and finance empirically demonstrate the continuance of colonial and post-colonial patterns of economic exploitation of the countries previously labeled 3rd World, semi-peripheral or peripheral (Arrighi 2007; Mohanty 2018; Ayers 2018; Bond 2018a). The redefinition of the North–South into 'global North and South' allows states like Russia and China to conceal geostrategic expansionist state strategies and rivalries, within an artificially created South–South frame called 'global South.' Such arbitrary dualism also adds grist to state-centric analyses that focus on how BRICS geostrategic strength as a bloc allows individual states to justify exploitative foreign policy measures and repressive domestic policies. More critical analysts agree that BRICS cuts away the hard-won gains on socioeconomic rights at the same time as it reinforces patterns of North—South domination (Mohanty 2018; Ayers 2018; Bond 2018a). The repressive/coercive/surveillance characteristics of BRICS are increasingly hard to ignore: China in administering social credit ratings, repression of activists in India, Russia, and in all likelihood, Bolsonaro's Brazil. The BRICS Think Tanks inability to grapple with developing the BRICS 'good governance frame' is fraught with dangerous consequences for society in general and activists in particular.

The validation of the official narrative occurs each year around the BRICS Summits through the Think Tanks. While attempting to retain legitimacy by asserting mild critique, the approaches that emerge from the Tanks endorse the lack of a development alternative. Magida (2018, 16), while otherwise critical in his analysis in the South African Think Tank publication *BRICS Academic Review*, is optimistic of the Bank, '...(t)he NDB... could offer the world not only a new way of doing business, but could also sow the seed of an alternative framing of the idea of development.' Buenaventura and Lucey (2018, 20) while mildly critical of the NDBs failure to deliver on promises of participation, add, '... the NDB offers the African continent promise of a new way of working that that is transformative, inclusive and participatory.'

Within the current conjuncture of social forces and processes in the world economic system, there is recognition from both liberal perspectives and more critical, Marxist, dependency, world system approaches that the Western developmental model is problematic and may even be the cause of the Modi/Temer/Bolsonaro effect, even more certainly for the Trump effect, on global geostrategic dynamics. Yet the 'problem' of development in the South is approached very differently from within the two framings. It is generally agreed that development progress, in both the North and South, is fraught with contagious global instability. Yet the dominant liberal economic model still holds onto the hope for developmental linearity at state level (Ayers 2018). This despite prevailing evidence in both the North and South, that capital crises are cyclical and more accurately predicted by critical GPE systems analysis (Harvey 2003; Arrighi 2007; Bond

2015; Lesufi and Thompson 2019). Added to this is the liberal conditionality that democratization is the *sine qua non* in terms of good governance
and development (Mohanty 2018; Ayers 2018). While bifurcated into two
distinct trajectories, both presuppose a linear progression toward being
globally recognized as 'developed.' Ayers points out,

> … (t)he highly specific notion of (neo)liberal democracy enjoined by the
> comparativists is located within a narrow conceptual framework based on a
> Weberian-Schumpeterian model of democracy, promulgated through Robert
> Dahl's conception of polyarchy…(s)ignificantly, comparativists presuppose a
> moral position (to) the notion of democracy… such a conception is heavily
> biased towards an understanding of democracy that is electorally based and
> highly elitist as well as "to some degree capitalist". (Ayers 2018, 3)

This morality to the liberal economic position is concealed in the technocratic policy discourse surrounding democratization and development,
which while stripping development and democracy to policy processes
(Crush 1995; Ferguson 1990; Mohanty 2018; Ayers 2018). The liberal
approach, even in its more critical variants, remains focused on the question
of tweaking development by refining expert knowledge (Mohanty 2018).

The 'Beyond Aid' discourse simply removes democracy and rights as
part of the 'no strings' aspect to IDA. IDA as a form of development
assistance focuses on technocratic flaws in applying the export-led growth
model of development, in addition to weighing up the economic and political 'science' of developmental choices relating to finance, trade and infrastructural investment in order to ensure better application of development
policies (Gomes and Esteves 2018).

The liberal bifurcation between the political and economic in terms of
policy creation leads to a discussion of foreign policy on the one hand and
economic development as a distinct policy set on the other. This type of
analysis is well illustrated by Alden and Schoeman who state that South
Africa's structural deficiencies, which include its inability to provide sufficient leadership on issues of security for example, hamper its aspirations as
regional and continental hegemon, yet,

> … (d)espite this weak record of effective leadership, Pretoria is continu-
> ally 'rewarded' with leadership positions in international groupings, such as
> BRICS, G20 and nearly consecutive terms on the UN Security Council. Far
> from being a reluctant hegemon, South African history is marked by a drive

to fulfil an ambition predicated on its 'manifest destiny' as Africa's leader. (Alden and Schoeman 2015, 241–42)

Here, the question of hegemony is defined in terms of the components of state structural power, but with the twist of adding the relational or following Joseph Nye, soft power (Strange 1988; Nye 2004). Alden and Schoeman (2015) emphasize that in South Africa's case, both forms of power are contingent on the state maintaining and enhancing its symbolic value to the North in terms of its geostrategic value and ability to act, and, as Bond (2015, 23) puts it, as an economic 'deputy sheriff' for the North. In addition, while South Africa does provide some IDA for the sub-Saharan region, it is by far the smallest of the BRICS in terms of growth, trade, and investment indicators.

For South Africa at state policy level, holding onto 'gateway' status to Africa in public development discourse is of great symbolic significance in foreign policy terms (Alden and Schoeman 2015). Maintaining the rhetoric of BRICS as an alternative has become a priority at Think Tank and government level, what the Head of the Think Tank describes as '... a distressing amount of cognitive dissonance as to the internal dynamics of BRICS.' Sitas describes the alternative that BRICS poses as follows,

> ...the BRICS initiative is beyond the obvious new trade winds – the creation of a world system with a cooperative set of relations, respectful of sovereignty and difference was appreciated... BRICS is not challenging the existing multilateral system, nor is it trying to subvert or create alternatives to the United Nations system's working institutions. What it is trying to do is to strengthen it, while at the same time create a multipolar framework for cooperation. How we understand the word "reconfiguration" must bear this in mind. (Sitas 2018, 16)

Sitas emphasizes the very weakness of the bloc: It is not challenging the global economic system, and indeed, it is enforcing the very patterns of North–South economic domination, in a different 'reconfiguration' and the alternative development policy frame supports the lack of any ideational differences to development.

BRICS Alternative Development as a Policy Construct

The OECD-DAC model is seen as an exemplar of the liberal good governance aid approach. BRICS, as part of the emerging powers solidarity network, is seen by some policy analysts (from both the left and right) as challenging the Northern developmental model, by bettering good governance as a frame by appealing to sovereignty. As Esteves and Gomes put it, '… the field of IDC as become a true battlefield in which the Western-centric discourse on international development grounded strongly in a belief in linear progress, has been questioned and defied' (Gomes and Esteves 2018, 138).

In hindsight, even liberal economic approaches recognize these distortions were often compounded by neoliberalism and the austerity policies that accompanied structural adjustment loans and their conditionalities. The approaches fail to go beyond a limiting discourse on how to mix the right combination of technocratic, expert knowledge, government capacity, and accountability, with infrastructural investment, industrialization, trade diversification, and technological innovation. Social and redistributive justice as concepts features largely in the local developmental discourse on participatory development (Mohanty 2018). This discourse has conceptual, theoretical, and policy limitations but does nonetheless emphasize inclusion of the marginalized, stressing that exclusion from the system of capitalist growth will entrench and extend economic inequalities. According to the critical liberal approach, good governance as a concept and as a way of configuring society can only be a myth if these distortions are not continually measured and addressed through increasingly reflexive and sophisticated policy innovations. From within this perspective, the notion of SSC is criticized because according to those involved in the policy debates,

> …the Global North wants the South to monetise cooperation to enable universal comparisons … the North calls for increased transparency, improved indicators and reliable statistics, but the South asks to respect its diversity of approaches. There is no unified position here either. Some developing countries, particularly in Asia, question the applicability of monitoring and evaluation to SSC. They also point out that the South needs to create its own monitoring vocabulary. Proponents of this view say that SSC is narrative and political, rather than institutional and practical. Therefore, it should be measured through case studies, not indicators…. (Turianskyi 2017)

Beyond Aid policy advocates interpret IDA innovations as enhanced by borrowing from international best practice, especially from examples in the South, and also from drawing on non-Western models and methods of South–South network building (Gu and Kitano 2018). Gomes and Esteves (2018, 129) refer to these 'new' SSC practices as '... the "BRICS effect" – an effect that ultimately destabilizes established positions and interaction patterns between agents.'

According to this perspective, the BRICS effect challenges the very concept of ODA, in particular, the unchanging and hierarchical donor and recipient relation. The adaptation of the Rostow's stages of development approach ensured that the North could determine the right policy paths and development trajectories for the less developed states in the South. According to Gomes and Esteves (2018), built into the OECD/DAC 'donorship credo' is a somewhat patronizing notion of responsibility in which 'advanced' or 'industrialized' economies determine the course for international development and (secondly) the societal welfare of developing states.

Esteves and Gomes refer to Bourdieu's conceptualization of this type of practical belief/knowledge as '*doxa*.'

> *Doxa* ultimately enables agency, generates classificatory schemas, structures positions, and guides practices, which become naturalized over time (Bigo 2011). In this sense in terms of development and good governance, ODA has become the main doxic practice of the North. While contingent and arbitrary, ODA transformed development into a set of fixed choices, "necessary requirements" that conditioned the differences between North and South and the parameters of what is considered to this day as developed and underdeveloped in liberal economic terms. (McEwan and Mawdsley 2012)

Gu and Kitano (2018, 5) argue in a similar way that

> ... (t)his has led governments, practitioners, and academics alike to ask whether it is indeed time to move development policy and practice 'beyond aid'. As noted above, this term is best understood in terms of the evolution and application of a broader notion of development assistance to embrace wider economic development and sustainable growth, including multilateralised financing, premised on principles equity, inclusivity, and partnership. At the centre of this evolution, China and other emerging powers have emerged as critical players... (f)rom discourse to cooperation modalities to new institutions, the emerging powers have served as an influential drivers of shifting

development paradigms (Qobo and Soko 2015). Furthermore, as a result of its overseas activity, development finance has diversified beyond official development assistance (ODA), entering recipient countries through other channels such as investment and trade.

The BRICS Think Tanks also claim a normative-ideational, if not explicitly ideological, distinctness from the North in relation to the development of economic policy. Transformation is still framed in very general, policy terms, for example '… (t)he long term BRICS vision is committed to exploring and shaping new modes of global governance that shall strive to achieve more equitable development and inclusive growth' (SABTT 2018).

Criticism of the BRICS is countered by the Think Tanks in terms of North-South ideological differences. The 2018 SABTT Agenda Setting Concept note illustrates this well,

> It is often said that BRICS is all about a self-serving agenda and a new way of harnessing an existing (or emerging) status quo or worse still, in creating a new rapacious status quo that will deplete the world of all resources, it has increasingly been receiving bad press in the dominant economic journals and newspapers in the USA and Britain, which continue to define the discourse for much of the world. From the Financial Times Steve Johnson asserting 'the BRICS are dead, long live the Ticks'(South Africa, Brazil and Russia out, Taiwan and South Korea in)… to the creation by the Economist of special blogs: China beyond BRICS, Brazil beyond BRICS etc…. (d)espite this negativity from the thought leaders of the North, the initiative continues to gain in strength and the array of projects and programmes under its auspices are increasing exponentially. Since it will be South Africa's turn to steer in 2018, how do we help co-steer such a reconfiguration on a virtuous path, not only to silence the constant criticisms about the initiative but to ask the deeper question: towards which ends or goals? (SABTT 2018)

Despite these defenses, the reality is that in the BRICS states, high levels of inequality and economic marginalization of poor communities are endemic. The BRICS states in the South not only fail to regulate the more exploitative aspects of global capital accumulation but also tend to enforce these patterns (Zhang 2017; Bond 2018a). This is evident by the gaps between the growth and development aspects of most of the BRICS trade and investment bilateral agreements.

While trade and investment among the BRICS states is very uneven, and managed through bilateral, rather than multilateral agreements, Amisi et al.

(2015) and Bond (2018a, b) provide numerous examples of their exploitative trade and investment patterns in the southern African region. This evidence highlights that the BRICS states (China in particular) advance the agenda of globalized economic liberalism, to legitimate market access. Critics of Chinese investment show that much of what Chinese bilateral forms of investment in Africa and South Africa demonstrate similar patterns of extractivism to those of the former colonizers. Amisi et al. (2015, 89) refer to this as '… accumulation by dispossession… (China) promot(es) the construction of railways, bridges ports… this infrastructure is often indistinguishable from colonial era projects meant to more quickly extract primary products for the world market.' These exploitative trends in Chinese trade and investment are not restricted to southern Africa.

BRICS rhetoric also emphasizes the development of local skills leading to stronger employment base where skills acquisition can occur in more geographically less developed areas. In support of these claims, Chinese success in developing the export zones such the Shenzhen SEZ in Guangdong Province in the 1970s is cited in relation to the growth in China's GDP and the creation of millions of jobs in the three decades thereafter that Shenzhen flourished.

IDA/IDC and SSC in Africa

The BRICS IDA/IDC and SSC positions are best to be described as a state diplomacy approach to development and aid, largely devoid of any theoretical or policy framing. It carries within the epistemological construction of development as a science and foreign policy as the realm of Realpolitik. It contains tenets of development that persist from Industrial Revolution in Britain until the present day, as quoted by President Harry S. Truman at the end of World War II,

> … greater production is the key to prosperity and peace. And the key to greater production is a wider and more vigorous application of modern scientific and technical knowledge. (Mohanty 2018, 7)

Escobar (1995) underlies that this application of scientific and technical knowledge requires experts and institutions to plan for the progress of society. In BRICS, these experts preside in the Think Tanks and in the NDB. Here, the BRICS bloc claims to be in the process of constructing not just an alternative vision of development, but an alternative policy framework for SSC. The lack of economic content to the 'Beyond Aid' debate is evident from its policy application in Africa and especially in the case of the BRICS 'leader,' South Africa.

One of the main development policy strategies that have been promoted as part of BRICS IDA, through China, is the establishment of special economic zones in BRICS states to address the problem of reliance on undiversified exports. The 2018 BRICS Summit Declaration (2018, 10) refers to export zones as priority development areas along with, '... establish(ing) BRICS networks of Science Parks.' FOCAC 2018 echoes the same focus on export-led growth through SEZs as a way of attracting FDI (FOCAC 2018).

The evidence of the influence of Chinese development assistance on South Africa has been in plain view for last five years. Rob Davies, Minister of the DTI and a member of the South African Communist Party (SACP) stated in 2015, 'China is one of South Africa's strategic partners... we need also to derive value from our cooperation with China on SEZs, particularly as we embark on our industrialization and beneficiation programmes' (http://www.southafrica.info/business/Chinese-South-Africa-trade, December 5, 2015; http://www.gov.za/sa-delegation-attend-SEZs, Seminar-in-China, May 10, 2016).

The SA-China Economic and Trade Association (Saceta) 2016 Report emphasizes (unsurprisingly) that South Africa requires increased infrastructure investment, in power and railways in particular. It boasts of China's success in the use of industrial and scientific parks and special economic zones, and this form of export-led development trajectory has been accepted by the DTI, as evident from interviews and the 2017 DTI SEZ Report (Klassen 2018). Such initiatives would improve production capacity, facilitate complementary transfers of technologies and skills, and utilize Africa's significant market capacity and relatively low labor costs.

China has driven the establishment of SEZs in BRICS over recent years. South Africa's regulatory environment offers some protection to workers. For example, minimum wage standards still apply within the zones, and trade unions activity is tolerated. In 2017/2018, the Beijing Automotive International Corporation (BAIC) invested R11 billion in the Coega SEZ. This investment has drawn attention back to the 'success' of Coega, and in 2016, Coega SEZ won DTI's parastatal of the year award as a result (Vilakasi, Brand and Corporate Communications CEO, Coega Development Corporation Interview, August 31, 2017). In 2018, Chinese Ambassador Lin Songtian declared Coega the most successful SEZ in Africa.

China is also the main funder of the establishment of the Musina-Makhado SEZ, in Limpopo Province, a significant investment initiative that indicates the shift toward combining IDA knowledge transfer with FDI. At FOCAC 2018, Ramaphosa entered into a much-publicized agreement with Bank of China for a US$1.1 billion (R15 billion) investment into SEZs and industrial parks. In tandem, the DTI also struck a deal with the National Development and Reform Commission of the People's Republic of China, targeting the Musina-Makhado SEZ. Underlining the lack of commitment to sustainable development in practice, the deal includes the construction of a 4.600 MW coal-fired power plant and investments in stainless steel plants and ferrochromium/manganese plants. According to Limpopo Premier Stan Mathabatha, the investment in Limpopo will be worth around $10 billion. Mathabatha maintains that the SEZ will benefit the 'people of South Africa' because it promises to employ 21,000 people. Given the area it will cover (60 km), it is bound also to have some environmental and livelihoods impact (Makone 2018).

Despite the rigorously enforced official BRICS and FOCAC narrative and corresponding pro-China arguments on trade and investment leading to value chains and product diversification, South Africa's trade with China and with BRICS consists of the export of primary products and the imports of final products. Where value is added in SEZs, the bulk of the profits is mostly remitted to the country of origin (Bond 2018a, b). Even more liberal orientated policy analysts such as Sheldon et al. (2017, 28) conclude that this has serious implications for South Africa's focus on industrial development and export promotion of value-added production and trade.

South Africa's SEZ success story, Coega, provides the perfect example of the gaps between development rhetoric and the desperate situation in which most communities remain mired. This is illustrated by the failure to generate more than the minimum of permanent employment opportunities over the 17 years of Coega's existence, at the staggering estimated cost per post of R1.2 million or US$86,000. At the same time, as in the rest of Africa, most of the communities in the areas surrounding the SEZ are unemployed or underemployed, and most of the social reproduction costs are carried by women. Most of the men employed in the SEZ from the main township areas are provided with skills through Coega's development program that ensure they remain underemployed, for example bricklaying, and learn to drive courses (DTI 2015).

These statistics call to question whether the success of SEZs in China and in South-East Asia is replicable (Yejoo 2013; Brautigam and Tang 2011, 2012). Despite Coega marketing, the unemployment statistics in the greater Port Elizabeth area show that the zone is failing to measure up to the skills and employment creation promises made at policy design level (NMBM 2017). Coega is hailed as the SEZ success story of Africa, yet most communities in the Nelson Mandela Bay Municipality lack the skills required to be able to take up more professionalized wage positions in the zones.

Coega's lack of success illustrates that, in the absence of extensive job creation and appropriate skills development, the IDA form of development assistance will exacerbate the exploitative, extractivist investment practices that characterize BRICS and Chinese FDI throughout the continent. Coega may be a good example of the potential for state corporations and private business to create the impression of the flourishing of South—South cooperation, despite the realities for local communities.

SUMMARIZING THE POLICY CONTENT OF BEYOND AID

Reflecting on the links between the narrative and policy, it is clear that 'Beyond AID' as an alternative to Western development aid is simply a form of policy fairy story that endorses bilateral forms of IDA where China negotiates the terms of win-win, so as to modify the flows of commodity and capital extraction from BRICS states. The Belt and Road Initiative (BRI) assists in spatially linking these flows. The model is still based on the Western developmental model that prioritizes linearity in development through industrialization toward greater economic capacity as defined in corporate capital terms (be these SoEs or private).

The Beyond Aid package of policies does the following:

- Decenters/removes democracy and social justice from the South—South International Development Aid narrative;
- Links all associations with the concept of good governance with Western paternalism and prescriptive development policy strategies;
- Constructs IDA as an alternative to Western developmental ideology and policy;
- Enforces an arbitrary construction of Global South that is tenuously geostrategically anchored;
- Reshapes trade, aid, and investment policies in favor of China;

- Constructs a new policy narrative of development that challenges critique on the basis of being pro-South and anti-North;
- Is still nonetheless based on the Western notion of linearity/progress;
- Conceals economic domination through the narrative on the non-conditionality of concessional loans that must still be repaid.

Despite these evident flaws, the evidence of the growing strength of the official BRICS narrative is plain to see in the aftermath of BRICS 2018 in Johannesburg and FOCAC 2018 in Beijing. As Esteves is quoted earlier reminding us, power is knowledge and the power to shape knowledge of development through IDA is an under-estimated feature of 'soft power.'

Missing Bricks: BRICS Alternative 'Inclusive Development'

A range of authors (Sitas 2018; Gomes and Esteves 2018; Gu and Kitano 2018; Thomas 2018, and others) support the official BRICS discourse on alternative development insofar as it represents a different model of aid, trade, and investment that breaks from the prescriptions and paternalism of the North. The South–South cooperation perspectives place emphasis on OECD/DAC/IMF/World Bank biased conditionalities attached to good governance, but also to austerity measures that affect the poor the most. These perspectives are also critical of the liberal economic standpoint, in that it ticks the boxes in terms of the types of development narratives of the likes of Christine Lagarde, the CEO of the IMF endorse.

Yet, if the BRICS policies on inclusive, collective, and economic development are broken down into its component parts, it would comprise the following:

- Growth (measured by GNP and GDP);
- Industrialization;
- Manufacturing and the creation of value chains (preferably through FDI);
- Export-led growth, boosted by FDI;
- Equity in the global economic system, in WTO terms, minimal or no tariff-based protectionism on imports, in particular, the main trading partners of BRICS states, the United States and the EU.

Skills and employment creation usually make it onto the BRICS inclusive development list. Rather like tomatoes or lettuce being added to a fast-food burger, these are tokenistically healthy in the eyes of the state and corporate elite players. It is clear in the implementation of BRICS policies that encouraging local skills and employment creation are not considered essential to the actual consumption of BRICS IDA.

Equally, the alternative model lacks the following policy elements:

- Policy content to the inclusivity promised at local levels of development;
- Democratic content, including a non-tokenistic attempt to include gender;
- Skills diversification as a collective (as opposed to national) policy component in Beyond Aid model;
- Recognition of the weaknesses of stronger economy (China) and its reliance on the United States;
- Redistributive policy components to deal with market failures.

On the last point, Mohanty in her incisive new book *Democratising Development—Struggles for Rights and Social Justice in India* reminds us that India's democratic development trajectory from early on included the concept of social justice. This state-led economic development approach (enforced by social forces and movements) recognized the need for redistributive policies and programs to ensure inclusion and redistribution of the benefits of development to the marginalized (Mohanty 2018, 3–5). Although India's democratic development trajectory has been far from linear, like Brazil, both states have robust policy examples of such social justice initiatives, for example, in India, the National Rural Employment Guarantee Act (NREGA) and associated policies, that has over the years, provided socioeconomic support for millions of the poor in India, and in Brazil, the Bolsa Familia program (Mohanty 2018).

Yet, BRICS as an alternative development approach poses threats to both procedural and distributive socioeconomic justice at a time when these forms of development are already under threat (Mohanty 2018, 2; Bond 2018a, b). The notion of development as a transformational force has been subverted by multiple centers of power and politics. While the marginalized do not accept these power dynamics quietly, the battle for resources and redistributive justice is endemic and the ideological content of the battle is not always shared or clear. In Brazil, India and South Africa social mobilization has been critical to democratizing development from below (Mohanty 2018, 5). Part of the problem with the entire development debate is that it has become a system of control. International development conceals, mostly poorly, a broader economic project: economic domination.

Bond (2015, 20) and Zhang (2017) draw on Marxist and dependency framings of global systemic economic domination to theorize that the expansion of the global capitalist system to include BRICS as regional gendarmes reframes historical moments of imperialism of the Industrial Revolution expansionism and forms of global systemic socioeconomic exploitation (e.g., Arrighi et al. 1989, 1999; Harvey 1982, 2003). It is not hard to find empirical evidence to support this claim, although of course many contingencies create a reconfigured, complex global economic system. Certain economic features remain the same. The core of the (neo)imperialism debate is that capitalism needs to expand to avoid crises of over-accumulation. State 'gendarmes' or deputies in the semi-periphery facilitate this expansion, as the same systemic economic fault lines manifest in their own economies, that are codependent on the historically imperialist powers. While their roles may differ in each regional (hinterland) context, they nonetheless play a role of both enforcing their own (usually somewhat precarious) political and economic hegemonic status by ensuring that global, nation-state (SoEs), and corporate elites are able to prioritize profit maximization. In this sense, the question mark raised by pro-China analysts as to South Africa's retaining its 'gateway' (gendarme) status in BRICS is both carrot and stick (Gu and Kitano 2018). In order for the government to ensure the symbolic hegemonic role referred to earlier, and to increase the ability of SOEs and South African corporates to extend their profit-making ventures into Africa, Chinese development policy narratives require deep assimilation into state development policies.

In Conclusion, the BRICS Transformatory Development Policy Agenda?

China's ideational influence on BRICS has been to promote what Kitano (2018) refers to as Da Yaunzhu or Grande Aid, drawing and adapting the Japanese model of trade, infrastructural investment (non-traditional aid) and imports that expanded its influence post-World War II, to include a more globalist reach, through the BRI. Chinese Da Yaunzhu decenters, in fact removes, democracy and social justice concepts from the form of aid altogether in favor of the policy slogans 'win-win,' mutual benefit and equitable South–South cooperation (BRICS 2018; FOCAC 2018).

The analysis confirms that the 'Beyond Aid' debate simply provides further legitimacy for BRICS authoritarian regimes and paradoxically and provides further grist to the North to argue that the BRICS alternative is a backward, 'anti-democratic' debate. The no strings attached nature of BRICS IDA is the Faustian twist, and the gains of rights-based movements may be lost along the way.

The chapter illustrates that, paradoxically, in terms of South Africa and Africa BRICS may further enforce the economic and geostrategic hegemony of the North through the Chinese led IDA 'Beyond Aid' form of development collaboration. A related, equally disturbing aspect is what could be called a 'captured' BRICS official development narrative. The BRICS development alternative is used to mask global adaptations of forms of capitalist economic exploitation under the guise of a new configuration of state forces referred to as the Global South.

This is not to endorse the conditionalities attached to OECD/DAC IMF/World/Bank development aid—these are unquestionably paternalistic, controlling and ultimately hugely detrimental to redistributive justice. BRICS as a bloc could work toward transformatory development that prioritizes redistributive justice, if the alternative development content of policies is re-orientated toward social justice and the transformation of the marginalization of the poor under existing development policies to focus on livelihoods and sustainability. It is unlikely that this will originate at state level. As Bond and Garcia (2015, 4) state, '… (t)he critical question for the future is whether social struggles in each of the BRICS countries will discover linkages of solidarity between peoples, on the basis of reversing the path of the elites and creating paths for another kind of development'.

Transformatory development policies, either within the context of SSC that prioritizes redistributive justice or nationally, occur through contestation and struggle (Crush 1995; Thompson and Tapscott 2010; Bond and Garcia 2015; Ayers 2018; Mohanty 2018). The official BRICS development policy narrative, described above, requires collective solidarity and resistance among the transnational collectivity known as 'BRICS from below.' Grassroots social forces and social movements that forge transnational solidarities and national and local resistances to exploitation and super-exploitation in the name of development are essential to redistributive justice. It is only through these resistances that the hope for development alternatives reflecting the realities of the excluded of the South will emerge.

REFERENCES

Alden, Chris, and Maxi Schoeman. 2015. "South Africa's Symbolic Hegemony in Africa." *International Politics* 52 (2): 239–54.

Alvares, C. 1992. "Science." In *The Development Dictionary: A Guide to Knowledge as Power*, edited by Wolfgang Sachs, 219–32. London: Zed Books.

Amisi, Baruti, Patrick Bond, Richard Kamidza, Farai Maguwu, and Bobby Peek. 2015. "BRICS Corporate Snapshots During African Extractivism." In *BRICS: An Anti-capitalist Critique*, edited by Patrick Bond and Ana Garcia, 86. London: Pluto Press.

Arrighi, Giovanni. 2007. *Adam Smith in Beijing*. London: Verso.

Arrighi, Giovanni, Terence Hopkins, and Immanuel Wallerstein. 1989. *Antisystemic Movements*. London: Verso.

Arrighi, Giovanni, Beverley Silver, and Iftikhar Ahmed. 1999. *Chaos and Governance in the Modern World Systems*. Minneapolis: University of Minnesota Press.

Ayers, Alison. 2018. *A Global Political Economy of Democratisation: Beyond the Internal-External Divide*. London: Routledge.

Bello, Waldo. 2006. "China and Southeast Asia: Emerging Problems in an Economic Relationship." *Focus on Global South*. Last modified January 12, 2011. http://www.focusweb.org/node/1096.

Bigo, Didier. 2011. "Pierre Bourdieu and International Relations: Power of Practices, Practices of Power." *International Political Sociology* 5 (3): 225–58.

Bond, Patrick. 2015. "BRICS and the Sub-imperial Location." In *BRICS: An Anti-capitalist Critique*, edited by Patrick Bond and Ana Garcia, 15–26. London: Pluto Press.

Bond, Patrick. 2018a. "Can the BRICS Re-open the 'Gateway to Africa'? South Africa's Contradictory Facilitation of Divergent Brazilian-Russian-Indian-Chinese Interests." In *Africa and External Actors*, edited by Charles Mutasa and Dawn Nagar. Cape Town: CCR Publication.

Bond, Patrick. 2018b. "Ecological-Economic Narratives for Resisting Extractive Industries in Africa." In *Environmental Impacts of Transnational Corporations in the Global South*, edited by Paul Cooney and William Sacher, 73–110. Bradford: Emerald Group Publishing.

Bond, Patrick, and Ana Garcia, eds. 2015. *BRICS: An Anti-capitalist Critique*. London: Pluto Press.

Brautigam, Deborah, and Xiaoyang Tang. 2011. "African Shenzen: China's Special Economic Zones in Africa." *Journal of Modern Africa Studies* 49 (1): 27–54.

Brautigam, Deborah, and Xiaoyang Tang. 2012. "Economic Statecraft in China's New Overseas Special Economic Zones: Soft Power, Business or Resource Security?" *International Affairs* 88 (4): 799–816.

BRICS. 2018. "10th BRICS Summit Johannesburg Declaration." http://www.brics2018.org.za/sites/default/files/Documents/JOHANNESBURG%20DECLARATION%20-%2026%20JULY%202018%20as%20at%2007h11.pdf.

Buenaventura, Marianne, and Amanda Lucey. 2018. "What Is New About the New Development Bank?" *BRICS Academic Review*, July 5. https://www.nihss.ac.za/sites/default/files/BRICS/BRICS_Academic_Review.pdf.

Crush, Jonathan. 1995. "Introduction, Imagining Development." In *The Power of Development*, edited by Jonathan Crush. London: Routledge.

Dooley, B. 2018. *China's Xi offers $60bn Africa aid, says 'no strings attached.'* https://www.dailymaverick.co.za/article/2018-09-03-chinas-xi-offers-60-bn-africa-aid-says-no-strings-attached/.

DTI. 2015. *SEZ Performance Analysis Bulletin.* Johannesburg: DTI.

Escobar, Arturo. 1995. "Imagining a Post-development Era." In *The Power of Development*, edited by Jonathan Crush. London: Routledge.

Ferguson, James. 1990. *The Anti-politics Machine, 'Development', Depoliticization and Development in Lesotho.* Cambridge: Cambridge University Press.

FOCAC. 2018. "Summit Declaration 2018." https://www.focac.org/eng/zywx_1/zywj.

Gomes, Geovana Zoccal, and Paulo Esteves. 2018. "The BRICS Effect: Impacts of South-South Cooperation in the Social Field of International Development Cooperation." In *Beyond Aid—The Future of Development Cooperation*, edited by Jing Gu and Naohiro Kitano, 129–45. IDS Bulletin.

Gu, Jing, and Naohiro Kitano. 2018. "Introduction: Beyond Aid—The Future of Development Cooperation." *IDS Bulletin* 49 (3): 1–12.

Harvey, David. 1982. *The Limits to Capital.* London: Verso.

Harvey, David. 2003. *The New Imperialism.* Oxford: Oxford University Press.

Kitano, Naohiro. 2018. "Estimating China's Foreign Aid Using New Data." In *Beyond Aid—The Future of Development Cooperation*, edited by Jing Gu and Naohiro Kitano, 49–72. IDS Bulletin.

Klassen, Thami. 2018. "Special Economic Zones." Department of Trade and Industry. Interview, March 19.

Lesufi, Ishmael, and Lisa Thompson. 2019. "China in Africa: South-South Solidarity or Imperialism in the 21st Century?" In *Contention, Assimilation and Co-optation*, edited by Justin Van der Merwe, Patrick Bond, and Nicole Dodd. London: Zed Books.

Lipton, Merle. 2017. "Are the BRICS Reformers, Revolutionaries or Counter-Revolutionaries?" *South African Journal for International Affairs* 24 (1): 41–59.

Magida, Soya. 2018 "BRICS Must Address Injustices at Home Before It Can Fix the World." *BRICS Academic Review*, July 5. https://www.nihss.ac.za/sites/default/files/BRICS/BRICS_Academic_Review.pdf.

Makone, Thabo. 2018. "Ramaphosa Strikes Deals in China to Bring Jobs, Factories to Musina-Makhado Corridor." *Sunday Times*, September 3. https://www.timeslive.co.za/politics/2018-09-03-ramaphosa-strikes-deals-in-china-to-bring-jobs-factories-to-musina-makhado-corridor/.

McEwan, Cheryl, and Emma Mawdsley. 2012. "Trilateral Development Co-operation, Power and Politics in Emerging Aid Relationships." *Development and Change* 43 (6): 1185–209.

Mohanty, Ranjita. 2018. *Democratizing Development: Struggles for Rights and Social Justice in India*. New Delhi: Sage.

Mosoetsa, Sarah. 2018. "Introduction." *BRICS Academic Review*, July 5. https://www.nihss.ac.za/sites/default/files/BRICS/BRICS_Academic_Review.pdf.

Nelson Mandela Bay Municipality (NMBM). 2017. "Integrated Development Plan (IDP)." https://www.nelsonmandelabay.gov.za/datarepository/documents/nmbm-integrated-development-plan-idp-second-edition-2018-19.pdf.

Nye, Joseph. 2004. *Soft Power: The Means to Success in World Politics*. New York: PublicAffairs.

Qobo, Mzukisi, and Mills Soko. 2015. "The Rise of Emerging Powers in the Global Development Finance Architecture: The Case of the BRICS and the New Development Bank." *South African Journal of International Affairs* 22 (3): 277–88. https://doi.org/10.1080/10220461.2015.1089785.

Sheldon, Mark, Willemien Viljoen, Talkmore Chidede, and Ron Sandrey. 2017. "BRIC-Africa Trade—Is It All About China's Trade with South Africa." Tralac Working Paper No. S17WP11/2017.

Sitas, Ari. 2018. "Reconfiguring the World System." *BRICS Academic Review* 1: 87–91.

South African BRICS Think Tank (SABTT). 2018. *Agenda Setting Concept Note*. Johannesburg: SABTT.

Strange, Susan. 1988. *States and Markets*. London: Pinter Press.

Thakur, Ramesh. 2014. "How Representative Are BRICS?" *Third World Quarterly* 35 (10): 1791–808.

Thomas, Ngangam. 2018. "Merging Tracks from Academia to Real Politik." *BRICS Academic Forum Review*, 2.

Thompson, Lisa, and Chris Tapscott, eds. 2010. *Citizens and Social Movements: Perspectives from the Global South*. London: Zed Books.

Thompson, Lisa, and Pamela Tsolekile de Wet. 2017. "BRICS Development Strategies: Exploring the Meaning of BRICS 'Community' and 'Collective Action' in the Context of BRICS State Led Cooperation in South Africa." *Chinese Political Science Review* 2 (1): 101–13.

Turianskyi, Yarik. 2017. "Beyond the Numbers: Measuring South-South Coopera-tion." *SAIIA Programme*, October 24. https://saiia.org.za/research/beyond-the-numbers-measuring-south-south-cooperation/.

Weiss, Thomas, and Adriana Erthal Abdenur. 2014. "Introduction: Emerging Pow-ers and the UN—What Kind of Development Partnership?" *Third World Quar-terly* 35 (10): 1749–58.

Yejoo, Kim. 2013. "Chinese-led SEZs in Africa: Are They a Driving Force of China's Soft Power?" Discussion Paper 1, Centre for Chinese Studies.

Zhang, Xin. 2017. "Chinese Capitalism and the Maritime Silk Road: A World Systems Perspective." *Geopolitics* 22 (2): 310–31.

CHAPTER 4

International Development Assistance: A Case Study of Brazil, a Member of the BRICS

Rogerio F. Pinto

INTRODUCTION

Transformations of the global economic and geopolitical order brought on at the dawn of the twenty-first century have had an effect on development assistance (DA) (Pinto 2013). Many emerging economies, among them those of the BRICS have come to aspire to global recognition, asserting themselves in their own right as emerging powers, leaders in their regions, and seeking sources of soft power by means of becoming players in the development assistance marketplace.[1] While some countries assert their identity on nationalistic grounds enhanced by DA on a bilateral basis, others seek to harness the dividends of globalization as a vehicle to assist lagging countries by bringing them into the global marketplace and community. Established rules of international relations among nation-states drive the approach to DA by the former, whereas the latter are driven by the emerging and still imperfect global governance (Kumar and Messner 2011, 8–9).

R. F. Pinto (✉)
International Consultant, Washington, DC, USA

© The Author(s) 2020   59
J. A. Puppim de Oliveira and Y. Jing (eds.), *International Development Assistance and the BRICS*, Governing China in the 21st Century,
https://doi.org/10.1007/978-981-32-9644-2_4

In the wake of global economic and geopolitical shifts, international development assistance has radically changed in character and scope. Critics describe today's aid architecture as "fragmented," overly complex, inefficient, and ineffective. The increasing numbers of emerging economies (EEs) as donors with their own goals and mechanisms have created an operational challenge increasingly difficult to manage. As DA goes from functional collective action to dysfunctional hyper-collective action, costs rise, efficiencies are lost, and intended benefits diminish overall.[2] An important contribution to resolving this complexity, alleviating its adverse effects would be to profile the DA landscape, by better grasping the roles, styles, and performance of these new donors.

As this increment adds to the complexity of the development assistance landscape, it will be crucial for the BRICS to invest more in the rational design and management of in- and outflows of DA and their governance. Most importantly, this design must be specifically consistent with the nature of the public goods now being transacted in international DA. In the current international geopolitical setting, and given the nature of threats and challenges to the international order and welfare, there is a premium on international public goods, which compete with national public goods in the international assistance marketplace (see Pinto and Puppim de Oliveira 2011).[3] Some observers, however, might argue that the increased focus on critical global public goods may displace the focus on lagging countries which attach a higher priority to their national public goods, hence creating a dilemma for DA which is increasingly concerned with the former.[4]

Despite these challenges, emerging countries, such as the BRICS, have gained prominence in the DA environment, adding to its diversity and innovativeness.[5] They are part of a larger group of countries that share certain key features: middle income, large and relatively large populations, representing a significant share of global GNP, and most importantly influential in their respective regions. None are members of OECD, while being members of the G-20.[6] These countries have become more active as both recipients and donors in bilateral DA transactions and have brought pressure to bear on the governing boards of multilateral aid organizations. Brazil in particular has favored its role in multilateral organizations, the destination of a large share of its official Development Assistance resources (Manning 2006; Kharas 2008).[7]

In order to frame the narrative of Brazil's experience with development assistance both in-and-out, a set of key conceptual questions are formulated, contributing to building a framework of pre-theoretical principles which might be helpful in understanding the dilemma of countries in similar situations. As we attempt to answer these questions with respect to the Brazilian case, it is hoped that a pre-theoretical conceptual framework may be derived.[8] These principles/questions and their answers are interspersed throughout the case study, as they regard Brazil's DA experience. It is hoped that this experience might also inform other emerging donors as they shape their own policies and institutional arrangements as suppliers and/or recipients of DA and partners in TCDC. Furthermore, the study also seeks to inspire them on how to navigate the increasing complexity of the DA environment.

As Brazil developed over recent years and has gained in geopolitical standing, it has become a provider of DA while continuing to receive it on a more cooperative basis from larger donors (N/S), partners and especially from multilateral organizations.[9] At the same time, it has become a key player in South–South DA among developing countries: Technical Cooperation among Developing Countries (TCDC).

Can N/S assistance coexist with S/S TCDC? Are they harmonious or do they clash? Can a recipient of N/S assistance also be a participant in TCDC?
Brazilian TCDC experience and strategy lead it to distance itself from the N/S model of international assistance and to reject the principles of the Paris resolution on Aid Effectiveness. The given reason for this position is that Brazil is not a donor country in the OECD sense. An official source states that Brazil's practice of TCDC coexists with its role as a recipient because it is still a developing country and continues to rely on N/S assistance. "They operate on different tracks", the source added.

This brief case study seeks to elicit this emerging country's experience by examining the evolution of its DA, its current trends, and the role of its lead agency, the ABC. By highlighting its comparative advantages and weaknesses, it provides a basis for a comparison with other country cases. It is hoped that the Brazilian experience may also inform other emerging donors as they shape their own policies and institutional arrangements as donors and/or recipients of DA and partners in TCDC. Furthermore, the study seeks to inspire them on how to navigate the increasing complexity of the DA environment.

CONCEPTUAL FRAMEWORK AND HISTORICAL BACKGROUND

International Development Assistance over time has been defined with respect to its sponsors: bilateral, trilateral and multilateral; but most importantly by its evolution and focus. Starting as a gap-filling resource to underdeveloped countries—which lagged in investment and skill capacities—filled by *financial and technical assistance* from bilateral or multilateral donors, it then moved to cover gaps in human welfare such as in education and health, acquiring a social/humanitarian and redistributive focus, by focusing on poverty reduction. More recently, it encompassed the critical reformulation of development policy by way of structural adjustment inspired in a liberal political/economic framework emerging from Western countries, mainly the USA and UK. Due to the discomfort of recipients with the uneven duality of *donor* and *recipient*, the politically correct concept of "partners" was adopted, despite the persistent power differential between the two, making for an uneven "partnership."

What is gained/lost by abandoning the concept of "donor and recipient of aid" (as articulated in N/S Aid models), as one embraces the more egalitarian notion of "partners who cooperate to achieve their mutual development" (as articulated by the TCDC model)?

Instead of a superior/inferior relationship between a donor and a recipient, the partnership is more harmonious, egalitarian and implies equal rights and mutual respect. To the detriment of the receiving party, what may be lost is the unavoidable differential between the party that needs/receives the assistance and the one that provides it. There are no donors and recipients in TCDC, only partners.

Through the UN-sponsored Buenos Aires Conference of 1978, the term Technical Cooperation between Developing Countries (TCDC) further deemphasized the notion of technical assistance as coined by the North donors, which were seen by some as neocolonialist.[10] Horizontality, solidarity, self-reliance, sustainability, respect for national sovereignty and authority became the main pillars of TCDC partnerships. By the end of the twentieth century, the term Technical Assistance was out and Technical Cooperation firmly in the lexicon of development assistance, and substantial resources started to flow from within this community of DA.[11]

Has the adoption of N/S assistance affected the flows of aid? Do the N/S practices really reflect colonialist attitudes and trample on recipient country sovereignty, authority and fail to show solidarity with recipients?
The Brazil case shows no evidence indicating that TCDC partnerships have benefitted more either partner from its assistance than its traditional N/S donor assistance. In fact resources for TCDC have shrunk considerably. Likewise of its sovereignty having been trampled on when it was the beneficiary of N/S assistance, mainly from the US. Yet by adopting the TCDC model of international assistance. Official statements of ABC reflect an explicit rejection of any policies that fail to recognize the sovereignty of its recipient or partner countries. Interestingly, it places itself as a recipient in regards to aid received by North donors, but does not consider itself donor vis a vis its partners of TCDC.

As a by-product of the non-alignment movement in the international order of the late 1970s—enabled by the UN—South/South Cooperation emerged as a challenge to N/S Assistance.[12] Clearly, the S/S model had ideological overtones reflecting the shifts in global geopolitics. However, the growing needs of the poor South did not abate, and increasing pressure for development assistance from the North persisted, as it was realized that the "light" Technical Cooperation modality did not go far enough in addressing the dire needs of developing countries in economic and humanitarian distress.[13] Furthermore, the type of assistance needed by the poor South required a volume of resources that other developing countries simply were not capable of bringing to the table within the framework of TCDC.

What is gained or lost by segmenting international aid by N/S and S/S. Is it only an illustrative categorization or are they mutually exclusive in their practices?
By staying away from N/S donors, developing countries with needs that may be met by international assistance are foregoing an important source of assistance. By welcoming TCDC, developing countries are gaining other development partners and strengthening their solidarity ties. Brazil seems to have been treading both paths, although advocating TCDC, which an official source says is not "a form of aid but a feature of its foreign policy".

The worldwide economic woes of the eighties saw a retraction of aid flows from the North, replaced with an aid-induced economic liberalization of lagging economies of the south.[14] Multilateral development banks, led by the Breton Woods entities, ushered in the era of structural adjustment as the foundation of N/S development assistance. "Trade not aid" and better economic governance were the preferred mottos that set the tone for the kind of cooperation being advocated, alongside with responsible fiscal policy.

As a result of the fatigue and discrediting of the Washington Consensus paradigm, multilateral agencies shifted the focus of aid to poverty reduction/eradication, with social programs at their core. In parallel, multilaterals returned to an assistance mode focusing on capacity building, institutional development, and good governance as essential companions of structural adjustment. It was common, at the time, for structural adjustment loans and grants from multilaterals to be combined with technical assistance projects focusing on these three elements (Berg 1993).[15] The emergence of information technology innovations with their hardware and software advances called for equivalent innovations in "human ware," hence the emphasis on assistance to develop human capital.

Still as part of the focus on financial assistance as the motor of development, the Monterrey Consensus recommended to DAC of OECD the creation in 2003 of a working group on Aid Effectiveness. This group put in place the High-Level Forum on Aid Effectiveness of 2006 which issued the Paris Declaration on Aid Effectiveness, now a landmark standard in the operational conceptualization of International Aid as practiced mostly by the aid giving developed countries of the North, as per the N/S model. While some 130 countries attended this important event, not all ratified it and subscribed to its principles.[16] Some in attendance—Brazil included—justified their position by arguing that the "principles" were driven by OECD donor members, and that they were not "donor" countries, hence becoming alienated.

Was the rejection of the Paris Resolution by some countries driven by objections to the intrinsic properties of these principles or driven by the same geo-political motivation of non-alignment with donor countries of the North?

The Brazil case suggests that the objections are not directed to the principles themselves but to their prescriptive tone which an official spokesperson says "do not apply to developing countries engaged in TCDC", which is based on horizontal relationships among equals rather than vertical ones between donors and recipients.

Despite these developments in the state of play of international DA, there is still a sense that its contribution to the development of poor countries has been marginal at best. David Philips in his provocative "Development without Aid" (Philips 2013) seeks to debunk the widely supported assumption among donors that development aid over the last 50 years has contributed significantly to growth of beneficiary countries and made a dent on poverty. He investigated how far the people of the poorest and most aid-dependent countries can begin to move beyond their need for foreign aid and thereby assume or resume sovereignty over their development process and destiny. He does that by offering a broad compilation of Official Development Assistance (ODA) shortcomings and their root causes and goes on to make overtures to how aid-dependent countries can break the shackles of aid addiction, seek alternative sources of capital and speed their development process. He compiles illustrations of Official Development Assistance (ODA) failures by reviewing its dimensions and highlighting its negligible volume of resources in aggregate terms, albeit proportionately large for small aid-dependent economies. He also points out that in 2010 ODA reached $130 billion, representing a mere 0.3% of donors' national income. He shows that 70% of ODA comes from bilateral donors and 30% from multilaterals, and that at its 50-year mark accumulated ODA was estimated at $4 trillion, covering a range of assistance including "hardware and software." In terms of ODA as a share of financial flows to poor countries, he shows that starting in the early 1990s it averaged 50% and has since decreased to 20%, as measured in 2007. In essence, the way out of this dependency, according to Mr. Phillips is by means of harnessing indigenous financing from remittances by the poor countries Diaspora, along with capital flows and skills of migrants to the developed world.

Another important factor determining the nature and scope of international DA of late is the emerging concern with global public ills only addressed by global public goods (Pinto and Puppim de Oliveira 2011). Among them, threats to the global environment particularly those of global warming caused by carbon emissions have inserted global public goods in the agenda of most donors (Diewald and Pinto 2006). The funding, formulation, and delivery of this type of international assistance have also challenged the conventional way of managing TCDC.

What effect, if any, do topical areas for international assistance/cooperation have on its segmentation and operations? For example, on the topic of carbon emissions and climate change, do either of the N/S, S/S-TCDC models maximize/minimize results and outcomes of the assistance provided?

(continued)

(continued)

The climate change agenda of development cooperation is unique in the sense that it has certain determinants intrinsic to its nature. For example, assistance for mitigation of global warming's adverse effects is usually provided by rich polluting countries of the north to less polluting countries of the south, so clearly a N/S modality. In terms of adherence to standards agreed in global conferences to achieve emission reductions and slow down global warming, clearly all developing countries share the benefits, so exchanging their experiences at achieving that in a collaborative manner calls for the TCDC modality. In Brazil these issues are not addressed as part of ABC's TCDC remit but independently by specialized ministries such Science and Technology, Agriculture, Energy and Mining etc. The export of bio-fuels technology by Brazil, where ABC did play a role, is a form of meeting the needs of developing countries searching ways to curb their carbon emissions. Brazil seems to have reached a good fit between both and benefited accordingly. New donors must take stock of their individual needs and not lock themselves into any models, by virtue of belonging to a given club. Caution, however, should be exercised to avoid inconsistency of behavior among partners. The mixed variety might best suit their needs and they should also keep pace with the recent emergence of global public goods designed to address global welfare needs. While the Brazil case shows its affinity on geo-political grounds with the SS TCDC model, new donors should not lock themselves into any particular mode on grounds other than maximum effectiveness of the assistance provided. While clustering of donors under one or another mobilizing principle or movement may lead to certain conformity with given standards and practices, individual countries should place assistance effectiveness high on their agenda. To the extent that TCDC is closer to the foreign policies of the engaged partners, the new donors should make an effort to seek a reasonable level of harmonization among these policies, and avoid inconsistencies among members of the group.

These developments set the tone, the terminology and the stage for the dynamics of development assistance towards the end of the twentieth century. It is at this stage that "new donors" such as the BRICS, among others, emerge. It is unclear the extent to which these new donors have effectively subscribed to the aid ideology of the S/S, TCDC model as discussed above. While it can be argued that DA is not philanthropy, its role, especially in the international public health area, is substantial and impactful in terms of raising levels of health across the world.[17]

THE BRAZIL CONTEXT FOR DEVELOPMENT ASSISTANCE

Following the end of World War II, Brazil, a member of the allied forces, became a privileged recipient of US aid, initially in the form of military cooperation and donation of military equipment, and later of infrastructure and industrial development assistance. Brazil was then seen as a potential bastion against the encroachment of communism in the region, hence the favored nation treatment by the USA. As a regional power, Brazil has foreign relations with a broad range of countries worldwide and a correspondingly large network of embassies and consular offices. In regard to its international assistance, it does favor those with which it shares a historical, language/cultural and ethnic heritage. With these factors as background, added to the breadth and depth of the knowledge and expertise of numerous national entities, Brazil has felt emboldened as a provider of assistance to this constellation of countries and beyond. It has chosen to channel such assistance in the form of the South/South development cooperation via the (TCDC) mode. In doing so, it shows a keen awareness of the sovereignty and self-determination of those countries that it has assisted as partners, not recipients of aid.

What is gained or lost by emerging economies to sustain concomitantly a role of donor and recipient of development cooperation?

To the extent that TCDC is a two way exchange of assistance where "partners" give and take assistance, it seems that they can only gain from the coexistence of the two directions of assistance. An official source in Brazil argued that it is not an emerging donor, but continues to be a recipient country that engages in TCDC a practice that emerges "progressively, as a component of bilateral relations among developing countries". As part of a bloc of countries or club such as the BRICS, that may be an issue as each member may take a different position, creating internal inconsistencies.

Despite ABC's[18] official position that the cooperation it provides is essentially beneficiary demand driven, it also acknowledges that its projects are largely dependent on the expertise and the operational approach of Brazilian specialized agencies that are made available to recipient countries, in an essentially supply driven approach. As it recognizes the demands of its TCDC partners, it follows that it is implicitly recognizing that these are recipients of aid. Donors articulate supply, not demand of aid.

Is TCDC supply or demand led? How do these options condition outcomes?

In the case of Brazil ABC claims that it is entirely demand led as part of the recognition of partners' needs and best interests. Yet the assistance actually provided has to be consistent with the capabilities and interests of the Brazilian entities executing the projects, a supply-led factor.

As a staunch supporter of TCDC, Brazil has resisted the principles laid out in the Paris.

By not subscribing to the guidelines of the Paris Resolution on grounds of principle, not on an assessment of its properties, Brazil is making a statement that shows solidarity with other non-aligned countries that favor TCDC. By doing so, Brazil is distancing itself from the code of best/modern practices adopted by the developed northern countries. Officially, it associates these principles with the requirements set by OECD donors for its recipients, hence its rejection.

TCDC has enjoyed some preeminence in Brazilian foreign policy. Since it promoted development cooperation in financial, technical, technological, educational, cultural, and humanitarian matters among its partners, Brazil drew numerous benefits, accruing to its own development. As Brazil intensified its diplomatic ties in Africa and Latin America, after several decades of being a recipient of international assistance, it turned to the role of lead partner within the policy frame of S/S development cooperation.[19] At the time no commercial dividends of such cooperation were sought, hence, free of conditionality. It is also noteworthy that the TCDC activities coordinated by ABC and implemented by a host of Brazilian specialized agencies and ministries are more germane to exchange and joint study programs where all benefit rather than a concerted effort to meet specific demands of the "recipient" country as is the case in N/S-TCDC programs and projects.

By the mid-1980s, the existing institutional set up for Brazil's international assistance was showing signs of fatigue and decreasing internal support. Consequently, early in 1987 the Subsecretaria Internacional (SUBIN) of the Ministry of Plan and Department of Development Cooperation (DCOPTD) of the Ministry of Foreign Affairs was abolished, and later in the same year, Agencia Brasileira de Cooperação, or Brazilian Cooperation Agency (ABC) was created. The clear loss of such a move was that development cooperation would no longer enjoy the inter-ministerial crosscutting coordination only possible from a ministry with the scope and coverage of the Ministry of Planning. Furthermore, the Ministry of Planning also has technical command of development matters. Yet international assistance was brought closer to its germane function of foreign policy and international relations, the mandate of the Ministry of Foreign Affairs.

Motivation of Brazilian TCDC

As seen above in the evolution of Brazil's experience with international assistance and its alignment with the bloc of countries ambivalent toward N/S assistance, which do not see themselves as donors, has to a certain extent defined its motivation to engage in TCDC. This stance would become ambiguous were Brazil to join the ranks of "new donors" that may agree on principles and rules incompatible with those that Brazil advocates. The reconciliation between being a new donor and engaging mostly in TCDC cooperation becomes problematic, as the latter would constrain its scope of action. Consequently, in today's international context—quite different from that prevailing in 1978, era of the Buenos Aires UN Conference on Development Cooperation—a clear role definition is required; especially should Brazil eventually join the ranks of the associated new emerging economies, subscribing to the New Development Assistance (NDA) modality. In the current environment, it may become untenable to be a donor, a recipient, a partner as well *as* an associate of the NDA at the same time. Among the many reasons, why it is so difficult is the increasing challenge for emerging countries' DA institutions of navigating the complex development assistance landscape, still lacking an overall rule framework.

The role and impact of TCDC on Brazil's foreign policy is an issue around which experts disagree. Although official documentation states that development cooperation plays an important role in policy, some interview respondents argue that this has not been the case over the years. Yet Brazilian foreign policy has clearly shifted with different governments depending on their assessment of the geopolitical global environment and their policy choices on how to insert Brazil in it. Development Cooperation strategies tended to reflect such views.

The recent populist, left-leaning governments of the Workers Party (PT) have used development cooperation and development finance to strengthen ties with Angola, Cuba, and Venezuela among others. In fact, a substantial portion of Brazil DA in the broad sense was enabled under PT governments through concessional loans by the National Social and Economic Development Bank (BNDES) to governments of "partner" countries that shared ideological leanings with the PT. Under this policy, BNDES was mobilized to subsidize financing for infrastructure projects in these countries, on the condition that they procured the construction from large Brazilian contractors—a venture which, along with other reprehensible features facilitated endemic corruption and the eventual unraveling of the Workers Party itself. This practice also ran counter to the officially sanctioned principle that Brazil's development assistance seeks no commercial advantage. These loans were at the time of writing under scrutiny by

Brazilian investigative bodies and the courts, on the grounds of massive systemic corruption.

It is further argued by observers that when governments engage in travel diplomacy and cooperation, such as that of the recent President Lula da Silva of PT who, with his Minister of Foreign Affairs promoted Brazil's Development Cooperation, there is a better fit between foreign policy and development cooperation.[20] By the same token, the Workers Party was supportive of Brazil's alignment with the resistance to OECD/DAC countries in regard to Development Cooperation. The more liberal government of the Social Democratic Party (PSDB) steered its Technical Cooperation along the lines of traditional diplomacy, as practiced by the somewhat independent and steady Ministry of Foreign Affairs, which advocates foreign policy as a matter of state and not to fluctuate with changes of government. Consequently, it did not favor countries as targets of TCDC on the basis of ideological affinity. Few, however, disagree that Brazil's engagement in development cooperation has benefited its own development, in addition to promoting the county's image as a generous, progressive and a reliable partner.[21]

The Lead TCDC Agency in Brazil: ABC

At the outset, ABC was subsumed in the Under-secretariat for Cooperation and Commercial Promotion of the Ministry of Foreign Relations (MRE),[22] as part of a Public Foundation. Its statutory mandate is to *"coordinate, negotiate, approve, monitor and evaluate development cooperation - with national scope - in all areas of knowledge received from other countries and international organizations, and that between Brazil and other developing countries."*[23] This mandate assigns to ABC the double responsibility over *outgoing and incoming* international assistance, clearly an overload for the agency.

What is gained/lost by combining in a single agency both incoming and outgoing assistance/cooperation?

While incoming bilateral and TCDC assistance have few things in common, the Brazilian case does not highlight any major issues. Official documentation is silent on this aspect, mostly because projects and activities under TCDC are of greater volume than the former. Aside from sharing staff and systems that may have a few factors in common, no other advantage is visualized. An official respondent argued for keeping both N/S and TCDC under the same agency, mostly on the grounds of managerial resources economy and cross fertilization between the two modalities under the same roof.

Although labeled an "agency," its Director on inception was in effect the Director of the Department of Technical and Scientific Cooperation, part of the top management of the Ministry of Foreign Affairs. As such, it did not enjoy the autonomy that the agency model would imply. In 2004, ABC became part of the Sub-Secretariat General of Cooperation and Brazilian Communities Abroad (SGEC), and currently, ABC's Director does not share his executive functions with any other MRE unit.

What is gained/lost by the autonomy of the official aid agency of a country? What are the advantages of autonomy *versus* those of connectivity/interface with other agencies and ministries within country?

Autonomy of Aid agencies provides the obvious advantage of flexibility, the ability to set its own legal and regulatory framework, its operational procedures, staffing standards and practices. In the case of the Brazilian ABC, failure to enjoy such flexibility has been given as a source of some of its most serious constraints. Among the disadvantages of autonomy is the loss of prestige and empowerment that comes with being inserted in a Ministry such as Foreign Affairs.

Designing the key features of an ideal institutional and organizational architecture for an aid agency raises a central issue: whether it should be organized geographically or topically. In the case of ABC, first there is the "Ministerial Executive Order" that sets the organizational structure of the Ministry of Foreign Affairs, where ABC is one of 15 Departments and many Divisions.[24] Second, there is the "Manual de Gestão da Cooperação Técnica Sul/Sul," (Manual of Management of South/South Cooperation). Third, there is the "Diretrizes para o Desenvolvimento da Cooperação Técnica Internacional Multilateral e Bilateral" (Directives for International Technical Cooperation of Multilateral and Bilateral operations). Despite all such institutional/organizational instruments, many Brazilian critics argue that ABC is institutionally weak because it lacks a dedicated Law of Technical Cooperation and does not cover the entirety of Brazilian DA. Such a law would only make sense if it were to selectively consolidate and replace the multiplicity of related legal and regulatory instruments which renders the framework dense and of difficult compliance.[25]

Should every new donor enact a dedicated law on International Cooperation incoming and outgoing?

The case of Brazil, which has a set of very dense regulatory and operational instruments applying mostly to the Ministry of Foreign Affairs, with areas of ambiguity, would probably benefit from a dedicated law that covers the essential elements of international assistance across the board. It however should be a replacement to some of these existing instruments and not an addition to the existing legal/regulatory framework. Moreover such law should also address the enhanced concept of DA, which goes beyond TCDC. Some officials at ABC have argued for a dedicated law. That said, it is unrealistic to expect such law to pass as long as ABC remains in the realm of the MRE, as it would clash with its statutes and regulations. An official respondent indicated that such legal framework if it were considered should include: Policy; Governance; Regulatory Instruments and Funding. No reference was made of the crucial broader DA concept Total Support to Sustainable Development (TOSSD).

ABC has four operational units: CGPD which oversees S/S (TCDC) cooperation, CGCB for bilateral incoming cooperation, CGCM for incoming assistance from multilateral organizations and trilateral arrangements, and CGAO for Administration and Budgeting (see Fig. 4.1). At first, it also had a project management unit which proved overwhelmed with operational tasks and ultimately was abolished. Project management responsibilities were subsequently assigned to Brazilian entities executing assistance projects. ABC's organizational design fits model 2 (Agency within Ministry of Foreign Affairs, with policy and implementation) of the organizational typology proposed by Nilima Gulrajani.[26]

Which are the key features of an ideal organizational architecture for an aid agency? Should it be organized geographically or according to topics of incoming and outgoing assistance?

Given the role of TCDC in foreign policy, it is important that the design and implementation process of such projects draw on country knowledge and be informed by the staff of the Ministry of Foreign Affairs that have greater exposure and influence over these factors. Therefore, these links must be preserved but not at the cost of full insertion of the incoming and outgoing assistance operations into this ministry. Autonomy and independence can and should be reconciled with access to sources of foreign affairs. Thematic expertise needs not be available in-house. In the case of Brazil, it is provided by the TCDC implementing agencies and assisted by the multiple specialized bodies within the Ministry of Foreign Affairs.

Fig. 4.1 Organizational chart

At first and for some 12 years, ABC relied on UNDP as a means to hire "consultants" via a procedure allowed only to international agencies operating in Brazil. This bypassing of local rules to induct civil servants was finally brought under question and in 2002 terminated through legal action against ABC and UNDP. This however did not stop UNDP from continuing to play a role in supporting ABC over the years (currently for a 5% annual fee). This support includes making available its offices around the world to support ABC operations abroad.

Operationally, a significant load of ABC's work is tied to the prospective (up-stream/pre-investment) tasks undertaken by ABC staff with occasional consultants, by way of field missions. Attendance at assorted gatherings and conferences also takes up considerable time and travel. Resources consumed in this part of ABC's workload seem to outweigh ABC's expenditures with actual assistance operations. This pattern could bring into question the agency's efficiency, which would be exposed in any credible evaluation exercise.

Procurement as well as budgeting has been an issue because government rules on the matter are somewhat inflexible when it comes to procuring and paying for goods and services internationally. For example, budgeted and allocated funds not spent during a given budget year have to be returned to the Treasury, therefore leaving multiyear projects unfunded. UNDP has assisted with this constraint, but always under the watchful eye of the CGU (General Accounting Office), given the problematic background. These issues strengthen the argument for a dedicated law on international cooperation, addressing them and including the broader international development assistance. Counterpart funding on the part of recipients/partners of cooperation projects is also an issue, as execution hinges on such availability and can paralyze a project.

Should foreign assistance have a dedicated financial/procurement system, separate and apart from that of the government?
In the case of Brazil standard budgeting and procurement norms and procedures proved to be a constraining factor accounting for delays in project set up and execution. This suggests that any dedicated legislation should correct this shortcoming by establishing ad hoc norms and procedures. It was noted by a respondent that this would be extremely difficult to accomplish, given Brazil's legal rigidities on public budgeting.

Funding for ABC

Funding for ABC is included in the Budget of the Ministry of Foreign Affairs and is minimal.[27] The diagram below shows its 2000–2014 Budget allocations, which include project funding and part of ABC's overhead estimated at 20% of them.[28] Personnel costs of project executing agencies are covered by them, while travel costs are covered by ABC (Fig. 4.2).

Contributions from international organizations and/or other countries (Japan, Germany, UK, and others) associated with bilateral or trilateral programs, which are not included in ABC's financial accounts, also fund ABC Cooperation projects. Still the figures on these budgets do not go far in funding TCDC operations.[29] Moreover, ABC projects require an unusually high number of international missions of medium duration. According

ABC - Agência Brasileira de Cooperação

Fig. 4.2 ABC financial execution 2000–2014 in US$ (These figures cover all expenses of ABC. Not included in these figures are contributions it makes to international organizations, programs and salaries of staff of technical entities and other government agencies and ministries mobilized for ABC projects, absorbed by these agencies. This explains in part the small amount of resources budgeted for DA under ABC)

to the ABC site, between 2003 and 2014 a total of 663 prospective, and M&E missions were carried out, which presumably did not include the actual delivery of the technical cooperation intended.[30] While no figures on mission costs were made available to this study, it is assumed that they take up most of its funding. The sharp decline from the peak of 2010 to 2014 is visible and is explained as a consequence of overall budget reductions across the Brazilian Federal Government.[31]

Funding during the decade of 1995–2005 was apportioned at 33.7% for Central America and Caribbean, 31.2% for each South America and Africa and the remaining 3.9% for other regions.[32] In terms of areas of project focus, 23.4% went to Agriculture and Livestock,[33] 16.5% to health, 11.1% to Environment, 9.2% to Education, 7.7% to Public Administration, 6.1% to Social Development, 4.2% to Energy and Biofuels, 4.2% to Professional Training, 3.1% to Industry, 2.3% to Transport, 1.9% to Mining, 1.5% to Labor relations, 1.5% to Entrepreneurial Development, 1.5% to Rural development, 0.8% to Information technology, and 5.0% to Others (Table 4.1).

ABC's funding pales when compared to the overall expenditures of Brazil in DA and related areas. ABC's budget for 2013 is a mere 9.8% of Brazil's overall expenditures for international development for the same year. These magnitudes suggest a minor resource role for ABC. By far, the

Table 4.1 Overall expenditures of Brazil with International Development Assistance, in US$[a]

Modalities/years	2009	2010	2011	2012	2013
Technical Cooperation	48,872,380	57,770,553	45,617,071	33,970,749	31,846,055
Educational Cooperation	22,236,954	35,544,099	20,689,408	22,251,006	23,809,864
Scientific/Tech. Cooperation		24,009,084	73,106,869	72,085,370	53,174,326
Humanitarian Cooperation	43,521,166	161,469,749	72,418,476	109,828,325	21,667,913
Refugee Assistance		590,469	4,710,229	4,122,857	1,819,718
Peace Maintenance	62,704,500	332,422,426	40,167,190	20,654,923	10,330,872
TOTAL	177,335,000	559,806,380	256,709,843	262,913,230	142,648,748

[a]IPEA, ABC/MRE, Acnur; AEB, Aisa/MS, Anvisa, CAIXA, Capes/MEC, Ceplac/Mapa, CGFome/MRE, CNPq/MCTI, Conab, Conare, CPRM, DCE/MRE, DNPM, Embrapa, Enap, Esaf, Fiocruz/MS, Ibama, Ibram, Inmet, Iphan, MCidades, MCTI, MDS, MME, MPA, MPS, MTE, MTur, Sain/MF, SDH/PR, Seain/MP, SESu/MEC e SVS/MS. Most of these acronyms represent the bulk government or quasi-government agencies that are either called on by ABC to implement TCDC activities or that engage in DA on their own

largest item of expenditure is Brazil's contributions to international organizations, listed below for 2005–2013 in US$, Table 4.2. Furthermore, these contributions are not channeled by ABC. *This leads to the conclusion that ABC is not the lead agency in the provision of Brazil's DA.* While this case study did not explore the remaining agencies, it did not uncover evidence that any government agency exercises oversight over the broader and more resourceful ODA function.[34]

Table 4.2 Brazil's contributions to international organizations in US$ thousands

2005	2006	2007	2008	2009	2010	2011	2012	2013
123,105	233,731	228,421	249,863	247,579	311,569	331,6422	250,857	254,157

Should the entire range of DA activities of a country, including TCDC, S/S activities as well as the much larger transfer of financial resources (TOSSD) under different concessional arrangements come under the scope of a single agency?

The Brazil case shows that ABC does not have supervisory authority over all DA activities. Instead, in addition to centralizing oversight of the substantial contributions to international organizations, mostly of the UN family, it oversees TCDC projects with a very limited amount of resources which are seen as an appendage of Brazil's Foreign Policy, hence the organizational location of ABC. The remainder and much larger volume of DA come under the scope of a range of government and quasi-government entities not surveyed by this case study. It is not clear whether such arrangements came into existence by design or as a result of a fortuitous evolution in Brazil's role in the DA environment. In any event, centralization of oversight of the entire range of DA activities and resources looms as a rather challenging task for any EE, with questionable gains in terms of increased effectiveness of DA.

Luijkx and Benn (2017)[35] report that among EEs, Brazil's contributions to DA in 2013 (when data available) amounted to US$ 316 million, below Kuwait, Mexico, Qatar, Russia, Saudi Arabia, United Arab Emirates, all oil/energy exporters, and China, India, and Turkey.

Among the BRICS, only China ranks higher in contributions to UN funds and specialized agencies. In regard to contributions to Regional Development Banks and the World Bank Brazil ranks third after China and Russia[36] (Table 4.3).

Considering that 68% of projects are on the average from 1 to 3 years of duration, these figures suggest an average cost of approximately $50.000 per project. Assessing the direct costs of IDA is important; however, it is also important to assess the indirect transaction costs to donors and recipients of IDA ensuring that these costs are offset by the benefits ultimately resulting to recipients.

In the absence of results evaluation in general, certain cooperation projects are "assessed" as having positive impacts, such as those in environmental matters and especially in the development and application of biofuels, which have important commercial potential.[37] Likewise, ABC documents indicate that no significant failures of projects have been reported. Shortfalls of projects are usually attributed to failures of recipients to come up with counterpart funding as per contractual arrangements. Discontinuity of recipient governments and generally low-absorptive capacity are also blamed for shortfall in certain cases. It is also argued that certain implementing agencies in Brazil attach low priority to cooperation activities and fall

Table 4.3 Number of projects by year and average expenditures by project

2004	2005	2006	2007	2008	2009	2010	2011	2012	2013	2013
67	87	179	246	375	555	737	783	736	472	385
$10,776	$10,410	$29,656	$14,880	$18,670	$34,925	$51,315	$34,487	26,919	29,538	$18,439

behind on their implementation responsibilities.[38] Given that certain multilateral aid agencies which provide financial assistance require that recipients improve their capacity to make use of these resources, such companion technical assistance operations raise the issue of undue conditionality. While the Brazil case study indicates that often poor absorptive capacity of its partners of TCDC accounts for project delay and shortcomings, it did not uncover instances of assistance to improve such capacities. It is entirely possible though that its Public Administration projects may actually address that. The position of an official respondent is that this requirement does not constitute conditionality.

Does international assistance depend primarily on the capacity of donor country/agency or does it also require capacity of the recipient country/beneficiaries? Can one compensate for the other?

The Brazil case shows that capacity at the delivery end of TCDC, while necessary, it is not sufficient. Absorptive capacity at the receiving end is equally critical, especially in regards to the integrity of the systems and staff at both ends of assistance operations. A respondent from ABC makes the point that sovereignty involves the capacity to take responsibility for properly managing cooperation partnerships for development. Furthermore, he claims that ABC has offered capacity building interventions directed to the management of development cooperation.

On the whole, there are plenty of reasons to justify a more robust evaluation (preferably independent) effort on the part of ABC. The ideal way to chart a path going forward for an entity such as ABC is to base it on results of an evaluative effort. As seen above, the agency has a low propensity to engage in results-based evaluation, so it effectively does not really know how it is performing, except for subjective statements that suggest that it is successful. Under such circumstances, its short- and long-term prospects are probably based on future governments, their respective foreign policies, and the extent to which they are willing to make space for development cooperation in the agenda of the Ministry of Foreign Affairs. It was reported to this study that plans for an evaluation policy are in the works.

Over the years, staffing issues have also affected ABC's effectiveness. At first, it operated entirely with staff from the Ministry of Planning and later the MFA (Ministry of Foreign Affairs). As staffing needs grew, ABC resorted to UNDP through a mechanism of hiring "consultants," which worked until this practice ceased by legal injunction, and "consultants" were terminated by October 2005.[39] At its peak in 2001, ABC had 181 staff. Currently (at the time of this writing), it is down to 123 following a significant drop in funding and operations of ABC. The predominant use of diplomatic staff at ABC frustrated expectations of diplomats to be posted abroad after 2 years of service in Brasilia, as part of their career path.

Is the task of delivering TCDC programs and projects consistent with the professional competency model of foreign affairs/diplomatic staff?
Aside from the clashes with career expectations of diplomats in terms of service at headquarters and abroad, their professional training is unlikely to include the skills and knowledge to serve as a Technical Cooperation officer. Exception to this is international relations, country and language knowledge that diplomatic staff is required to have. Part of this gap is filled with on-the-job training offered by ABC. The Brazil case suggests that for effective conduct of international assistance, both incoming and outgoing, it is not enough to be trained in the skills of diplomacy. International relations, development in general, in addition to language skills and country knowledge are necessary but not sufficient. Understanding development in its economic and institutional implications, as well as international management skills and genuine empathy/vocation to be of assistance to those in need, are also required. Independent evaluations of ABC projects would cast some light on this issue.

Given these personnel issues, ABC started recruiting dedicated staff with appropriate skills through competitive selection as per government personnel rules. By 2004, most such new hires were on the job. Despite these measures, an initiative to create and train a new personnel track of Technical Cooperation for ABC with specialized training was proposed but rejected by the MFA. Reason given was that of an alleged incompatibility with diplomatic service standards and encroaching on the career rights of diplomats. This suggests that preserving the career interests of diplomatic staff of MFA ranks higher than making staffing consistent with TCDC requirements.

Are civil servants of ministries and agencies implementing TCDC projects a suitable conduit to deliver the expertise required by them. How are the issues of conflicting allegiances to home and target country resolved?
Probably not and therein is one the most salient vulnerabilities of ABC's TCDC delivery. This can only be assessed through independent evaluations centered on results.

CONCLUSIONS

In the current environment of new donors, one may question whether these countries can/should remain tied to the principles of TCDC, S/S cooperation or they should aspire to become more like the N/S model of

OECD/DAC countries by selectively adopting some of their standards and practices. While the Brazil case shows its affinity on geopolitical grounds with the SS TCDC model, new donors should not lock themselves into any particular mode on grounds other than maximum effectiveness of the assistance provided.

The case shows that Brazil has favored its role in multilateral organizations, a destination of a large share of its official DA resources. As this increment adds to the complexity of the development assistance landscape, it is crucial that the BRICS invest in the rational design and management of in-and-outflows of DA and their governance. Most importantly, this design must be particularly consistent with the nature of the public goods now being transacted in international DA. In the current international geopolitical setting and given the nature of threats and challenges to the international order and welfare, there is a premium on international public goods, which compete with national public goods in the international assistance marketplace (Pinto and Puppim de Oliveira 2011).[40] Some observers however may argue that the increased focus of critical global public goods may displace the focus on lagging countries which attach a higher priority to their national public goods, hence creating a dilemma for DA which is increasingly concerned with Global Public Goods.[41]

The clustering of donors under one or another mobilizing principle or movement may lead to a certain conformity with given standards and practices; however, individual countries should put *assistance effectiveness* higher on their agenda. To the extent that TCDC better assimilates to the foreign policies of the engaged partners, new donors should seek a reasonable level of harmonization among these policies, to avoid inconsistencies among members of the group. Furthermore, unless there are policies, operational or managerial restrictions associated with the principles of the Paris Resolution, which did not transpire in the Brazilian case, emerging donors should reconsider them on the basis of their merit.

Development Cooperation as practiced by Brazil is not equivalent to N/S Development Assistance in the sense that it is not focused on the transfer of technical and financial resources to countries in need of them, accompanied by governance reforms among others. Instead, because of its insertion in the Ministry of Foreign Affairs (MRE), ABC plays a role of accessory to foreign policy by emphasizing numerous missions consisting of diplomatic staff inter alia, focusing on rapprochement, exchanges of information and experiences around topics of common interest: a "Para-diplomatic" mandate. Because of the frequency, size, and duration of these missions, they represent a potential load on recipient countries human resources. They stretch their scarce professional staffs who would otherwise be dedicated to their domestic development tasks. Given the load on recipient countries caused by the sharp increase of donor and partner countries with multiple missions and demands, it becomes critical to give preference to those modalities likely to be least onerous on the former. David Phillips in op. cit. describes the impact that such activity has on the public services of recipient countries. In some instances, counterpart civil servants use such missions to seek opportunities for personal advantages in the form of fellowships and study tours to the donor countries. In other instances, donors set up project management units which cannibalize the more qualified civil service staff, depriving them of such valuable resource. Though none of these features came up specifically in this study, it is a real risk only detrimental to the ultimate objectives of DA.

In sum, this brief case study raises a number of issues that imply lessons relevant to other BRICS members as they perfect their DA systems; mainly viz., (a) No integrating legal/regulatory framework and no policy framework discerned; (b) significant difficulty in assessing the real financial magnitude of DA; (c) lack of a culture of evaluation to take stock of input costs, outputs, and efficiency and effectiveness in terms of results/impact; and (d) no effective focal point with total coverage of TOSSD. Finally, while the large collection of DA-executing agencies across government is indeed a real asset to build upon, these issues must be addressed before Brazil will be able to join any network of EEs in a concerted DA effort. Perhaps a role for NDA should be to assist potential BRIC members to address such issues.

Acknowledgements The author wishes to acknowledge the assistance provided by Dr. Scarlet do Carmo from FGV, Brazil in the drafting of this chapter.

NOTES

1. In addition to being an active member of the BRICS club, Brazil had earlier sought—under a separate cluster—an association with India and South Africa, known as IBAS, covering a menu of topics for cooperation among them, which suits their shared technological and scientific aspirations.
2. Philips compiles illustrations of the shortcomings of Official Development Assistance (ODA). In: Philips, David A. 2013. *Development Without Aid: The*

Decline of Development Aid and the Rise of the Diaspora. London: Anthem Press.

3. These refer to health, security, climate change, poverty, refugees, and immigration, among others.

4. On the case for public goods, see, e.g., "Global Public Goods: A Framework for the Role of the World Bank" a report to the Bank's Development Committee, October 2007, DC2007-0020.

5. Also known as "rising states", "emerging powers", or "great peripheral countries". Together they represented in 2009 6.4% of total ODA. While none of the BRICS are members of the OECD, Brazil has recently (May 30, 2017) applied to accede. OECD estimates that in 2014 EEs contributed 17% of total global DA or approximately US$32 billion. Although heavily weighted by contributions of the United Arab Emirates and Saudi Arabia, if a broader concept of contribution to DA is used, this figure might grow tenfold.

6. Not included in the BRICS, yet meeting some of the emerging donor criteria are: Turkey, Mexico, Chile, and South Korea (OECD/non-DAC). Non-OECD and falling in no other categories are: Thailand, Indonesia, and Malaysia.

7. Manning, Richard. 2006. "Will Emerging Donors Change the Face of International Co-operation?" *Development Policy Review* 24 (4): 371–85, and Kharas, Homi. 2008. "The New Reality of Aid." In *Global Development 2.0*, edited by Brainard and Chellet, 53–73. Washington: Brookings Institution Press report that among the 60 bilateral donors, emerging countries are estimated to provide between 2 and 8 billion dollars of ODA.

8. It would be somewhat presumptuous to assume that these principles would qualify as "theories" as their validity and applicability are still rather tentative with universality yet to be tested.

9. In 2009, Brazil received an estimated 200 million US$ in bilateral aid, of which some 40% was for the protection of the Amazon forest, a global asset, 22% for agriculture, 12% for health, 10% for industry, 10% for social sectors and 6% for public administration. Souza, S.-L. J. (2009). "Brazil as a New International Development Actor, South-South Cooperation and he IBSA initiative," www.nsi-ins.ca/english/events/DAW/2_depercent20Sousapdf.

10. The UNDP through its Special S/S Cooperation Unit on TCDC of 1996 became the focal point to assist countries wishing to engage in such modality of aid practices.

11. The UN reports that TCDC in 2013 had reached a volume of 20 billion US$, in SG Report (E/2016/65), p. 11. The China Development Bank and its Export-Import Bank extended 110 billion $ in loans to other developing countries and their companies during 2009–2010, as reported by Chaturvedi et al. in "Development Cooperation and Emerging Powers".

12. Historical precursors to these events were: The 1955 First Conference of Asian and African Countries held in Bandung, Indonesia aimed at political cooperation to overcome neocolonialist tendencies of the north to continue to dominate the south under the guise of development assistance, launching the non-aligned movement. Later in 1964, the First UN Conference on Trade and Development, the creation of several middle eastern entities dedicated to international development, such as the Kuwait Arabic Development Fund, the Islamic and the Arabic Development Banks, culminating with the G-77 at the UN and the associated New Economic order, ushered in the concept of collective self-reliance among countries that shared this aspiration of resisting Northern dominance. Cuba, a strong advocate of this movement was already sending doctors and teachers around the underdeveloped world to promote human welfare, along with ideological proselytizing.

13. It was only in 2000 that the first Forum of Cooperation China-Africa took place, followed by the 2003 Forum India-Brazil-China, South Africa IBAS, launching China's pro-activity in limited partnerships for TCDC, later expanded to the BRICS, with the inclusion of Russia.

14. Greatly inspired by the leadership of Ronald Reagan in the USA and Margaret Thatcher in the UK.

15. See Eliot Berg, Coordinator, Rethinking Technical Cooperation: Reforms for Capacity Building in Africa, Regional Bureau for Africa UNDP, 1993 for a treatment of this conceptual and operational shift in DA.

16. Principles are Ownership, Alignment, Harmonization, Management for Results, and Mutual accountability.

17. See, for example, the Bill and Melinda Gates Foundation and the Clinton Foundation.

18. "Agência Brasileira de Cooperação".

19. Because of its strong official advocacy of the TCDC modality of DA, official respondents do not see Brazil as a "donor" and resent this designation. Furthermore, donor countries bring substantially more resources to the table, which Brazil lacks. TCDC is a way to do DA economically for the donor. However, as TCDC involves numerous missions, it only adds to the costs of recipient countries to entertain such missions and tie up valuable local government/partner staff resources that could be dedicated to other more productive activities.

20. In fact, the populist social policy of direct payments to very low-income families with children, known as "Bolsa Família" (Family Welfare Payments) became an attractive topic for social development cooperation as it became a topic for assistance. A similar effect was caused by the success of Brazil's campaign to fight HIV/AIDS, which became a much sought area for Brazilian cooperation with countries that were also struggling with HIV/AIDS.

21. Areas with the largest number of assistance projects are Agriculture, Health, Education, Environment, and Public Administration, availed by over 100

countries mostly in Africa, Latin America and the Caribbean, but including Asia, and the Middle East, with which Brazil has cooperated. Of late favored areas are biofuels and energy. The availability of specialized technical units within the Ministry of Foreign Affairs has facilitated this topical diversity

22. Ministério das Relações Exteriores.
23. With the caveat that outgoing assistance is in the form of Development Cooperation in the model of TCDC.
24. Portaria 212 of 2008.
25. While this brief case study cannot assess the consistency and effectiveness of such elaborate institutional and legal framework, they appear to be potentially redundant and of cumbersome application.
26. Model 2 does not fully fit the case of ABC to the extent that project implementation was actually shifted to the executing Brazilian agencies providing the required technical assistance. Public Administration and Development, Wiley and Sons, 35, 125–64, 2015.
27. In 2015, ABC's budget of approximately 10 million US$ was equivalent to 2.4% of the Budget of the Ministry of Foreign Affairs. In 2016, it was approximately 10 mill US$ and in 2017, approximately US 6 mill US$ (ABC site).
28. From 1995–2005, budgets averaged approximately 1.27 million US$ yearly (ABC site).
29. ABC interview.
30. See Agência Brasileira de Cooperação website: http://www.abc.gov.br/.
31. ABC's budget for 2016 was USD 6,553,052.37.
32. Focal countries in South America have been Bolivia, Peru, Ecuador, Venezuela, and Colombia. In the Caribbean and Central America: Cuba, El Salvador, Costa Rica, and Guatemala. In Africa: Angola, Mozambique, São Tome and Principe, Cape Verde, Guiné-Bissau, and Namibia.
33. EMBRAPA, Brazilian Company for Agricultural Research is by far the most active project implementer representing 5.5% of all expenditures in TCDC between 2011 and 2013 with 11,6 mil R spent in staff time. Lately, it implemented some 12 projects in Africa and Latin America with a total budget of approximately 78 mill US$. The Cotton-4 project in Togo is by far the largest one.
34. These figures suggest that ABC delivers only a fraction of what Brazil spends on these categories, and that the bulk is via contributions to International Organizations.
35. Their data are at variance with official data, suggesting unreliability of data in general.
36. *The Economist* stated in 2010 that: "the value of all Brazilian development aid broadly defined could reach $4 billion a year. That is less than China, but similar to generous donors such as Sweden and Canada". A table in that

article clarifies that only USD 1.2 billion is "direct aid". The other part consists of commercial loans from the Brazilian Development Bank, BNDES. However, even the USD 1.2 billion is well above the figure published by the Brazilian government itself of USD 923 million, not to mention the OECD estimates that indicate that USD 500 million out of the USD 923 million would be eligible for reporting as ODA.

37. Large Projects are submitted to independent evaluations, while others are internally evaluated.
38. Distribution of implementation time for projects is: <1 year, 17.2%, 1–2 years 34.9%, 2–3 years, 33.3%, 3–4 years, 8.8%, +4 years 5.7%
39. Apparently, the practice is again being utilized as the 29 Technical Analysts on the staff of ABC were hired via this mechanism.
40. These refer to health, security, climate change, poverty, refugees, and immigration, among others.
41. On the case for public goods, see, for example, "Global Public Goods: A Framework for the Role of the World Bank" a report to the Bank's Development Committee, October 2007, DC2007-0020.

BIBLIOGRAPHY

Berg, Eliot. 1993. *Rethinking Technical Cooperation: Reforms for Capacity Building in Africa.* New York: United Nations Development Programme (UNDP).

Diewald, Christoph, and Rogerio Pinto. 2006. "Brazil Country Survey on Alignment of Global Programs with Country Planning and Operational Frameworks." Background Report for a Study by the Global Programs and Partnerships Group of the World Bank.

Gulrajani, Nilima. 2015. "Dilemmas in Donor Design: Organizational Reform and the Future of Foreign Aid Agencies." *Public Administration and Development* 35 (2): 152–64.

Kharas, Homi. 2008. "The New Reality of Aid." In *Global Development 2.0*, edited by Lael Brainard and Derek Chellet, 53–73. Washington: Brookings Institution Press.

Kumar, Ashwani, and Dirk Messner. 2011. "Introduction: Global Governance: Issues, Trends and Challenges." In *Power Shifts and Global Governance: Challenges from South and North*, edited by Ashwani Kumar and Dirk Messner, 3–30. London: Anthem Press.

Lima, João Brígido Bezerra, ed. 2016. *Cooperação Brasileira para o Desenvolvimento: 2011–2013 (COBRADI)*. Brasília: Instituto de Pesquisa Econômica Aplicada (IPEA).

Luijkx, William, and Julia Benn. 2017. "Emerging Providers—International Cooperation for Development." OECD Development Cooperation Working Paper, 33.

Manning, Richard. 2006. "Will Emerging Donors Change the Face of International Cooperation?" *Development Policy Review* 24 (4): 371–85.

Philips, David A. 2013. *Development Without Aid: The Decline of Development Aid and the Rise of the Diaspora*. London: Anthem Press.

Pinto, Rogerio F. 2013. "Implementing Development Cooperation." In *Global Review*, edited by Shanghai Institutes for International Studies, Spring.

Pinto, Rogerio, and Jose Antonio Puppim de Oliveira. 2011. "Institutional and Policy Implementation of International Public Goods: The Case of Global Commons." In *Power Shifts and Global Governance: Challenges from South and North*, edited by Ashwani Kumar and Dirk Messner, 65–92. London: Anthem Press.

World Bank. 2007. *The Role of IDA in the Global Aid Architecture: Supporting the Country-Based Development Model*. Washington, DC: World Bank. http://documents.worldbank.org/curated/en/415801468331269146/The-role-of-IDA-in-the-global-aid-architecture-supporting-the-country-based-development-model.

PART II

BRICS and Development Banks

The New Development Bank vs The Asian Infrastructure Investment Bank: A Comparative Perspective on Their Past, Present and Future

Shigehisa Kasahara

INTRODUCTION

Many emerging economies and developing countries have long voiced their concerns about the inadequacy (quantity and quality) of international development finance, and the slow pace of governance reforms in the traditional financial institutions. Their multifaceted frustration was one major factor that led to the recent establishment of two multilateral financial institutions: the New Development Bank (NDB) and the Asian Infrastructure Investment Bank (AIIB). Yet, the preparatory negotiations for these institutions were somewhat contrasting. The negotiations for the NDB

S. Kasahara (✉)
The International Institute of Social Studies, The Hague, The Netherlands
e-mail: kasahara@iss.nl

Erasmus University Rotterdam, Rotterdam, The Netherlands

© The Author(s) 2020   91
J. A. Puppim de Oliveira and Y. Jing (eds.), *International Development Assistance and the BRICS*, Governing China in the 21st Century,
https://doi.org/10.1007/978-981-32-9644-2_5

were long, intense and exclusive—within a small circle of five emerging economies, the BRICS members (Brazil, Russia, India, China and South Africa)—over the 2012–2014 period. Those for the AIIB were shorter and more subdued—mostly bilateral, between China (as the finance provider) on the one hand and numerous Asia countries (as beneficiaries) on the other—intermittently, just over several months from late 2014.

The novelty of these institutions has drawn much attention, and many scholars have looked into their background and implications. However, only a few have compared and contrasted these institutions, and yet even a fewer have attempted at contemplating—as scenarios with specific numerical estimates—the prospect of scaling-up in their funding operation. This is partly because these institutions are still very new, not having as yet built much of the track record on which researchers can base their estimation. This chapter presents a comparative analysis of the NDB and the AIIB by looking into the different paths that led to their establishment, and perhaps more importantly discusses the organizational and functional prospect of scaling-up of these institutions.

The rest of the chapter consists of the following sections. Second section briefly traces the respective diplomatic background that led to the creation of these new institutions. Third section highlights their major similarities and differences on selected issues as stipulated in their respective official documents and observed in their initial institutional development and operation. Fourth section, a sequel to the previous one, presents a comparison of the prospect of their scaling-up. And the final section, the conclusion, sums up the key issues of our discussions and analyses.

New Institutions: Diplomatic Background and Initial Operation

The New Development Bank (NDB)[1]

In April 2010 when the first meeting of the national development banks from Brazil, Russia, India and China was held, the participants signed a Memorandum of Understanding (MoU) of mutual cooperation. Since then the governors of these banks (with South Africa as well from 2011) have met in what is known as the BRICS Financial Forum, parallel with the BRICS Summits (He 2016, 3). However, it was in the broader BRICS diplomatic context between 2012 and 2014 that the idea of establishing a South-led development bank was nurtured and concretized into an institutionalized entity. Specifically, at the 2012 BRICS Summit, the host country, India, proposed the idea of establishing such a bank. China also became more active in the preparatory process of creating new institutions, particularly after President Xi Jinping came to power in 2012 (He 2016, 3). At the 2013 BRICS Summit, the host country, South Africa, showcased a new multilateral bank as the centrepiece of discussions, and the BRICS leaders agreed to the idea of creating such an institution.

In the lead-up to the 2014 Summit (Fortaleza, Brazil), the BRICS members were engaged in the last phase of assiduous negotiations—most of all, between China and India—on the basic operation and governance structure of the new institution (Cooper 2016). Subsequently, on 15 July 2014, their leaders formally signed the *Agreement of the Establishment of the New Development Bank* (the NDB Agreement). The ratification of the NDB Agreement by each of the five Founding Members' legislative bodies—which had occurred by March 2015—led to its formal establishment, in the wake of the 2015 BRICS Summit (Ufa, Russia). With the Headquarters Agreement with the Chinese central government as well as the MoU with the Shanghai municipal government (the host city) in February 2016, the NDB became operational. As of this writing (July 2018), the NDB has still remained as an institution for the five founders.

The NDB aims at financing infrastructure and sustainable development projects in the Global South by forgoing partnerships with various—national, regional and multilateral—financial institutions. The NDB began its operation with an authorized capital of US$100 billion, of which US$50 billion has been subscribed *equally* by the five BRICS founders, i.e. each with the US$10 billion subscription. The remaining US$50 billion is to be subscribed in the future. According to official sources, during the inaugural year of 2016, the NDB approved its first set of loans—four projects, one each in Brazil, India, China and South Africa—totalling US$850 million.

Asian Infrastructure Investment Bank (AIIB)[2]

During the official visit to Kazakhstan in September 2013, China's President Xi Jinping disclosed his country's ambitious idea of Eurasian development by reviving "the Silk Road Economic Belt", thereby linking the country with Central Asia, the Middle East and Europe. In the following month, at the Asia-Pacific Economic Cooperation (APEC) meeting in Indonesia, President Xi also revealed yet another large undertaking, "the twenty-first Century Maritime Silk Road", to link China with Southeast

Asia and, later, Europe and East Africa via the Indian Ocean. These projects then quickly merged into the "One Belt, One Road" (OBOR) or Belt and Road Initiative (BRI), to connect all of the economies along the inland and maritime routes of the Silk Road. In late 2013, the drive to create a multilateral institution to finance this huge initiative gained momentum, and in March 2014 China officially proposed the idea of establishing the AIIB. The proposal was discussed in May 2014 on the sidelines of the annual Board of Governors meeting of the Asian Development Bank (ADB) held in Astana, Kazakhstan. This new institution—together with the US$40-billion Silk Road Fund (established in December 2014 as China's public institution for bilateral financing)—was expected to play the central role for the OBOR initiative.

On 24 October 2014, after the initial consultation meetings 22 Asian countries signed the MoU to support the idea of establishing the AIIB. Despite the United States' appeal against, the British announced its intention to join the AIIB in mid-March 2015 (against the deadline—to be a Founding Member—of the end of the month), which incidentally induced similar announcements by many non-Asian members. By the time of the deadline, 57 countries (37 Asian and 20 non-Asian)—known then as "the Prospective Founding Members"—had indicated their commitment to the preparatory process for the AIIB. Ongoing negotiations on the *Articles of Agreement* (the AIIB Agreement) ended in May 2015 (Etzioni 2016, 174), and on 29 June 2015, 50 out of these 57 Prospective Founding Members signed the AIIB Agreement in Beijing.[3]

The AIIB became operational in December 2015 when a legally sufficient number of members—holding together more than 50% of the initial subscriptions of the authorized capital—notified their ratifications. On 16 January 2016, the AIIB was officially inaugurated. The AIIB began its operation with authorized capital of US$100 billion, and virtually all of it had been subscribed by (or allocated to) the Founding Members. Purportedly, the AIIB approved, in its inaugural year of 2016, US$1.73 billion in financing nine projects in seven countries in Asia, of which six are co-financing with other institutions, and the remaining three are standalone. As of this writing (July 2018), the AIIB's membership has grown to 80 including those whose financial contributions are under consideration.

COMPARATIVE ANALYSIS (1): WHAT THE *ARTICLES* OF *AGREEMENT* STIPULATE

The NDB and the AIIB show similarities and differences. In this section, we compare these institutions' official documents, most of all, their *Articles of Agreement*, under the following three broad headings: (1) overall institutional characteristics, (2) decision-making and (3) operational modality.

Overall Institutional Characteristics

The issue areas under this heading include (i) purposes & functions, (ii) membership, (iii) governance structure and (iv) authorized & subscribed capital. Table 5.1 presents some concrete elements that these official documents explicitly stipulate on them.

Purposes & Functions
While their wordings somewhat differ, their respective *Articles of Agreement* specify that their institutional mandate is to finance such projects that will enhance infrastructure and sustainable economic development in the Global South. These institutions are expected to forge partnerships with national development banks as well as existing multilateral and regional development banks, through co-financing projects of the private and public sectors. While not as yet seen, it is likely that in the long run the NDB's operation will be more geographically and sectorally dispersed than the AIIB's counterpart which will be more Asia-centric and connectivity-focused.

Membership (Eligibility and Configuration)
Give that the NDB membership is open to the member countries of the United Nations (UN), and the AIIB membership to the members of the World Bank or the Asian Development Bank, both of these new institutions are likely to grow into universal institutions.[4] However, they have so far shown a clearly contrasting membership configuration. The NDB started with the five BRICS founders in 2016, and its membership has since not expanded at all. On the other hand, the AIIB began with 57 signatories in 2016, and its membership has since grown rapidly to 80 (as of July 2018). Despite its official name, many non-regional countries (mostly as donors) have also joined the AIIB. Interestingly, AIIB members (presumably, central governments) can apply for the membership of their non-sovereign

Table 5.1 Purposes/functions, membership, governance structure, authorized capital

	NDB	AIIB
Purposes and functions	To "mobilize resources for infrastructure and sustainable development projects in BRICS and other emerging economies and developing countries, complementing the existing efforts of multilateral and regional financial institutions for global growth and development" (Art. 2)	(I) To "foster sustainable economic development, create wealth and improve infrastructure connectivity in Asia by investing in infrastructure and other productive sectors"; (Art. 1) (II) to "promote regional cooperation and partnership in addressing development challenges by working in close collaboration with other multilateral and bilateral development institutions" (Art. 1)
Membership eligibility	Open to the UN members countries, as a borrow or non-borrower (Art. 5-b, 5-c)	Open to the members of the World Bank and the ADB (Art. 3-1); AIIB members can apply for the membership of their "non-sovereign entities" (Art. 3-3)
Membership: size & configuration	5 (Brazil, Russia, India, China and South Africa); no additional members (as of November. 2017)	57 Founding Members (37 regional and 20 non-regional members); it has grown to 80, with some are in pipeline
Governance structure	(I) the Board of Governors (all members) (Art. 11-a) (II) the Board of Directors (5 seats of 2-year-term, one each from BRICS) (Art. 12-c); it may increase up to 10 (Art. 12-b)	(I) the Board of Governors (all members) (Art. 22-1) (II) the Board of Directors (12 seats): 9 are from Asia (Art. 25-1-i)

	NDB	AIIB
	(III) President selected from BRICS on the rotational basis; 4 Vice-Presidents from the remaining BRICS (Art. 13-c), and the number may increase in the future (Art. 13-b-ii)	(III) President (with senior management), chosen from Asia (Art. 29-1)
	(IV) other officials and staff	(IV) other officials and staff
Authorized capital	US$100 billion (Art. 7-a): 20% in paid-in capital; 80% in callable capital (Art. 7-c) (see Table 5.3 for details)	US$100 billion (Art. 4-1): 20% in paid-in capital; 80% in callable capital (Art. 4-2; Art. 5-1) (see Table 5.3 for details)

Source The author's compilation based on official documents, including AIIB (2017a, b) and NDB (2014)

entities as in the case of Hong Kong. While not totally clear, an implication of this provision could allow—at least theoretically—non-sovereignty,
or quasi-sovereign entities (such as provincial/local governments and perhaps state-owned enterprises) to become the AIIB members (see further
discussion below).[5]

Governance Structure
The NDB and the AIIB share the similar governance structure, consisting
of a Board of Governors, a Board of Directors, a President (with senior management), and other officials and staff. The Board of Governors, which is
represented by all member countries at the Ministerial level, is responsible
for most important decisions to these institutions. The Board of Directors—a non-resident, non-paid entity consisting of government officials
from member countries—is responsible for overseeing the general operation of these institutions (most importantly, granting the approval to each
financing) as well as those functions delegated by the Board of Governors.
The President—the legal representative of the institution, and also Chairman of the Board of Directors without a voting right except the casting
vote—is the chief manager, who is assisted by senior management (vice-
Presidents) and other officers and staff. Due to its smaller scale of membership and operation, the NDB's governance structure is much simpler than
the AIIB's. Let us note that Russia, India and China have their country
presentation at the Board of Directors meetings in both institutions.

The NDB began with the five-member (BRICS) Boards of Governors
and Directors. The Board of Directors may increase its seats up to 10
in order to accommodate new members. The President, chosen from the
BRICS on a rotation basis, heads the credit and investment committee,
which is composed with the four Vice-Presidents (and possibly more in the
future). The first President is K.V. Kamath, an experienced Indian commercial banker. The posts of the Vice-Presidents are occupied by each of
the BRICS members that are not represented as President, and the number
may rise in the future with new members.

The AIIB's Board of Governors began with 50 of the 57 founding signatories (due to the ratification process), and its Board of Directors is composed of 12 seats, of which nine are elected by the regional (Asian) members, and three by the non-regional members. The President—presently,
Jin Liqun of China—is chosen from the regional members for five years.
Each of the five Vice-Presidents—initially from three regional members
and two non-regional members—is responsible for (i) Policy and Strategy,

(ii) Investment Operations, (iii) Finance, (iv) Administration and (v) the Corporate Secretariat, respectively.[6]

Authorized and Subscribed Capital

The NDB and the AIIB commonly began with a total authorized capital of US$100 billion. But they differ greatly regarding how much of it has been subscribed among members. In both institutions, the members' subscription consists of 20% paid-in capital and 80% callable capital. As shall be discussed later, the level of authorized capital has bearings on these institutions' potential lending capacity, and the distribution of their subscribed capital greatly affects the configuration of voting power among the members.

Decision-Making

This subsection presents a comparison between the NDB and the AIIB with regard to voting power. Table 5.2 presents some concrete elements that these institutions' official documents postulate on this matter.

Voting Power

The NDB and the AIIB markedly differ from each other in the distribution of voting power in the Boards of Governors and Directors, where the NDB is at present much simpler and much more "egalitarian" than the AIIB. The NDB's five BRICS founders have the equal voting power (20% each) concomitant with their subscribed capital, and no single member has veto power. While new members would dilute the BRICS members' voting power as a group, the distribution among the Founding Members would remain equalitarian, unless the NDB Agreement should be amended.

The distribution of voting power is far more complicated in the AIIB where each member's voting power consists of: (i) basic votes, (ii) share votes and (iii) Founding Member votes (in the case of a Founding Member). The basic votes, equally distributed to all members,[7] are 12% of the grand total of all votes, i.e. the aggregation of the basic votes, share votes and Founding Member votes of the institution's members. The number of the share votes for a member is equal to its contributions to the AIIB's capital stock. In addition, each Founding Member is allocated a fixed amount of 600 additional votes. Among the three components, the share votes occupy the largest portion, followed by the basic votes and then the Founding Members votes.

Table 5.2 Voting power

	NDB	AIIB
Overall system	"The voting power of each member shall be equal to the number of its subscribed shares in the capital stock of the Bank". (Art. 6-a)	"The total voting power of each member shall consist of the sum of its basic votes, share votes and, in the case of a Founding Member, its Founding Member votes". (Art. 28-1)
Equality elements	BRICS with equal subscription (20% each) share equal voting power (20% each) No veto power to any members	Equal distribution of "basic votes" (12% of grand total) divided up among all members (Art. 28-1-i) Equal distribution of 600 votes to each of the 57 Founding Members (Art. 28-1-iii). But this is a small (and diminishing) portion of total votes
Inequality elements	The consent of 4 out of BRICS, together with 2/3 of the total vote, is required for important matters (Art. 6-b) No new members will enjoy the same voting power as BRICS (see Safeguards below)	Share votes, the heaviest weight in the total votes, are proportional to the members' contributions (Art. 28.1.ii) China, the largest capital contributor, holds veto power (> 25%)—a case of Super Majority—on substantive matters (Art. 28-2-i)
Safeguards to favour a certain group (country)	Ensuring BRICS' dominance, against non-BRICS and non-borrower (donor) members (I) voting power of the BRICS as a group will remain above 55% of the total voting power regardless of additions of new members (Art. 8-c-i); (II) voting power of the non-borrowing members, presumably developed countries, as a group cannot exceed 20% of the total voting power (Art. 8-c-ii) (III) voting power of any single non-BRICS member cannot exceed 7% of the total voting power (Art. 8-c-iii)	Ensuring the dominance of the regional members (particularly China) at least 75% of total voting power (Art. 5-2), against non-regional (and/or non-borrower) countries

Source The author's compilation based on official documents of these institutions, most of all *the Articles of Agreement*

Both institutions also safeguard the special status of certain groups, namely, the BRICS members in the NDB, and the Asian members in the AIIB. According to the NDB Agreement, the BRICS members can retain their dominant position by making future "non-borrowers" remain minor importance with a limited voting power.[8] The AIIB's safeguard provisions allow the regional (Asian) members collectively to retain their "dominant" position (75%) against non-regional members. China, the largest capital contributor in the AIIB, holds veto power (> 25%)—a case of Super Majority—on substantive matters at the Board of Governors. China is followed by India (7.5%), Russia (5.9%), Germany (4.1%) and South Korea (3.5%).

Operational Modality

This subsection section presents two interrelated issue areas: (i) modality of disbursement and (ii) fund sourcing. Table 5.3 presents some concrete elements that the NDB and AIIB Agreements postulate regarding them.

Modality of Disbursement
The NDB and the AIIB are similar in many aspects of funding modality. They are authorized to provide loans, guarantees, equity participation and other financial instruments as well as technical assistance related to development projects in the Global South. These institutions are expected to maintain reasonable diversification of funding activities, thereby not disproportionally benefiting any particular members. The NDB's lending activities are more geographically diverse covering the three major regions of the Global South (Asia, Africa and Latin America), whereas the AIIB, as its name indicates, prioritizes its activities for Asia. These institutions are also expected to treat public sector projects and private ones equally, as in the case of the Inter-American Development Bank.[9] They are allowed to provide services by themselves as well as together with existing institutions, but the lack of in-house manpower and track record are likely to oblige them for a while to be engaged in co-financing those projects that have been already evaluated by others.

While details are not elaborated on, the NDB Agreement postulates that the new institution's overall loaning activities consist of "ordinary operation"—presumably for non-concessional loans—which is financed from the ordinary capital resources, and "special operation"—for concessional loans—which is to be financed from the Special Funds resources. It is anticipated that once poorer countries particularly those in Africa begin to join

Table 5.3 Operational modality: service provision and fund sourcing

	NDB	AIIB
Provision of services (financial and technical)	It provides "loans, guarantees, equity participation and other financial instruments" (Art. 3.i) and "technical assistance for the preparation and implementation of … projects to be supported by the Bank" (Art. 3.iii)	It (i) makes, co-finances or participated in direct loans; (ii) invests funds in the equity capital of an institution or enterprise; (iii) guarantees loans for economic development; (iv) deploys Special Funds resources in accordance with the agreements determining their use; (v) provided technical assistance. (Art. 11-2)
Co-cooperative financing	They provide service by themselves as well as together with existing national, regional and international financial institutions	
Concessional assistance	No concessional lending as such, so far, as no low-income countries are members. Future low-income members (particularly in Africa) will demand such lending. This also depends on these institutions' track record	
Private sector lending	They provide services to public and private projects	
Fund sourcing: subscription, paid-in capital & others	Only half (US$50 billion) of total authorized capital has been subscribed by BRICS (each by US$10 billion)	Virtually all of total authorized capital (US$100 billion) has been subscribed by the Founding Members
	BRICS are expected to make their paid-in capital payment over a time (about 7 years) (Art. 9-a)	The members are expected to make their paid-in capital payment over a time (about 5 years) (Art. 6-1)
Fund sourcing: borrowing	Borrowing is the major source of the NDB's lending activities, presumably from the BRICS capital markets	Borrowing (rather than the members' subscription) is the major source of AIIB's lending, presumably from the international capital markets

Source The author's compilation based on official documents of these institutions, most of all *the Articles of Agreement*

the NDB, they will ask for concessional loans. Similarly, while far from clear the AIIB Agreement also contains the provision on Special Funds, again presumably for concessional loans.

Fund Sourcing

As noted earlier, the NDB and the AIIB commonly were set up with authorized capital of US$100 billion. They differ greatly, however, regarding how much of it has been subscribed among members. At the time of inauguration, the NDB's subscribed capital (US$50 billion)[10] was about one half of the NDB's counterpart (US$98 billion).[11] Furthermore, while the NDB's subscribed capital is equally allocated among the BRICS founders, the AIIB's subscribed capital is dominated (nearly 30%) by China, a country with 26% of total voting power.

As noted earlier, in both institutions, each member's subscription consists of paid-in capital (20%) and callable capital (80%).[12] Paid-in capital, which entails the actual payment over a period of several years, is used—especially at the early period of operation—to cover the sink costs for institutional build-up and associated administrative costs. Callable capital is the member governments' guarantee, and its activation occurs only when the institutions must meet obligations incurred on borrowing funds. We may anticipate that some members—especially China as the wealthy "host" country for both institutions—may voluntarily make extra-budgetary contributions, additionally and separately from their paid-in capital subscription.[13] In any case, these institutions have to wait some time before reaching the position to generate any operational profits and recycle them.[14]

The new institutions, just like the majority of multilateral financial institutions, raise their loanable funds by *borrowing* from international capital markets, by issuing bonds, against the collateral of their capital stock (paid-in capital at hand and callable capital) and retained profit earnings/reserves from past operational profits (Humphrey 2014; Kapur and Raychaudhuri 2014; Nelson 2013). The NDB Agreement sets at 100% as the statutory limit on its gearing ratio.[15] Thus initially (with little capital reserves and surplus), the NDB's lending cannot exceed its total subscribed capital of US$50 billion, and most of fund sourcing is from borrowing. In theory, the NDB is authorized to borrow up to US$50 billion and lend out by the same amount.[16] But the "retained" NDB's paid-in capital may or may not decline depending on its use for covering organizational build-up and administrative costs as well as portfolio investment. Whether the NDB can borrow such large amounts at reasonably low interest rates depends on the selection of appropriate projects, and this process could present cumbersome political questions.

Unlike many other parts, the AIIB Agreement is extremely sketchy regarding fund sourcing, such as its gearing ratio. This is in a way understandable since preparatory consultations, including the negotiations on this document, were mostly bilateral between China (as the finance provider) and Asian countries (as recipients). Perhaps, the latter group was much careless about the sourcing of the AIIB's loanable funds, since this would presumably be the task of China. In any case, the AIIB may raise funds, "through borrowing or other means, in member countries or elsewhere, in accordance with the relevant legal provisions" (Art. 16-1). The AIIB's larger membership, including many non-regional traditional donors with a high credit-rating status, makes it easier (than the NDB) to tap "more efficiently" on the international capital markets.

Concessional loans (Special Accounts) with below market-based terms are to be financed separately from the ordinary account, and this is likely to be financed through period replenishments by member countries in the voluntary basis. So far, this operation has not taken place, it may take some time to get it underway.

Comparative Analysis (2): Prospects of Scaling-Up

Given the fluid world situation, contemplating the future of the NDB and the AIIB, particularly their prospects of scaling-up, can be a risky attempt. Nonetheless, let us proceed with our discussion by focusing on three broad issue areas: (i) membership, (ii) lending activities and (iii) South-South cooperation. Table 5.4 tabulates our discussion.

Membership

The NDB has taken the gradualist approach with regard to membership build-up in order not to overly strain its nascent capacity. As a result, its membership has not shown any expansion beyond its five initial members. On the other hand, thanks to the Chinese initiative and the willing response from many non-regional donors, the AIIB's large initial membership of 57 has further grown to 80 as of this writing (July 2018), and its presence has already eclipsed the NDB's (Cooper 2016, 78; Humphrey 2015).

Now the NDB is at the stage of soliciting new membership. Which countries does it prioritize as favourable new members? Perhaps, its initial

Table 5.4 Prospect of scaling-up: membership, institutional cooperation, service provision

	NDB	AIIB
Membership: pace of expansion	The NDB has taken the "gradualist approach", not overly straining its capacity. It seeks to ensure geographical diversity and a "reasonable mix" of advanced, middle-income and lower-income countries	The AIIB observed an initial rush for membership, but it has slowed down somewhat. Its future membership, particularly that of non-Asian members, will be affected by the track record of its operation. The majority of Asia countries (with a notable exception of Japan) have already joined the institution, though they are different in enthusiasm
	South Africa's regional office, which was established in 2017, will encourage African countries' participation	Japan has remained outside, but has recently indicated its guarded interest in joining the institution
	In the future, the similar offices in Brazil (for Latin America), India (for South Asia) and Russia (Central Asia) may bring forth comparable effects	Some African countries, particularly those that are facing the Indian Ocean, have joined the institutions. Most of the Latin American and Caribbean countries have remained outside
Institutional cooperation	Many official agreements (binding and non-binding) with national and international institutions, not just for co-financing but for many other areas of institutional cooperation. The networks of cooperation appear to be widening	
Service provision: geographical scope	Membership expansion will widen the institution's geographical scope of activities beyond BRICS	Many non-Asian developing countries may not join the institution as its lending activities are geographically prioritized

(continued)

Table 5.4 (continued)

	NDB	AIIB
Service provision: other matters	*Co-financing*: Gradual reduction of heavy reliance on co-financing as the institutions generate a good track record *Project size*: The average size of the projects is likely to grow with their track record of operation *Private sector projects*: While it may not be seen much first, the share of private sector project is likely to grow *Concessional Loans*: No concessional lending so far, as no low-income countries are members. Future low-income members (particularly in Africa) will demand such lending. This also depends on the institution's track record	The AIIB's large membership provides a wider choice of firms for implementing the approved projects Firms from non-regional, non-borrower members (i.e. developed countries) will likely participate actively in projects' procurement biddings Chinese firms, in particular, will be challenged in open biddings
Procurement: agents of project execution	The NDB's limited membership (thus limited locations of projects) may limit who implements them BRICS's collective dominance as procurement sources will inevitably decline as new members (particularly donor countries) join the institution BRICS (and their firms) are likely to retain their collective dominance in the NDB's project implementation	

Source The author's own judgement after the consultation with various sources targets will be other emerging economies and developing countries over developed countries, as the former groups will likely consolidate its pro-South solidarity vis-à-vis traditional financial institutions. In this regard, South Africa's regional office, which was established in 2017, will encourage African countries to join the institution. Likewise, the establishment of similar offices in Brazil (for Latin America), India (for South Asia) and Russia (for Central Asia) may engender comparable effects. Between non-BRICS emerging economies and developing countries, the priority probably may lie in the former group, as they can provide the NDB with larger capital contributions, less risky investment opportunities and more reliable capital markets. While no traditional donor countries have so far indicated their intention of participation, the BRICS founders (and future borrower members) may feel that the NDB should welcome their participation as they would augment its capital base and raise its credit rating, thereby improving its access to international capital markets. However, their membership, even as minority stakeholders, is also likely to dilute the concept of the NDB as an institution of South-South cooperation. In any case, non-borrower countries may consider that they should not harry to join the NDB, preferring to take a wait-and-see stance.

In our view, countries that are very likely to join the NDB are those that are *not* major beneficiaries of the AIIB, namely the non-Asian developing economies, particularly those in Africa and Latin America. Their participation in the NDB will heavily depend on effective solicitation by South Africa and Brazil in their respective region. One possible implication of the likelihood of new membership from Africa and Latin America is the rise of influence of South Africa and Brazil in the NDB's decision-making process. This is because the South African and Brazilian Directors are likely to represent their respective region's smaller members in the Board of Directors.

The AIIB's initial membership of 57 Founding Members has been already a good indication for the future prospect. However, only a few non-regional developing countries—including two BRICS members, Brazil and South Africa—have joined the AIIB. They may perceive that the AIIB's large membership (thus the intense competition among beneficiaries) and Asian-centric operation would put them in a disadvantaged position in benefiting from the institution. Indeed, non-borrower/non-regional members may pressure the AIIB management to intensify its efforts to diversify its membership beyond regional emerging economies and developing countries. One major non-borrower that may join the AIIB in the foreseeable future is an important Asian stakeholder, Japan, a country that has increasingly contemplating the value of positively engaging with—and affecting—the AIIB.

Lending Activities (Quality and Quantity)

Many observers used to expect that the NDB and the AIIB would be alternatives to the traditional multilateral institutions, as their loans would be purportedly free of a strong dosage of prescribing political conditions. However, as these institutions are increasingly co-financing with others and sourcing their loanable funds widely (and cheaply) from international capital markets, they are progressively adhering the conventional banking standards. As for the AIIB, even if its major Asian members (including possibly, China) were willing to let the new institution take high risks, many non-regional/non-borrowers—which are represented by several Vice-Presidents—would likely oblige its loan contracts to stick with conventional prudential conditionality. In any case, most of the AIIB's projects are those located in countries related to China's "One-Belt, One-Road" initiative, and no non-regional members have so far overtly suggested that the AIIB should divert its attention away from this initiative.

Though it is difficult to come up with accurate estimates of these institutes' lending, some observers have attempted at estimating their potential lending based on different methodologies and assumptions. Many of these estimates are optimistic. One observer enthusiastically, or unrealistically, concludes that these institutions could have "a discernible impact on multilateral lend, and thus on global governance" (Reisen 2015, 302). Our estimates are more modest than these referred estimates.

Griffith-Jones, one of the first scholars that bravely ventured into speculating, estimates that the NDB will lend (with average maturity of ten years) about US$5 billion per year during the first 10 years, and US$7 billion annually thereafter (Griffith-Jones 2014). These figures show an extremely large size of lending by a new institution. Reisen (2015) estimating the loan portfolios (outstanding and undisbursed) of the NDB when their respective members' pay-in capital is completed. Reisen (2015) argues that the NDB will cover potential borrower groups similar to the World Bank, and that the institute will potentially have the loan portfolio of US$109 billion in several years. Amazingly, this implies that the NDB's loan stock will potentially reach about two-thirds of the World Bank's present stock. Humphrey (2015) presents scenarios of the NDB's activities based on more detailed and additional assumptions, where even the most optimistic ones turn out to be smaller in scale than those presented by Griffith-Jones and Risen. In fact, Humphrey's estimates for the NDB's *cumulative* loan portfolio are in the range of US$45–65 billion over the first seven years as opposed to Griffith-Jones' estimates of US$5 billion per year during the first ten years and US$7 billion/year during the second ten years, or Reisen's estimate of US$109 billion in seven years after launching operations. Humphrey (2015, 30) thinks that the amounts of the NDB will be "relevant but fairly modest" in relations to existing multilateral development banks, and will not be a global "game-changer". In our view, the NDB will make loans of a few billion dollars at most a year for several years. When emerging economies and developing countries begin applying for membership, the NDB will face a real opportunity of raising its lending capacity substantially. Otherwise, its lending will remain rather limited, at most a few billion dollars.

An estimate of the loan portfolio of the AIIB by Reisen (2015) indicates that the institute will have the portfolio (outstanding and undisbursed) of US$ 127 billion when the paid-in capital is completed (in several years). This is based on the assumption that the AIIB will follow the lending practice of the ADB. This means that the AIIB's loan stock will reach more than one and a half times the ADB's present stock. Based on different assumptions, Humphrey (2015) presents several scenarios of the AIIB's outstanding loan portfolio over the 2016–2025 period and states that the outstanding loan portfolio in 2025 will amount to be somewhere between the lowest sum of US$65.3 billion to the highest of US$127.6 billion.

South-South Cooperation

One big political issue, which this chapter has not discussed, is the outlook of cohesiveness of the Global South as a crucial factor underpinning these new institutions. Perhaps, this is more pertinent to the NDB than the AIIB. It is wondered whether seemingly dwindling BRICS political solidarity would possibly lead to the disintegration of the NDB. Indeed, such weakening could be a crippling effect to the NDB's operation at the early stages of development when there are no or few buffer states/members within the institution that could cushion serious differences among contending members. In this regard, the membership build-up may bring forth the merit of creating conciliatory buffers to the BRICS founders. But we also see that the NDB's management (and the Board of Directors) will try to maintain the institution's technocratic (business) stance and try not to prevent political issues from interfering in the institution's operation.

We recognize the possibilities that some BRICS members may become less willing to keep themselves engaged, and some may officially leave the institution, but the NDB does not require, for its continued existence, the full BRICS membership. In this regard, the only absolutely critical member of the NDB (and to a lesser extent, the AIIB as well) is China, the only Founding Member with political and financial clout and commitment. As for the AIIB, South-South solidarity—as opposed to intra-Asian solidarity—may not be so significant. In fact, the institution's continued operation seems to hinge on the balancing acts of non-regional and/or non-borrower members which can curb China's overwhelming influence in it.

It is wondered whether South-South cooperation as such is related to concessional loans, often through an autonomous (or semi-autonomous) soft loan window. So far, the NDB and the AIIB provide loans carrying interest rate and repayment requirement similar to commercial lending as the main line of operation. But it is anticipated that concessional loans will soon occupy important parts of their operation vis-à-vis low-income countries, particularly those in Africa that may begin to join the NDB (Reisen and Zattler 2016, 3).[17] Given that the BRICS members have increasingly been involved in concessional lending in their bilateral South-South relations, they may not find much merit in bringing the issue of such lending with presumably more time-consuming negotiations to the NDB's operation. Thus, the BRICS members may prefer concessional lending to be handled on a bilateral basis.[18] Some low-income aid recipients themselves may prefer to rely on bilateral channels rather than switch to multilateral channels, but others may view that the NDB can provide an institutional merit of diluting bilateral donors' political influence over recipients' decision-making.

The AIIB Agreement contains the provision on Special Funds, presumably concessional loans, but the wording lacks clarity. As noted earlier, if the AIIB should follow the lending modalities of the major regional development banks, then it would be a matter of time for the AIIB to establish a concessional window to handle "special funds" just as some regional development banks have done earlier. However, the institutionalization of a soft loan window would likely entail a new phase of consultations among the AIIB members at the level of the Boards of Governors and Directors. The main issue of contention—particularly between non-regional (donor) members and the main contributor, China—would be the task allocation of additional contributions (replenishments) to the Special Funds. Arguably, China may prefer to keep its concessional loan operations in its own bilateral channel, rather than bring them under multilateral scrutiny of the new institution.

In sum, the comparative analyses presented in the two preceding sections point to the following issues during next several years. The new institutions are unlikely to induce extremely large impacts on infrastructure financing (a few billion dollars a year). The NDB may thrive to be as pro-development as a South-South institution could be. The AIIB, however, may have to compromise in this regard due to the sizeable and increasing participation of Northern donors. Yet, neither of them is likely to grow to be alternatives—in the sense of replacing—to the existing multilateral financial institutions. We foresee that the NDB's membership, institutional building and lending activity will expand beyond the BRICS parameter, but for various reasons (internal and external), this process will likely happen only slowly, and patchy, mostly in Africa and Latin America. Meanwhile, the AIIB is likely to enjoy its rapid expansion, but only as a contemporary version of traditional regional bank.

CONCLUSION

Given that aid commitments from traditional donors and their development institutions have not been able to effectively address the infrastructure bottlenecks in the Global South, any additional funds, including those from the NDB and the AIIB, should be welcome. These institutions should be encouraged to promote the process of overcoming these bottlenecks so that the fund recipients can tap their development potentials more effectively. After all, the stock of productive assets—particularly a wide range of transport and energy-related infrastructure assets—are likely to bring about positive impacts. Here, one major point of contention is the question of additionality, i.e. to what extent the financing by the NDB and AIIB can constitute a net addition to the international financial flows for infrastructure development in the Global South. The answer to the question of additionality may have a lot to do with the perception regarding whether the financing activities of these new institutions should be seen as alternative or supplementary to the traditional institutions' resources.

The NDB founders—the BRICS members—have often advocated horizontal, South-South solidarity as the institution's ideational foundation, which has offered a comforting rhetoric to many developing countries which may be interested in joining them. In fact, the NDB has been institutionalized so far, as a partnership organization of equals among its Founding Members, where each BRICS member is entitled with an equal amount of capital subscription. If this equality principle should persist, its capital stock will be heavily determined by the weakest BRICS member, South Africa. Thus, unless this smallest BRICS member cannot manage to obtain funds—say, for example, from other BRICS members—to cover the payment of its subscription, the new institution will remain too small to make a serious difference. In that event, one way to make the NDB large enough to matter is to encourage major Northern donors' participation, but this will make the NDB, as in the case of the AIIB, resemble existing multilateral institutions. If the NDB should decide to raise its lending but at the same time to eschew the option of extensively admitting non-borrower countries, then it will have to compromise the principle of equality by letting China— the only one with the financial clout among the BRICS members—raise the NDB's overall capital stock. In that event, it is very likely that China—as the United States did for the World Bank in the 1940s and 1950s—will ask for more commensurate power in the institution's governance (Kapur and Raychaudhuri 2014, 16)

The AIIB has begun its operation with a large membership, arguably the largest (with 57 members) at the time of birth among all regional organizations. In contrast to the NDB, its lager membership has also contributed to a larger operational and lending scale. However, the participation of many traditional donors (mostly as non-regional members) has complicated the task of resolving internal differences and forging a coherent package of institutional strategies that are acceptable to all. Prior to the European announcements of participation, some early observers viewed the AIIB as a manifestation of South-South cooperation, hoping that it would manage its own operations differently from the mainstream development institutions. Now, few observers stress the merit in the management of the AIIB of sustaining the principle of non-interference, a major element of South-South solidarity.

Some observers still expect that both the NDB and the AIIB will continue to refrain from imposing severely intrusive conditions of political and economic nature on their member countries. This is because such conditions (particularly, in the case of the NDB) may appear to contradict the principle of respecting national sovereignty (most importantly, country-ownership of reform). However, as these new institutions undertake large-scale commercial activities around the world, the attitude of ignoring the issue of helping loan-recipient countries build effective states may prove to be a disadvantage rather than an advantage of their operation. Obviously, all contemporary financial institutions—whether national, multilateral or regional types—have to take into consideration various issues of political and regional security issues (see Lipton 2017). The future participation of traditional donor in these institutions (already in the AIIB) will make these institutions resemble the mainstream multilateral institutions.

China, India and Brazil have been among the top borrowers from the World Bank. China and India are also similarly among the top borrowers of the Asian Development Bank. Then it is wondered to what extent the NDB and the AIIB will reduce these emerging economies' reliance on these traditional institutions. We do not expect a major reduction, particularly in absolute terms in the near future. We foresee that these new institutions will, in the foreseeable future, continue to supplement (particularly through co-financing) rather than replace existing institutions. Senior staff of these new institutions are expected to be engaged regularly in exchanges of views on best practices with their counterparts of major multilateral financial institutions. Such exchanges will be important not only to avoid various risks, such as inefficiencies, occupational overlap, and perhaps most importantly the turf war, but also to cause a greater convergence of operation mode. These new institutions, particularly the AIIB, may consequently end up with the same role which they have often accused the existing institutions of playing.

In sum, we recognize that official assistance from traditional donors (bilaterally or multilaterally) has failed to meet financial needs of many developing countries to overcome their infrastructure bottlenecks. In this regard, the expansion of lending activities of the NDB and the AIIB will enable the increasing number of developing countries to cope with their infrastructure deficits and tap their development potentials. We certainly expect that the operational scale of the new institutions will be widened, but at the same time we foresee that this will be a slow and unsteady process. The most optimistic forecasts indicate that these institutions' lending will amount to a fraction of the overall need of infrastructure development in the developing countries. It is unrealistic to expect that poor countries with few natural resources will suddenly be able to get access to sizeable, additional lending from them. If developing countries should perceive that the new institutions (particularly the NDB) fail to create recognizable impacts on the infrastructure bottlenecks and/or bring forth significant changes in the international financial architecture, they would question the merit of reinventing the wheel. Even worse, they may even regard these new institutions as an institutionalized smokescreen to the advantage of the emerging economies—particularly China with overwhelming foreign reserves and active construction firms—to hide their acts of exploitation in fellow developing countries.

NOTES

1. For the background of the NDB, see, for example, Cooper, Andrew F. 2016. *The BRICS: A Very Short Introduction*. Oxford: Oxford University Press; Cooper, Andrew F., and Asf B. Farooq. 2016. "The Role of China and India in the G20 and BRICS: Commonalities or Competitive Behaviour?" *Journal of Current Chinese Affairs* 45 (3): 73–106; Griffith-Jones, Stephany. 2014. "A BRICS Development Bank: A Dream Coming True?" UNCTAD. Discussion Paper No. 215; Kasahara, Shigehisa. 2017. "The New Development Bank (NDB) vs The Asian Infrastructure Investment Bank: An Analytical Comparison from a Critical Perspective". Conference Paper No. 19. Moscow, Russia: The 5th International Conference of BICAS; Latino, Agostina. 2017. "The New Development Bank: Another BRICS in the Wall". In *Accountability, Transparency and Democracy in the Financing of Bretton Woods Institutions*, edited by Elena Sciso, 51–75. London: Springer; and Stuenkel, Oliver. 2015. *The BRICS and the Future of Global Order*. Lanham: Lexington Books.
2. For the background of the AIIB see Chin, Gregory T. 2017. "Asian Infrastructure Investment Bank: Governance innovation and practices". *Global Governance* 22 (1): 11–26; Mishra, Rahul. 2016. "Asia Infrastructure Investment Bank: An Assessment". *Indian Quarterly* 72 (2): 163–79; Weiss, Martin A. 2017. "Asian Infrastructure Investment Bank (AIIB)". Congressional Research Service R44754; Yang, Hai. 2016. "The Asian Infrastructure Investment Bank and Status-Seeking: China's Foray into Global Economic Governance". *Chinese Political Science Review* 1 (4): 754–78; and Yu, Hong. 2017. "Motivation Behind China's 'One Belt, One Road' Initiatives and Establishment of the Asian Infrastructure Investment Bank". *Journal of Contemporary China* 26 (105): 353–68.
3. The Agreement does not reflect the concerns of all Founding Members, particularly those of the non-regional members that missed the earlier consultations. If these donors had been given fuller opportunities of participating in formulating the Agreement, it would have elaborated more on specifications of the new institution's organizational arrangement and operational modalities.

4. It is not clear what this difference in membership eligibility may imply, as the UN, the World Bank and the ADB heavily overlap in membership, with the notable differences being Hong Kong and Taiwan.

5. China rejected the application of Taiwan, a full member of the ADB, to be a "Founding Member", purportedly stating that Taiwan's case could be considered after the establishment of the AIIB, only if Taiwan should ask China's Ministry of Finance to apply for its membership. See Weiss, Martin A. 2017. "Asian Infrastructure Investment Bank (AIIB)". Congressional Research Service R44754: 10.

6. According to official sources, the AIIB has additionally established a Senior Management Team to assist the President. The team consists of five Vice-Presidents together with the General Council and the Chief Risk Officer.

7. Basic votes are intended to enhance the voting power of poorer members with small contributions (thus small share votes). As the scale of the AIIB rises, the collective amounts of basic votes (12% of the total) will also grow, but Founding Member votes (a fixed amount at 600 votes for each Founding Member) will decline in terms of relative weight.

8. While not imminent, the following situation is a possibility; if new members are judged to threaten the 55% majority threshold of the BRICS members, then the NDB management will have to consider either new members' applications (including the size of their shares), or the increase of the founders' shares.

9. They are far less private sector oriented that the European Bank for Reconstruction and Development (EBRD) which was established in 1991 to facilitate the market-oriented transition in the former Eastern bloc countries.

10. The BRICS members have subscribed US$50 billion of the NDB's total authorized capital, and the "headspace" of another US$50 billion will allow them and future members to subscribe additional capital shares.

11. The AIIB's authorized capital was almost fully (more than 98%) subscribed by the Founding Members, with 3/4 being subscribed by 37 regional members, and 1/4 by 20 non-regional ones ("Schedule A" attached to the AIIB Agreement).

12. In the NDB, each founding member's subscribed capital (US$10 billion) is divided into paid-in capital of US$2 billion (20%) and callable capital of US$8 billion (80%). Thus, initially the institution's subscribed paid-in capital and callable capital amount to US$10 billion (US$2 billion times 5) and US$40 billion (US$8 billion times 5), respectively.

13. The Shanghai and Beijing municipalities, the host cities, may provide sizable financial contributions separately to supplement these institutions' funds to cover organizational build-up and administrative costs.

14. According to official sources, the AIIB members as a whole had made the payment of US$6,775,305,000 for the total paid-in capital of

US$18,064,400, or more than 30% by the end of 2016, much faster than the stipulation of the AIIB Agreement.

15. The NDB Agreement states: "The total amount outstanding in respect to the ordinary operations of the Bank shall not at any time exceed the total amount of its unimpaired subscribed capital, reserves and surplus included in its ordinary capital resources" (Art. 20-a).

16. When the US$50 billion headspace of authorized capital is subscribed by the BRICS founders and new members, the amount of borrowing (and thus total lending) can rise up to US$100 billion (and possibly more, if profits should be made from past loans meanwhile) without amending its Agreement.

17. The World Bank started its operation in 1946 to provide "non-concessional" lending to middle-income countries and creditworthy low-income governments, but pressure from developing countries made the major Western powers agree to create a soft loan window, the International Development Association (IDA)—which has so far not raised any funds in the international capital markets—to provide concessional loans and grants to low-income countries. In fact, major regional development banks have established their soft loan window, whose is rather small relative to non-concessional counterpart, and its resources come mostly from periodic replenishments by donor countries (rather than bond issuances); Reisen, Helmut, and Jürgen Zattler. 2016. "Shaping the Landscape of Development Finance Institutions—World Bank reform as another component of a new world order?" *KFW Development Research. View on Development* (1): 3.

18. As stated above, the NDB's concessional lending window is likely to operate with the replenished funds by the members and retained earnings. Since the latter option is not possible at the early stages of operation when the institute has not generated profits, poorer countries may choose to not to join the institution until the institution becomes able to finance such preferential financing.

References

AIIB. 2017a. "AIIB Annual Report and Accounts 2016: Connecting Asia for Future." Asian Infrastructure Investment Bank. https://www.aiib.org/en/news-events/news/2016/annual-report/.content/download/Annual_Report_2016.pdf.

AIIB. 2017b. "Inaugural Meeting of the Board of Governors: Summary Proceedings." Asian Infrastructure Investment Bank, January 16–17. https://www.aiib.org/en/about-aiib/governance/board-governors/.content/index/_download/20160816034745788.pdf.

Cooper, Andrew F. 2016. *The BRICS: A Very Short Introduction*. Oxford: Oxford University Press.

Cooper, Andrew F., and Asf B. Farooq. 2016. "The Role of China and India in the G20 and BRICS: Commonalities or Competitive Behaviour?" *Journal of Current Chinese Affairs* 45 (3): 73–106.

Etzioni, Amitai. 2016. "The Asian Infrastructure Investment Bank: A Case Study of Multifaceted Containment." *Asian Perspective* 40 (2): 173–96.

Griffith-Jones, Stephany. 2014. "A BRICS Development Bank: A Dream Coming True?" UNCTAD. Discussion Paper No. 215.

Kapur, Devesh, and Arjun Raychaudhuri. 2014. "Rethinking the Financial Design of the World Bank." Center for Global Development Working Paper 352.

Kasahara, Shigehisa. 2017. "The New Development Bank (NDB) vs The Asian Infrastructure Investment Bank: An Analytical Comparison From a Critical Perspective." Conference Paper No. 19. Moscow, Russia: The 5th International Conference of BICAS.

He, Alex. 2016. "China in the International Financial System: A Study of the NDB and the AIIB." CIGI Papers No. 106. Waterloo, Ontario: Centre for International Governance Innovation (CIGI).

Humphrey, Chris. 2014. "The Politics of Loan Pricing in Multilateral Development Banks." *Review of International Political Economy* 21 (3): 611–39.

Humphrey, Chris. 2015. "Developmental Revolution or Bretton Woods Revisited? The Prospect of the BRICS News Development Bank and the Asian Infrastructure Investment Bank." Working Paper 418. Overseas Development Institute (ODI).

Latino, Agostina. 2017. "The New Development Bank: Another BRICS in the wall." In *Accountability, Transparency and Democracy in the Financing of Bretton Woods Institutions*, edited by Elena Sciso, 51–75. London: Springer.

Lipton, Merle. 2017. "Are the BRICS Reformers, Revolutionaries or Counter-Revolutionaries?" *South African Journal of International Journal* 24 (12): 41–59.

Mishra, Rahul. 2016 "Asia Infrastructure Investment Bank: An Assessment." *Indian Quarterly* 72 (2): 163–79.

NDB. 2014. "Agreement on the New Development Bank." Fortaleza: New Development Bank, July 15. https://www.ndb.int/wp-content/themes/ndb/pdf/Agreement-on-the-New-Development-Bank.pdf.

Nelson, Rebecca M. 2013. "Multilateral Development Banks: Overviews and Issues for Congress." Congressional Research Service R41170.

Reisen, Helmut. 2015. "Will the AIIB and the NDB Help Reform Multilateral Development Banking?" *Global Policy* 6 (3): 297–304.

Reisen, Helmut, and Jürgen Zattler. 2016. "Shaping the Landscape of Development Finance Institutions—World Bank Reform as Another Component of a New World Order?" *KFW Development Research. View on Development* (1): 3.

Stuenkel, Oliver. 2015. *The BRICS and the Future of Global Order*. Lanham: Lexington Books.

Weiss, Martin A. 2017. "Asian Infrastructure Investment Bank (AIIB)." Congressional Research Service R44754.

Yang, Hai. 2016. "The Asian Infrastructure Investment Bank and Status-Seeking: China's Foray into Global Economic Governance." *Chinese Political Science Review* 1 (4): 754–78.

Yu, Hong. 2017. "Motivation Behind China's 'One Belt, One Road' Initiatives and Establishment of the Asian Infrastructure Investment Bank." *Journal of Contemporary China* 26 (105): 353–68.

CHAPTER 6

Sustainable Development and the New Development (BRICS) Bank: The Contribution of the BRICS Countries

Alexandr Svetlicinii

Introduction: International Development Discourse and the BRICS

The current narrative and meaning of the key concepts in the international development assistance continue to be shaped by the norms and standards originated in the institutions such as the Development Assistance Committee (DAC) of the Organization for Economic Cooperation and Development (OECD)[1] and the World Bank, which have been traditionally dominated by the founding countries of the Bretton Woods institutions and Washington consensus (Serra and Stiglitz 2008). An illustrative example of this influence can be seen in the continuous use of the developed/developing country dichotomy, which draws a dividing line between countries based on various economic criteria (Guillaumont 2009).[2] It also

A. Svetlicinii (✉)
Faculty of Law, University of Macau, Macau, China
e-mail: AlexandrS@um.edu.mo

© The Author(s) 2020   119
J. A. Puppim de Oliveira and Y. Jing (eds.), *International Development Assistance and the BRICS*, Governing China in the 21st Century,
https://doi.org/10.1007/978-981-32-9644-2_6

perpetuates the donor-beneficiary relationship and provides justification for the conditional development aid thus strengthening an unequal relationship between the parties by highlighting the "ignorant arrogance" of the "developed countries" and the "averted responsibility" of the "developing countries" (Neuwirth 2010, 7). The "developing country" terminology criticized by legal scholars (Neuwirth 2013, 2017)[3] has infiltrated the official discourse including the United Nations development agenda which stated that "Millennium Development Goals are critical for meeting the basic needs of people in developing countries."[4] Similarly, the subsequent Sustainable Development Goals (SDG) agenda that "is applicable to all, taking into account different national realities, capacities and levels of development and respecting national policies and priorities" divides the nations into the developed and developing ones.[5] The United Nations Conference on Trade and Development continues to use the designations "developing", "transition" and "developed" in its official reports (UNCTAD 2016, xiii). The classification used by the United Nations Development Programme, the World Bank, and the International Monetary Fund (IMF) has been also criticized as "lacking in clarity with regard to their underlying rationale" (Nielsen 2011). The first timid steps toward the abandonment of the developed/developing country dichotomy can be seen in the World Bank's 2016 edition of the Development Indicators motivated by the SDG agenda: "there is no longer a distinction between developing countries (defined in previous editions as low- and middle-income countries) and developed countries (defined in previous editions as high-income countries)" (Fantom et al. 2016).

The uncritical use of this development terminology has been also adopted by the BRICS countries,[6] which are regarded by some as potential challengers of the Bretton Woods institutions and their development philosophy (Ban and Blyth 2013). In their annual summit declarations, the BRICS continuously referred to themselves as "emerging markets and developing countries" (EMDCs), appealing thereby to the growing potential of the South–South cooperation (Farber 2013).[7] However, there is hardly any agreement among the BRICS countries as to what the criteria for such classification are. For example, in its official development assistance policy China regards itself as a developing country[8] in line with the World Bank's classification.[9] Brazil has recently lodged a formal application for its membership in the OECD,[10] which would bring it, at least formally, into the rank of "emerging economies" together with Mexico, Chile, and Turkey, that had been admitted to this organization earlier. Russia is often classified in the UN documents as an "economy in transition" together with other former Soviet republics (United Nations 2017, 164). While it was engaged in the accession negotiations with the OECD, this process was interrupted in 2014 following the events in Eastern Ukraine and Crimea.[11] The scholars also argue that among the BRICS Russia should not be considered a developing country due to its higher level of income and a more advanced stage of development as well as due to its status of a former superpower and that of the industrialized economy (Nayyar 2016, 576).

A similar lack of clarity follows another, less divisive, concept of "sustainable development" adopted as an official discourse of the SDG agenda. Its origins can be traced back to the 1987 Report of the World Commission on Environment and Development which defined sustainable development as "a process of change in which the exploitation of resources, the direction of investments, the orientation of technological development and institutional change are all in harmony and enhance both current and future potential to meet human needs and aspirations" (World Commission on Environment and Development 1987, para 15). Since then, numerous definitions of sustainable development have been proposed including the "triple bottom line" concept which places an equal importance on environmental, social, and economic considerations in the decision-making (Pope et al. 2004, 597). The BRICS countries have also incorporated the concept of "sustainable development" into their official discourse: "we call for a large-scale mobilization of resources from a variety of sources and for the effective use of financing in order to give strong support to *developing countries* in their efforts to promote *sustainable development*."[12] The Strategy for BRICS Economic Partnership contains among its principles a commitment "to supporting *sustainable development*, strong, balanced and inclusive growth, financial stability, and balanced combination of measures ensuring social and economic development and protection of the environment."[13] The same is true for the national development aid policies of the BRICS countries. For example, although China's national policy on development aid mentions the term "sustainable development," it does not provide any definition of this concept.[14]

While the exact and uniform definition of "sustainable development" may not be practically achievable, there seems to be a universal consensus that infrastructure is crucial for achieving the SDGs. Bhattacharya, Oppenheim, and Stern define sustainable infrastructure as "infrastructure that is socially, economically, and environmentally sustainable" (Bhattacharya et al. 2015, 11). The social component includes respect for human rights and inclusiveness. Economic sustainability reflects a positive impact on GDP per capita and job outcomes. Environmentally sustainable infrastructure mitigates carbon emissions and caters for the climate change. The authors believe that the multilateral development banks (MDBs)[15] have the potential to play a leading role in mobilizing the much-needed capital required for the sustainable infrastructure development (Bhattacharya et al. 2015, 19). The Addis Ababa Action Agenda on Financing for Development concludes that "development banks can play a particularly important role in alleviating constraints on financing development, including quality infrastructure investment" (United Nations 2015, para 75). At the same time, it was noted that the existing MDBs and the bilateral development assistance are providing very limited infrastructure financing, especially for the green-field projects (Chin 2014, 368; Morozkina 2015).

The development of infrastructure has been labeled as one of the drivers of the BRICS' economic rise with economists mentioning the following features of the BRICS economies: significant growth in mobile telephony, intense electricity consumption, greater access to basic sanitation, increased access to water sources, and increased number of infrastructure projects (Santana et al. 2014, 262). However, a study on the efficiency analysis of the BRICS group to transform productive resources and technological innovation into sustainable development indicated significant discrepancies among the BRICS countries in terms of its economic, social, and environmental applications (Santana et al. 2014).[16] For example, in relation to SDG7 "affordable and clean energy," the 2017 UN report indicates that "progress in every area of sustainable energy falls short of what is needed to achieve energy access for all and to meet targets for renewable energy and energy efficiency."[17] The key challenge will be in increasing the share of renewable energy in the heating and transport sectors, which currently account for 80% of the world energy consumption.[18] As reported in 2013, China, India, Russia, Brazil, and South Africa were ranked first, fourth, fifth, sixth, and twelfth, respectively, in global greenhouse gas emissions (Santra 2017, 1). As suggested by the ecology economists, the BRICS countries should be advised to "repudiate the perspective that rapid growth rates are necessary to achieve sustainability, and strive toward a stable state while pursuing equitable access to resources" (May 2008, 3).

While the BRICS have consolidated as a global grouping relatively recently,[19] their individual approaches to development assistance have been already shaped by the prevailing development assistance narrative and their domestic development agendas, which displayed certain heterogeneity and lack of clarity as to the meaning of the key concepts such as developed/developing countries and "sustainable development." Nevertheless, aligned in the understanding of the importance of infrastructure in the economic development, the BRICS countries made a decisive step forward in their cooperation by establishing their own MDB with the aim to mobilize additional financial resources for sustainable development in the BRICS and beyond. The following section reviews the establishment of the BRICS development bank and highlights its institutional and functional features when compared to the existing international financial institutions.

The Establishment of the New Development Bank

The BRICS countries have addressed the problem of under-investment into infrastructure projects (Wang 2016, 41–54) in their 2012 New Delhi Declaration: "We have considered the possibility of setting up a new Development Bank for mobilizing resources for infrastructure and sustainable development projects in BRICS and other emerging economies and developing countries, to supplement the existing efforts of multilateral and regional financial institutions for global growth and development."[20] The agreement to establish the development bank was confirmed in 2013 at the BRICS Summit in South Africa.[21] The New Development Bank (NDB) was unveiled at the BRICS Summit in Fortaleza, Brazil: "we are pleased to announce the signing of the Agreement establishing the New Development Bank (NDB), with the purpose of mobilizing resources for infrastructure and sustainable development projects in BRICS and other emerging and developing economies."[22] The support for the NDB as a new actor in the field of development financing was reiterated in the 2015 Ufa Declaration: "We reiterate that the NDB shall serve as a powerful instrument for financing infrastructure investment and sustainable development projects in the BRICS and other developing countries and emerging market economies and for enhancing economic cooperation between our countries."[23] In order to facilitate the intra-BRICS investment cooperation, the national development banks of the BRICS nations concluded a Memorandum of Understanding on cooperation with the NDB.[24]

It is a rather symbolic coincidence that the Agreement on the New Development Bank was signed on July 15, 2014, which marked the 70th anniversary of the signing of Bretton Woods accord establishing the IMF and the World Bank. The symbolism of the change is also reflected in the fact that the Bretton Woods institutions are headquartered in Washington while the NDB has been hosted in Shanghai, China's international financial center.[25] Thus, in the same way as the economic crisis prompted the association of the BRIC countries in 2009, the slow pace of reforms within the IMF and other Bretton Woods institutions was regarded as one of the catalysts for the establishment of the NDB (Sarkar 2016; Khanna 2014; Tang et al. 2015, 44–49; Martins et al. 2017, 200–220).[26] According to the NDB's former Vice President Paulo Nogueira Batista, "the BRICS would not have gone so far as to create their own development bank if they were fully satisfied with the existing institutions."[27] Nevertheless, the leaders of the Bretton Woods institutions generally welcomed the establishment of the new MDB. The IMF Managing Director Christine Lagarde stated: "I would like to congratulate you on hosting a successful meeting of the BRICS leaders in Fortaleza, Brazil, and especially on establishing the Contingent Reserve Arrangement" (Jha 2014). The World Bank's President Jim Yong Kim also supported the establishment of the NDB (Goforth 2014). The BRICS countries have also chosen a rather cooperative tone urging the NDB to "fully leverage its role and enhance cooperation with multilateral development institutions including the World Bank and the Asian Infrastructure Investment Bank as well as with the BRICS Business Council, to forge synergy in mobilizing resources and promote infrastructure construction and sustainable development of BRICS countries."[28]

The establishment of the NDB is also notable because it represents the first step toward the institutionalization of the BRICS cooperation as opposed to the initial "BRICS way" of non-binding declarations, multi-level meetings, and sectoral dialogues (Qobo and Soko 2015). Some scholars have labeled the establishment of the NDB as a litmus test of cooperation and coordination among the BRICS members. They highlight the diverging national interests reflected in the compromises reached in the NDB Agreement and the pressure to deliver sensible results that put the "mortar" onto the BRICS, which were traditionally regarded as a loose association (Cooper and Farooq 2015). The founding members have decided to share equal stakes in the newly established bank, which reflects the principle of equality among the BRICS countries and their desire to distinguish the NDB from the traditional MDBs where higher capital share carry greater voting rights (Shelepov 2016, 56). This feature alone makes the NDB different from the existing MDBs including the recently established Asian Infrastructure Investment Bank (AIIB), which reproduces the traditional template of the MDB governance with the prominent role of China having a veto power over major decisions with its 29.8% of voting rights (Menegazzi 2017, 231).[29]

While its current members are the BRICS countries, the membership in the NDB is open to any member of the United Nations.[30] At the same time, the NDB Agreement restricted the potential role of the non-BRICS countries in the NDB's decision-making: (1) the BRICS countries will maintain at least 55% of the total voting power; (2) the non-borrowing members will not have more than 20% of the total voting power; (3) any single non-BRICS member cannot have a voting power in excess of 7%.[31] This way the BRICS countries will remain in control and will preserve their equal shares in the NDB governance, participating equally in its eventual successes and failures. The NDB Agreement also stipulated that the president of the NDB shall be elected from one of the founding members on a rotational basis and there shall be at least one vice president from each of the other founding members. Another innovative feature of the NDB was the decision to issue green bonds denominated in the BRICS national currencies. The first such bond in the amount of CNY 3 billion was issued in July 2016[32] and the bond proceeds were invested according to the Green Bond Principles of the People's Bank of China.[33]

At the same time, the academics have expressed their concern that, being increasingly confident in their decision-making abilities, the BRICS will be less willing to accept any advice from international financial institutions and they will also promote their own development models celebrating exceptionalism and uniqueness (Peerenboom and Bugaric 2015, 110–111; Ferchen 2013). The comparative studies on the origins and rhetoric of the BRICS countries' national development assistance programs as well as their administrative arrangements and institutional structures indicate substantial degree of heterogeneity (Rowlands 2012). Common trends such as lack of conditions attached to concessional loans have been noted in the national development aid practices of the BRICS countries (Fisher 2016, 144). For example, this common feature has been observed in the BRICS countries' development cooperation with African states, which "increased their ability to take the necessary decisions to pursue their own development objectives and not those of their donors, ending decades of almost unilateral dependence on Western donors" (Thiam 2017, 120). This is in line with China's principles of foreign aid: (1) helping recipient countries build up their self-development capacity; (2) imposing no political conditions; (3) adhering to equality, mutual benefit and common development;

(4) remaining realistic while striving for the best; and (5) keeping pace with the times and paying attention to reform and innovation.[34]

Professional background of the NDB leadership may be helpful for understanding of the complementarity and potential cooperation of the NDB with other international financial institutions. The NDB's current President K. V. Kamath made a career in the private sector banking leading ICICI, India's largest private sector bank. NDB's former Vice President Paulo Nogueira Batista, a Brazilian economist, served as Executive Director representing Brazil and ten other countries at the IMF from April 2007 to June 2015. Vladimir Kazbekov, NDB's Chief Administrative Officer, worked for Russian National Development Bank—Vnesheconombank. NDB's Chief Operations Officer Xian Zhu served as Vice President and Chief Ethics Officer at World Bank Group from 2012 to 2015. Since 2002, he has been working as Strategy and Operations Director for South Asia, Country Director for Bangladesh, Pacific Islands, Papua New Guinea, and East Timor. Finally, NDB's Chief Financial Officer Leslie Maasdorp worked as Managing Director and President of Bank of America Merrill Lynch for Southern Africa and as Vice Chairman of Barclays Capital. In 2002, he was the first African to be appointed as International Advisor to Goldman Sachs International.[35] The professional background of the NDB leadership made some scholars doubt as to whether the NDB would represent a real alternative to the Bretton Woods institutions (Bond 2016, 617; Cao 2016; Chossudovsky 2017),[36] claiming that the establishment of the NDB would only exacerbate human, ecological, and economic problems of the World Bank's development financing (Bond 2013). At the same time, the leadership composition could signify the intention of the BRICS countries to cooperate with the existing MDBs and other international financial institutions.

While both expectations and concerns about the future performance of the NDB in the field of international development financing have been numerous, the following section aims to understand the approach of the BRICS countries toward the concept of "sustainable development" as it has been articulated in the NDB's documents and financing practices up to date. This section provides an analysis of the environmental and social policies formulated by the NDB as well their initial implementation in the already approved projects and future-oriented strategies, which would allow to define its approach toward "sustainable development," due diligence and impact assessment.

New Development Bank and Its Approach to "Sustainable Development"

Whereas other regional MDBs such as AIIB and Asian Development Bank were called to "formulate differentiated yet complementary portfolios in line with their distinct mandates" (Ji 2017, 269), the NDB expressed its focus on sustainable development through green infrastructure from the outset. While the AIIB also focused its initial investment projects on infrastructure, these were made primarily in the field of transportation[37] and conventional energy.[38] The majority of the NDB's investment projects were made into the renewable energy.[39]

The term "sustainable development" appears in the description of the NDB's purpose to "mobilize resources for infrastructure and sustainable development projects in BRICS and other emerging economies and developing countries, complementing the existing efforts of multilateral and regional financial institutions for global growth and development."[40] Although it is mentioned seven times in the NDB Agreement and its Articles of Agreement, the founding documents do not provide an explicit definition or explanation of this term. In its development strategy for 2017–2021, the NDB pledged "to become an important player in helping BRICS and other EMDCs achieve the UN's 2030 Sustainable Development Goals, as well as those of the Addis Ababa Action Agenda on Financing for Development and the 2015 Paris Agreement on Climate Change."[41] This may indicate the declaratory adherence to the international standards without losing flexibility as to its own investment policies.

The Environment and Social Framework of the NDB is aimed to "ensure environmental and social soundness and sustainability of projects."[42] In the management of social and environmental risks, the NDB relies on the existing country and corporate systems, provided they are consistent with the key requirements of the NDB's Environment and Social Policy as well as Environment and Social Standards.[43] The proposed projects are ranked into three categories based on their potential environmental impacts: Category A (significant adverse environmental and social impacts); Category B (potential adverse environmental and social impacts which are less adverse than Category A); and Category C (minimal or no adverse environmental impacts).[44] For Category A and B projects, the client is required to conduct an environmental and social impact assessment as well as to develop some management plans to address these impacts. The coverage of environmental assessment should be in accordance with the country's international agreements and national laws including the following: biodiversity assessment, biodiversity impacts, critical habitats, natural habitats and protected areas, sustainability of land use, climate change, pollution prevention, resource efficiency, and greenhouse gases.[45] The social impact assessment covers vulnerable groups, gender equality, access to land and natural resources, cultural resources, community safety and health, and labor protection.[46] Then, the NDB carries the due diligence review of the client's reports and if the financing is granted, it monitors and supervises the client's compliance with the environmental and social obligations.[47]

The Environmental and Social Exclusion List contains the following types of projects that the NDB shall not support: illegal products or activities under national and international laws; trade of wildlife regulated under Convention on International Trade in Endangered Species of Wild Fauna and Flora[48]; trans-border movement of waste prohibited under the Basel Convention on the Control of Transboundary Movements of Hazardous Wastes and their Disposal[49]; weapons and munitions, including paramilitary materials; alcoholic beverages, excluding beer and wine; tobacco; gambling and casinos; un-bonded asbestos fibers; activities prohibited by national law or by international conventions related to the protection of biodiversity resources or cultural heritage[50]; commercial logging operations; marine and coastal fishing practices harmful to vulnerable or protected species in large numbers which are damaging to the marine biodiversity and habitats; shipment of oil or other hazardous substances in tankers that do not comply with the International Maritime Organization's requirements.[51]

It should be noted that, apart from the international instruments that have been ratified by the BRICS countries, the only additional item on the negative list directly related to the sustainable infrastructure development is the production and use of un-bonded asbestos fibers. It is hardly unlikely that the borrowing countries will request financing for the commercial logging operations and fishing practices that damage marine biodiversity. Thus, the Environmental and Social Exclusion List adds little to the internationally accepted norms and standards related to the environmental and social impact of development projects. For example, it was noted that the NDB may be willing to support large hydroelectric dams and coal-fired power stations, which could raise criticisms as to the sustainability of the development projects which the NDB supports (Bertelsmann-Scott et al. 2016, 20; Hochstetler 2014). Similar exclusion lists adopted by other MDBs appear to be more extensive. For example, the AIIB pledged not to support projects involving products containing polychlorinated biphenyl, pharmaceuticals, pesticides/herbicides and other hazardous substances subject to international phase-outs or bans, ozone-depleting substances, trans-boundary movements of waste prohibited under the international law, wood or other forestry products other than from sustainably managed forests, etc.[52]

When it comes to transparency and public participation in the NDB projects, the NDB's Environment and Social Framework is rather concise. It requires the beneficiary "to conduct a meaningful consultation process that is compliant with national laws and regulations."[53] It also requires the client "to establish and maintain a fair and effective grievance redress mechanism to receive and facilitate timely resolution of affected peoples' concerns and grievances about ... environmental and social performance."[54] Both obligations refer to the national legislation and standards unless they are incompatible with the NDB's policy. However, the NDB's own standards on these two issues are so succinct that they hardly allow for an objective assessment as to whether national standards are compliant with the NDB's ones or not.[55]

At the time of writing of this paper, the NDB has approved twenty-two projects benefiting all BRICS countries in the amount of USD5.5 billion. Table 6.1 summarizes the geographic, financial and sectoral profile of the approved projects.

The first NDB loan of USD81 million issued on December 21, 2016 funded the construction of the solar photovoltaic power plant with the total capacity of 100 MW in Lingang Industrial Area of Shanghai.[56] According to the NDB's President K. V. Kamath, this "project would benefit end users in the industrial area, people of Shanghai in particular and people of China in general, due to production of electricity in an environmentally sustainable manner leading to reduction in emissions."[57] Another green energy project financed by the NDB in China concerned the Putian Pinghai Bay offshore wind power project in Fujian province. In early 2017, the NDB approved a USD300 million loan to the Brazilian National Bank for Economic and Social Development (BNDES) to finance some renewable energy projects. In South Africa, the NDB supported the state public utility Eskom with a loan of USD180 million for the construction of transmission lines connecting various renewable energy plants to the national electricity grid (Cohen 2017).[58] In Russia, the NDB joined forces with the Eurasian

Table 6.1 New Development Bank's projects

No.	Project	Amount (in USD million)	Borrower	Target sector	Development impact
1	Canara (India)[a]	250	Canara Bank	Renewable energy (wind, solar, etc.)	500 MW renewable energy; avoided 815,000 t CO_2/year
2	Lingang (China)	81	PRC Government	Renewable energy (solar rooftop PV)	100 MW Solar; avoided 73,000 t CO_2/year
3	BNDES (Brazil)[b]	300	National Bank for Economic and Social Development	Renewable energy (wind, solar, etc.)	600 MW renewable energy; avoided 1,000,000 t CO_2/year
4	ESKOM (South Africa)	180	ESKOM	Renewable energy (transmission)	670 MW renewable energy evacuated (transmitted); avoided 1,300,000 t CO_2/year
5	EDB/IIB (Russia)[c]	100	Eurasian Development Bank/International Investment Bank	Renewable energy (hydro-power) + green energy	49.8 MW renewable energy; avoided 48,000 t CO_2/year
6	Madhya Pradesh (India)	350	Government of India	Upgrading major district roads	About 1500 km of MDRs will be upgraded
7	Pinghai (China)	298	PRC Government	Renewable energy (wind power)	250 MW Wind; avoided 869,900 t CO_2/year
8	Hunan (China)	300	PRC Government	Water, sanitation and flood control, environment	Improved water quality and flood control in the main streams and tributaries of Xiang River
9	Jiangxi (China)	200	PRC Government	Energy conservation	Savings of 95,118 t of coal equivalent; Annual CO_2 emissions reduction is 263,476 t

No.	Project	Amount (in USD million)	Borrower	Target sector	Development impact
10	MP Water (India)	470	Government of India	Water supply and sanitation, rural development	Project covers more than 3400 villages and will benefit over 3 million rural population
11	Judicial support (Russia)[d]	460	Government of RF	Social infrastructure	Increased judicial transparency and efficiency and enhanced protection of judicial rights of citizens
12	Rajasthan Water (India)	345	Government of India	Irrigation, agriculture	Additional 1.25 mil acre feet of water available for land cultivation; 33,312 hectares of water-logged area rehabilitated for cultivation; Water use efficiency improved by 10%
13	Ufa Eastern Exit (Russia)[e]	68.8	Government of RF	Transportation	Reducing congestion and aiding faster commute for residents; Enhanced safety of traffic by diverting dangerous goods away from city center; A balanced spatial residential and industrial development; Strengthening Ufa's position as a strategic transportation hub

(continued)

Table 6.1 (continued)

No.	Project	Amount (in USD million)	Borrower	Target sector	Development impact
14	Volga (Russia)	320	Government of RF	Water supply and sanitation, sustainable development	Increased operating efficiency of water supply and sanitation systems Reduced growth of utilities tariffs for the population Reduced investments in capital repairs for rehabilitation of water supply and sanitation systems Significant reduction of environmental damage of Volga river Increased health security for citizens with improved quality of water supply
15	Small Historic Cities (Russia)	220	Government of RF	Urban infrastructure, sustainable development	Better preserved and exhibited cultural heritage sites Upgraded basic urban infrastructure and incidental services

No.	Project	Amount (in USD million)	Borrower	Target sector	Development impact
16	Durban Container Terminal Berth Reconstruction Project (South Africa)	200	Transnet SOC Ltd.	Transport infrastructure	Expansion of the Durban Port's capacity, allowing to safely accommodate larger vessels with gross tonnage of 9000+ TEUs Trading volume growth for local businesses Creation of over 18,000 job opportunities Additional fish stocks due to increased intertidal and subtidal habitat in the Durban Port's area
17	Pará Sustainable Municipalities Project (Brazil)	50	Government of the State of Pará	Sustainable infrastructure, urban development	Provide all-weather connectivity within the city to residents of the municipalities Decreased flooding Improved sanitation Reduced road maintenance costs Improved health of residents

(continued)

Table 6.1 (continued)

No.	Project	Amount (in USD million)	Borrower	Target sector	Development impact
18	Maranhão Road Corridor—South–North Integration (Brazil)	71	Government of the State of Maranhão	Sustainable infrastructure, transport	Reduced time of road travel Reduced logistics costs between the agricultural area and the Itaqui Port Integration of the North and South of Maranhão, linking municipalities that are now isolated Enhanced economic development of the State of Maranhão
19	Chongqing Small Cities Sustainable Development Project (China)	300	PRC Government	Urban infrastructure, sustainable infrastructure	Improved spatial layout Increased connectivity and accessibility Reduced traffic congestion Enhanced ecological environment Enhanced tourism sector in some of the sub-project cities Improved living conditions through integrated urban planning and urban regeneration

No.	Project	Amount (in USD million)	Borrower	Target sector	Development impact
20	Bihar Rural Roads Project (India)	350	Government of India	Sustainable infrastructure, transport	Enhanced farm productivity Increased income Improved access to economic, social and educational centers Enhanced economic growth for the populace in the interior regions of the state, resulting from increased transport capacity and efficiency
21	Luoyang Metro Project (China)	300	PRC Government	Sustainable infrastructure, urban transport	Increased transport capacity Lower carbon environment Reduced congestion Faster commute with improved mobility Enhanced comfort, safety and reliability of traffic in the city-improved connectivity contributing to a balanced city spatial development More robust socio-economic development of Luoyang

(continued)

Table 6.1 (continued)

No.	Project	Amount (in USD million)	Borrower	Target sector	Development impact
22	Greenhouse Gas Emissions Reduction and Energy Sector Development Project (South Africa)	300	Development Bank of Southern Africa	Clean energy and sustainable development	Reduction in carbon dioxide emissions Increase in generation capacity from renewable energy sources Increase in the efficiency of the overall energy sector in South Africa Unlock private sector investment

Source New Development Bank (http://www.ndb.int/projects/list-of-all-projects/) (as of July 26, 2018)

[a]See "BRICS Bank Disburses $250 Million Loan for Renewable Energy Project to Canara Bank." *The Economic Times*, April 15, 2016

[b]See BNDES. 2017. "BNDES Signs Contract of US$300 Million with the New Development Bank to Finance Alternative Renewable Power." April 26. https://www.bndes.gov.br/SiteBNDES/bndes/bndes_en/Institucional/Press/Noticias/2017/20170426_alternative_renewable_power.html

[c]See Eurasian Development Bank. 2017. "EDB and New Development Bank Sign Loan Agreement for US$50 Million to Finance the Construction of Hydroelectric Power Plants in Karelia and Other 'Green' Projects." August 15. https://eabr.org/en/press/news/edb-and-new-development-bank-sign-loan-agreement-for-us-50-million-to-finance-the-construction-of-hy/

[d]See "Russia Received a Loan from BRICS Bank for the Development of Artificial Intelligence in Courts." *ACQUISITION.RU*, September 11, 2017. http://acquisition.ru/?p=2080

[e]See "Ufa Eastern Exit Construction Is Financed by New BRICS Development Bank." *Bashinform*, June 6, 2017. http://www.bashinform.ru/eng/1007921/

Development Bank and International Investment Bank to support the construction of small hydropower plants in the Russian northwestern region of Karelia.[59] Finally, India received five NDB loans: USD250 million to India's Canara Bank for renewable energy projects, USD350 million for the upgrading of major district roads in the land-locked state of Madhya Pradesh in the central region of the country, USD470 million for improving water supply and sanitation in the same province, USD345 million for investing in irrigation systems in the state of Rajasthan, and USD350 million for transportation infrastructure in the state of Bihar.

The above overview demonstrates that so far India, China, and Russia have been the primary beneficiaries of the NDB development financing with the loans totaling USD2765, 1479, and 1168.8 million, respectively. Eight out of total twenty-two loans issued by the NDB have been in the renewable energy sector. Most of the capital has been borrowed by the governments of the respective BRICS countries, while lesser amounts have been disbursed to the national development banks (Brazil), state-owned companies (South Africa), and MDB consortia (Russia). The focus on the green energy infrastructure was reiterated in the NDB's General Strategy for 2017–2021, which pledged to dedicate two-thirds of the NDB's financing commitments to "sustainable infrastructure development." The latter is understood as "infrastructure projects that incorporate economic, environmental and social criteria in their design and implementation."[60] As a result, the second batch of the NDB's loans has been directed toward the financing of urban infrastructure (including water and sanitation systems) and the transport infrastructure (upgrading of urban and rural roads, and port terminals).

At the initial stage of the NDB's activities, it received numerous suggestions as to the focus of its financing activities. For example, Muhammad Yunus, the Bangladeshi Nobel Peace Prize-winning economist and banker, has proposed four priorities for NDB: (1) mobilize the power of the young generation, (2) technology, (3) building social businesses, and (4) human rights and good governance (Yunus 2015). The Oxfam, an international charity confederation, suggested that "the new Bank must direct its efforts towards ending extreme poverty, deprivation and hunger, and ensuring human rights for all; so that everyone has their essential needs met, and can access the resources, capabilities and freedoms needed for human well-being" (Oxfam 2014, 6). Nevertheless, the emerging financing practice of the NDB and its General Strategy 2017–2021 indicates a preference of the founders to take one step at a time and focus on the financing of the green infrastructure projects that would fit into the national development policies of the BRICS countries. It is also indicative that significant amounts have been disbursed to the national development banks that carry out their countries' national development agenda. This confirms the earlier concern that the NDB's work would be influenced by the national development agendas of the BRICS countries (Abdenur 2014, 98).[61]

Conclusion: The BRICS for the Global Development Agenda

In the field of international development finance, the BRICS countries are relative newcomers despite the significant advances of their national development agendas and bilateral development aid programs. As a result, the international discourse and standards in this domain continue to be dominated by the traditional Western donors and Bretton Woods institutions. Although the BRICS have been hailed by some as challengers of the existing regulatory frameworks and builders of the future economic governance, at least in the field of development cooperation they seem to follow rather than to challenge the existing trends. The above analysis demonstrated that the BRICS countries and the NDB, their first institutional creation, have adopted the rhetoric of developed/developing country dichotomy. In this regard, we should note that the universal SDG agenda represents a unique challenge and an opportunity for the mutual learning in the field of international development cooperation both for the established and emerging development cooperation actors such as BRICS countries. While the differences in approaches and terminology of the development cooperation persist, the academics and practitioners should be encouraged to "work together to identify the necessary criteria and specific mechanisms to be put in place to ensure more transparency, efficacy and effectiveness in this changing environment of aid provision" (Gu 2015, 9).

The same is true for the understanding of "sustainable development" and "sustainable infrastructure." At this point, in time, the NDB has not yet made any substantial steps to clarify these terms or to develop its own "sustainable development" approach that would add to the existing international standards and practices developed by other international financial institutions. With the reference to the NDB's focus on infrastructure financing, the scholars noted at least partial incompatibility between the infrastructure projects and "sustainable development" pointing to the adverse environmental and social impacts of the large infrastructure development projects (Hochstetler 2014). In this sense, it should become imperative for the NDB to acknowledge the existence of this partial incompatibility and then to develop the standards that would allow for the balancing between various objectives. It appears that currently this balancing is left to the beneficiary countries.

As noted by Nayyar, "[the NDB's] success or failure as an institution will perhaps be the most important litmus test for BRICS in terms of their willingness and ability to contribute to development elsewhere and improve global governance" (Nayyar 2016, 588). That is why the expansion of the membership could be crucial for the NDB to make a difference. The scholars noted diverging national interests of the BRICS nations during the establishment and the initial period of the NDB's work (Chin 2014, 371).[62] The above analysis also demonstrated the influence of the national development aid policies of the BRICS countries on the NDB's policies. Although the expansion of NDB's membership was planned for 2017–2018 (Zhang 2016), no new members had been reported at the time of writing.

The continuous control of the BRICS countries over the NDB's activities and their equal share in this control, at least formally, places special responsibility on the BRICS in relation to future advances in the field of international development finance. By learning from their national experiences in the infrastructure building and sustainable development reforms, as well as from the practices of the existing MDBs, they are expected to make a meaningful contribution to the SDG agenda both in their own countries and beyond. In this sense, the recently established NDB could become a driving force in formulating the "BRICS approach" to the "sustainable development" that could encourage more South–South cooperation and supplement the efforts of various international organizations and development banks.

Acknowledgements The author acknowledges the support from the University of Macau Multi-Year Research Grant MYRG2016-00116-FLL "Global Governance through Transnational "Inter-Regime Coopetition" and the BRICS Countries."

Notes

1. See OECD Development Assistance Committee, http://www.oecd.org/development/developmentassistancecommitteedac.htm.
2. For example, the classification of the "least developed country" used by the United Nations includes the following indicators: gross national income

per capita, Human Assets Index, Economic Vulnerability Index. See United Nations, Committee for Development Policy. "LDC Identification Criteria and Indicators." https://www.un.org/development/desa/dpad/least-developed-country-category/ldc-criteria.html.

3. The scholar urged to abandon the developed/developing country terminology and to replace it by more differentiated methodological approaches, such as the stage theory as a method of scientifically studying "change" in the form of development.

4. United Nations, General Assembly. 2013. "Outcome Document of the Special Event to Follow Up Efforts Made Towards Achieving the Millennium Development Goals." A/68/L.4, October 1, para 4.

5. United Nations, General Assembly. 2015. "Resolution 70/1 'Transforming our world: the 2030 Agenda for Sustainable Development.'" A/RES/70/1, October 21.

6. The term BRICS refers to Brazil, Russia, India, China, and South Africa. The term BRIC was used in Jim O'Neill (2001).

7. See VII BRICS Summit Ufa Declaration, July 9, 2015, para 11. Farber divides the emerging economies into two large groups: One that is enjoying rapid economic growth and begins to see a trajectory toward developed country lifestyles, and another that is lagging behind and is still more similar to the developing country residents. As a result, the author argues in favor of differentiated responsibilities of the emerging economies.

8. Information Office of the State Council of the People's Republic of China, China's Foreign Aid, April 2011. http://english.gov.cn/archive/white_paper/2014/09/09/content_281474986284620.htm.

9. "Yet China remains a developing country (its per capita income is still a fraction of that in advanced countries) and its market reforms are incomplete." See "World Bank, China: Overview" *The World Bank*. April 8, 2019. http://www.worldbank.org/en/country/china/overview.

10. Presidency of the Republic of Brazil, 2017. "Brazil Formalizes Request to Join OECD." May 30. http://www.brazil.gov.br/about-brazil/news/2017/05/brazil-formalizes-request-to-join-oecd.

11. OECD. 2014. "Statement by the OECD Regarding the Status of the Accession Process with Russia & Co-Operation with Ukraine." March 13. http://www.oecd.org/newsroom/statement-by-the-oecd-regarding-the-status-of-the-accession-process-with-russia-and-co-operation-with-ukraine.htm.

12. VII BRICS Summit Ufa Declaration, July 9, 2015, para 66.

13. The Strategy for BRICS Economic Partnership, July 9, 2015, para I.2.

14. See Information Office of the State Council, China's Foreign Aid, July 2014. http://english.gov.cn/archive/white_paper/2014/08/23/content_281474982986592.htm.

15. See Overseas Development Institute. 2015. "Multilateral Development Banks: A Short Guide." December. https://www.odi.org/sites/odi.org.uk/files/resource-documents/10650.pdf.

16. According to the study based on the 2001–2007 data, Brazil had the highest average economic efficiency, while China was classified as the country with the lowest environmental efficiency. With regard to social efficiency, Brazil was on the top followed by Russia, South Africa, China, and India.

17. UN Economic and Social Council. 2017. "Report of the Secretary General 'Progress Towards the Sustainable Development Goals.'" E/2017/66, May 11.

18. Ibid.

19. The first BRIC Summit was held in Yekaterinburg (Russia) in 2009 and South Africa joined the group in 2011 at the BRICS Summit in Sanya (China).

20. 4th BRICS Summit, New Delhi Declaration, March 29, 2012, para 13.

21. See Statement by BRICS Leaders on the Establishment of the BRICS-Led Development Bank, March 27, 2013.

22. 6th BRICS Summit, Fortaleza Declaration, July 15, 2014, para 11.

23. 7th BRICS Summit, Ufa Declaration, July 9, 2015, para 15.

24. Memorandum of Understanding on Cooperation with the New Development Bank, July 9, 2015, was concluded at BRICS Summit in Ufa between Banco Nacional de Desenvolvimento Econômico e Social (Brazil), Bank for Development and Foreign Economic Affairs (Russia), Export-Import Bank of India, China Development Bank Corporation, and Development Bank of Southern Africa.

25. The NDB's Africa Regional Center was established in Johannesburg in August 2017. The NDB also announced its intention to open regional offices in Brazil, Russia, and India. See NDB. 2016. "NDB 2016 Annual Report." https://www.ndb.int/wp-content/uploads/2017/10/NDB-ANNUAL-REPORT-2016.pdf, p. 17.

26. Another set of reasons for the establishment of the NDB refers to the domestic economic realities of the BRICS countries: huge financing gap for basic infrastructure investment and the lack of productive investment options for their foreign exchange reserves.

27. "World Powers 'Misuse' World Bank, IMF: BRICS Bank Exec", *ZeeNews*, October 5, 2016, http://zeenews.india.com/business/news/international/world-powers-misuse-world-bank-imf-brics-bank-exec_1937157.html.

28. 9th BRICS Summit, Xiamen Declaration, September 4, 2017, para 31.

29. The similar tendency can be observed in other MDBs with the United States holding 16.45% voting rights in the World Bank and Japan having a majority of 12.78% in the Asian Development Bank.

30. NDB Agreement, Article 2(2).

31. NDB Articles of Agreement, Article 8(c).
32. As stated by NDB's CFO Leslie Maasdorp: "The NDB will continue to explore further local currency bond issuances in China as well as other member countries. We intend to actively promote the development of green finance and become a frequent issuer in the Chinese interbank market." In *NDB 2016 Annual Report*. https://www.ndb.int/wp-content/uploads/2017/10/NDB-ANNUAL-REPORT-2016.pdf, p. 32. In contrast, the AIIB has announced the plan to issue its first US dollar-denominated bond in 2018.
33. People's Bank of China Announcement No. 39/2015, December 15, 2015.
34. Information Office of the State Council of the People's Republic of China, China's Foreign Aid, April 2011. http://english.gov.cn/archive/white_paper/2014/09/09/content_281474986284620.htm.
35. The resumes of the NDB's senior management are available at http://www.ndb.int/about-us/organisation/governance/.
36. Bond: "Given the South African BRICS bankers' backgrounds, it is reasonable to ask whether Pretoria was ever serious about challenging the Bretton Woods system, dollar hegemony and other structures of global power." Also, Cao regards the establishment of the NDB and the yuan-denominated Russia-China natural gas deal as signs of erosion of the US dollar hegemony. At the same time, Chossudovsky points out that India, Brazil, and South Africa are heavily indebted countries and their contributions to the NDB could be financed either by depleting their dollar-denominated central bank reserves or by borrowing the money and thus running up their dollar-denominated external debt.
37. For example, in 2016 the AIIB financed the following transportation infrastructure projects: Tajikistan: Dushanbe-Uzbekistan Border Road Improvement Project, Pakistan: National Motorway M-4 Project; Oman: Duqm Port Commercial Terminal and Operational Zone Development Project; Oman: Railway System Preparation Project. The list of AIIB projects is available at https://www.aiib.org/en/projects/approved/index.html.
38. The examples include: Myanmar: Myingyan Power Plant (gas-fired) Project; Azerbaijan: Trans Anatolian Natural Gas Pipeline Project (TANAP); Bangladesh: Natural Gas Infrastructure and Efficiency Improvement Project; Turkey: Tuz Golu Gas Storage Expansion Project.
39. "We note with appreciation the approval of the first set of loans by the New Development Bank (NDB), particularly in the renewable energy projects in BRICS countries. We express satisfaction with NDB's issuance of the first set of green bonds in RMB." 8th BRICS Summit, Goa Declaration, October 16, 2016, para 4.
40. NDB Agreement, Article 1(1); NDB Articles of Agreement, Article 2.
41. NDB. 2017. "NDB's General Strategy: 2017–2021." June 30, pp. 12–13.

42. NDB. 2016. "NDB Environment and Social Framework." March 11, pp. 3–4.
43. Ibid., p. 6.
44. Ibid., pp. 7–8.
45. Ibid., pp. 16–17.
46. Ibid., pp. 18–19.
47. Ibid., p. 11.
48. 993 UNTS 243. All BRICS countries have ratified the Convention.
49. 1673 UNTS 126. All BRICS countries have ratified the Convention.
50. Convention on the Conservation of Migratory Species of Wild Animals (1651 UNTS 333), Convention on Wetlands of International Importance (996 UNTS 245), Convention Concerning the Protection of the World Cultural and Natural Heritage (1037 UNTS 151), and Convention on Biological Diversity (1760 UNTS 79).
51. NDB. 2016. "NDB Environment and Social Framework." March 11, p. 13.
52. AIIB. 2016. "Environmental and Social Framework." February. https://www.aiib.org/en/policies-strategies/_download/environment-framework/20160226043633542.pdf, p. 46.
53. NDB. 2016. "NDB Environment and Social Framework." March 11, p. 10.
54. Ibid., p. 11.
55. The definitions of "meaningful consultation" and "grievance mechanism" occupy two paragraphs in the NDB's Environment and Social Standards. See ibid., p. 15.
56. See NDB. 2016. "NDB Signs First Loan Agreement for Financing Shanghai Lingang Distributed Solar Power Project." December 21. http://www.ndb.int/press_release/ndb-signs-first-loan-agreement-financing-shanghai-lingang-distributed-solar-power-project/.
57. See NDB. 2016. "Speech for the Signing Ceremony—Shanghai Lingang Distributed Solar Power Project." December 21. http://www.ndb.int/president_desk/speech-signing-ceremony-shanghai-lingang-distributed-solar-power-project/.
58. The implementation of this project was delayed because Eskom subsequently refused to sign agreements with renewable energy projects in terms of the Renewable Energy Independent Power Producer Programme, arguing that they were not cost-effective.
59. See International Investment Bank. 2016. "Construction of Hydropower Plants in Russia's Republic of Karelia—First Joint Project of IIB and EDB." August 4. https://www.iib.int/en/articles/stroitelstvo-ges-v-karelii-pervyi-sovmestnyi-proekt-mib-i-eabr.
60. NDB. 2017. "NDB's General Strategy: 2017–2021." June 30, p. 7.
61. Abdenur argues that China's impact on the NDB could result in putting off the table the issues such as human and labor rights, environmental conditions, and other dimensions of social well-being.

62. For example, it was noted that South African officials urged the NDB to allocate significant funding to finance the development of African countries. Other BRICS countries, however, believe that the initial focus of the NDB should be on financing their own development projects.

BIBLIOGRAPHY

Abdenur, Adriana Erthal. 2014. "China and the BRICS Development Bank: Legitimacy and Multilateralism in South-South Cooperation." *IDS Bulletin* 45 (4): 85–101.

Ban, Cornel, and Mark Blyth. 2013. "The BRICs and the Washington Consensus: An Introduction." *Review of International Political Economy* 20 (2): 241–255.

Bertelsmann-Scott, Talitha, Cyril Prinsloo, Elizabeth Sidiropoulos, Lesley Wentworth, and Christopher Wood. 2016. "The New Development Bank: Moving the BRICS from an Acronym to an Institution." South African Institute of International Affairs, Occasional Paper No. 233, June. https://saiia.org.za/research/the-new-development-bank-moving-the-brics-from-an-acronym-to-an-institution/.

Bhattacharya, Amar, Jeremy Oppenheim, and Nicholas Stern. 2015. "Driving Sustainable Development Through Better Infrastructure: Key Elements of a Transformation Program." Global Economy & Development Working Paper No. 91, July 10. https://www.brookings.edu/wp-content/uploads/2016/07/07-sustainable-development-infrastructure-v2.pdf.

Bond, Patrick. 2013. "Sub-Imperialism as Lubricant of Neoliberalism: South African 'Deputy Sheriff' Duty Within BRICS." *Third World Quarterly* 34 (2): 251–270.

Bond, Patrick. 2016. "BRICS Banking and the Debate Over Sub-Imperialism." *Third World Quarterly* 37 (4): 611–629.

Cao, Lan. 2016. "Currency Wars and the Erosion of Dollar Hegemony." *Michigan Journal of International Law* 38: 57–118.

Chin, Gregory T. 2014. "The BRICS-Led Development Bank: Purpose and Politics Beyond the G20." *Global Policy* 5 (3): 366–373.

Chossudovsky, Michel. 2017. "BRICS and the Fiction of 'De-Dollarization'." *Global Research* 10.

Cohen, Tim. 2017. "Eskom's Brics Bank Loan on Ice Until 2018." *Business Day*, August 17.

Cooper, Andrew F., and Asif B. Farooq. 2015. "Testing the Club Dynamics of the BRICS: The New Development Bank from Conception to Establishment." *International Organisations Research Journal* 10 (2): 32–44.

Fantom, Neil, Tariq Khokhar, and Edie Purdie. 2016. "The 2016 Edition of World Development Indicators Is Out: Three Features You Won't Want to Miss." *Blog of the World Bank*, April 30. https://blogs.worldbank.org/opendata/

2016-edition-world-development-indicators-out-three-features-you-won-t-want-miss.

Farber, Daniel. 2013 "Beyond the North-South Dichotomy in International Climate Law: The Distinctive Adaptation Responsibilities of the Emerging Economies." *Review of European Community & International Environmental Law* 22 (1): 42–53.

Ferchen, Matt. 2013. "Whose China Model Is It Anyway? The Contentious Search for Consensus." *Review of International Political Economy* 20 (2): 390–420.

Fisher, Tamara. 2016. "China and the New Development Bank: The Future of Foreign Aid." *Loyola of Los Angeles International and Comparative Law Review* 38: 141–168.

Goforth, Sean. 2014. "Coming to Terms with the BRICS Bank—Analysis, Eurasia Review." *Eurasia Review*, August 9.

Gu, Jing. 2015. "China's New Silk Road to Development Cooperation: Opportunities and Challenges." Nueva York: United Nations University Centre for Policy Research. http://i.unu.edu/media/cpr.unu.edu/attachment/1803/UNUCPR_ChinasNewSilkRoad_Gu_.pdf.

Guillaumont, Patrick. 2009. *Caught in a Trap: Identifying the Least Developed Countries.* Paris: Economica.

Hochstetler, Kathryn. 2014. "Infrastructure and Sustainable Development Goals in the BRICS-Led New Development Bank." CIGI Policy Brief No. 46. https://www.cigionline.org/sites/default/files/cigi_pb_46_0.pdf.

Jha, Lalit K. 2014. "IMF Welcomes Establishment of BRICS Bank." *Outlook*, July 17.

Ji, Xianbai. 2017. "Promoting Regional Development Bank Complementarity: Challenges to Asia and Lessons from Europe." *Asia Europe Journal* 15 (3): 261–281.

Khanna, Parag. 2014. "New BRICS Bank a Building Block of Alternative World Order." *New Perspectives Quarterly* 31 (4): 46–48.

Martins, Cristiane Itabaiana, Lier Pires Ferreira, and Ricardo Basilio Weber. 2017. "The BRICS Bank: On the Edge of International Economic Law and the New Challenges of Twenty-First-Century Capitalism." In *The BRICS-Lawyers to Global Cooperation*, edited by Rostam J. Neuwirth, Alexandr Svetlicinii, and Denis De Castro Halis. Cambridge: Cambridge University Press.

May, Peter H. 2008. "Overcoming Contradictions Between Growth and Sustainability: Institutional Innovation in the BRICS." *Chinese Journal of Population, Resources and Environment* 6 (3): 3–13.

Menegazzi, Silvia. 2017. "Global Economic Governance Between China and the EU: The Case of the Asian Infrastructure Investment Bank." *Asia Europe Journal* 15 (2): 229–242.

Morozkina, Alexandra. 2015. "The New Development Bank in the Global Financial Architecture." *International Organisations Research Journal* 10 (2): 68–80.

Nayyar, Deepak. 2016. "BRICS, Developing Countries and Global Governance." *Third World Quarterly* 37 (4): 575–591.

Neuwirth, Rostam J. 2010. "A Constitutional Tribute to Global Governance: Overcoming the Chimera of the Developing-Developed Country Dichotomy." European University Institute Working Paper LAW 2010/20. http://cadmus.eui. eu/handle/1814/15704.

Neuwirth, Rostam J. 2013. "Global Governance and the Creative Economy: The Developing Versus Developed Country Dichotomy Revisited." *Frontiers of Legal Research* 1 (1): 127–144.

Neuwirth, Rostam J. 2017. "Global Law and Sustainable Development: Change and the 'Developing-Developed Country' Terminology." *European Journal of Development Research* 29 (4): 911–925.

Nielsen, Lynge. 2011. "Classifications of Countries Based on Their Level of Development: How It Is Done and How It Could Be Done." IMF Working Paper WP/11/31, February 1. https://www.imf.org/en/Publications/WP/Issues/2016/12/31/Classifications-of-Countries-Basedon-their-Level-of-Development-How-it-is-Done-and-How-it-24628.

O'Neill, Jim. 2001. "Building Better Global Economic BRICs." Goldman Sachs Global Economics Paper No. 66, November 30. http://www.goldmansachs. com/our-thinking/archive/archive-pdfs/build-better-brics.pdf.

Oxfam. 2014. "The BRICS Development Bank: Why the World's Newest Global Bank Must Adopt a Pro-Poor Agenda." *Oxfam Policy Brief,* July 11. https://www.oxfam.org/sites/www.oxfam.org/files/bp-brics-development-bank-110714-en_0.pdf.

Peerenboom, Randal, and Bojan Bugaric. 2015. "Development After the Global Financial Crisis: The Emerging Post Washington, Post Beijing Consensus." *UCLA Journal of International Law and Foreign Affairs* 19: 89–112.

Pope, Jenny, David Annandale, and Angus Morrison-Saunders. 2004. "Conceptualising Sustainability Assessment." *Environmental Impact Assessment Review* 24(6): 595–616.

Qobo, Mzukisi, and Mills Soko. 2015. "The Rise of Emerging Powers in the Global Development Finance Architecture: The Case of the BRICS and the New Development Bank." *South African Journal of International Affairs* 22 (3): 277–288.

Rowlands, Dane. 2012 "Individual BRICS or a Collective Bloc? Convergence and Divergence Amongst 'Emerging Donor' Nations." *Cambridge Review of International Affairs* 25 (4): 629–649.

Santana, Naja Brandão, Daisy Aparecida do Nascimento Rebelatto, Ana Elisa Périco, and Enzo Barberio Mariano. 2014. "Sustainable Development in the BRICS Countries: An Efficiency Analysis by Data Envelopment." *International Journal of Sustainable Development & World Ecology* 21 (3): 259–272.

Santra, Swarup. 2017. "The Effect of Technological Innovation on Production-Based Energy and CO_2 Emission Productivity: Evidence from BRICS Countries." *African Journal of Science, Technology, Innovation and Development.* https://doi.org/10.1080/20421338.2017.1308069.

Sarkar, Rumu. 2016. "Trends in Global Finance: The New Development (BRICS) Bank." *Loyola University of Chicago International Law Review* 13 (2): 89–103.

Serra, Narcis, and Joseph E. Stiglitz, eds. 2008. *The Washington Consensus Reconsidered: Towards a New Global Governance.* New York: Oxford University Press.

Shelepov, Andrey. 2016. "Comparative Prospects of the New Development Bank and Asian Infrastructure Investment Bank." *International Organisations Research Journal* 11 (3): 51–67.

Tang, Lingxiao, Ouyang Yao, and Zexian Huang. 2015. "The Foundation for the Establishment of the BRICS New Development Bank: Immediate Impetus and Theoretical Rationale." *Social Sciences in China* 36 (4): 40–56.

Thiam, Alioune Badara. 2017. "China-Africa and the BRICS: An Insight into the Development Cooperation and Investment Policies." In *The BRICS-Lawyers' Guide to Global Cooperation,* edited by Rostam J. Neuwirth, Alexandr Svetlicinii, and Denis De Castro Halis, 106–122. Cambridge: Cambridge University Press.

UNCTAD. 2016. *Trade and Development Report 2016.* New York and Geneva: United Nations. http://unctad.org/en/PublicationsLibrary/tdr2016_en.pdf.

United Nations. 2015. *Addis Ababa Action Agenda of the Third International Conference on Financing for Development.* New York: United Nations. http://www.un.org/esa/ffd/wp-content/uploads/2015/08/AAAA_Outcome.pdf.

United Nations. 2017. *World Economic Situation and Prospects 2017.* New York: United Nations. https://www.un.org/development/desa/dpad/wp-content/uploads/sites/45/publication/2017wesp_full_en.pdf.

Wang, Hongying. 2016. "New Multilateral Development Banks: Opportunities and Challenges for Global Governance." In *Global Order and the New Regionalism,* edited by Miles Kahler, C. Randall Henning, Chad P. Bown, Hongying Wang, Erik Voeten, and Paul D. Williams, 41–54. New York: Council on Foreign Relations.

World Commission on Environment and Development. 1987. *Our Common Future.* http://www.un-documents.net/our-common-future.pdf.

Yunus, Muhammad. 2015. "A New Bank for a New Era." *The Hindu,* July 8.

Zhang, Maggie. 2016. "BRICS New Development Bank Hopes to Expand by Drawing Other Nations as Members." *South China Morning Post,* July 21.

CHAPTER 7

The BRICS' New Development Bank at the Crossroads: Challenges for Building Development Cooperation in the Twenty-First Century

Laura Trajber Waisbich and Caio Borges

INTRODUCTION

The New Development Bank (NDB) was set up by the BRICS countries (Brazil, Russia, India, China, and South Africa) in 2015 with the purpose of mobilizing resources to finance infrastructure and sustainable development in emerging economies and in the developing world. Already during NDB's inception stages, an intense debate spurred in academic and

L. T. Waisbich (✉)
University of Cambridge, Cambridge, UK
e-mail: lt442@cam.ac.uk

C. Borges
University of São Paulo, São Paulo, Brazil

© The Author(s) 2020   149
J. A. Puppim de Oliveira and Y. Jing (eds.), *International Development Assistance and the BRICS*, Governing China in the 21st Century,
https://doi.org/10.1007/978-981-32-9644-2_7

policy-making circles on the potential the BRICS-led NDB and the China-led Asian Infrastructure Investment Bank (AIIB)—these two twenty-first-century multilateral development banks (MDBs)—had to accelerate the democratization of global economic governance and promote alternative paradigms of social and economic development, allegedly more responsive to the needs of the South.

Calling itself "New," the NDB has also sparked debates on the exact nature of innovations required to serve the developmental needs of emerging markets and developing countries (EMDCs). For some, like Dani Rodrik, there was disappointment with the BRICS countries' choice to focus their cooperation on infrastructure finance: an approach that would be bringing back a "1950's view of economic development" (Rodrik 2013). Others expected the NDB to adopt a "pro-poor agenda" (Oxfam 2014); become an "engine for sustainable development" without reproducing "old development models" (Kweitel and Krishnaswamy 2016); or even refrain from replicating "corporate-driven capitalism" (Bond and Garcia 2015).

The NDB is now fully operational. As of April 2019, it has already approved more than thirty projects, worth over US$9.2 billion,[1] as well as a set of fundamental operational policies and its first five-year strategy. Against this backdrop, this chapter aims to investigate whether and how the NDB transforms current international development cooperation (IDC) architecture and its underlying institutional and normative practices. Our approach is twofold. First, we map out the key innovations brought by the NDB in domains such as institutional governance (including decision-making processes), management structure, accountability mechanisms, policy framework, lending instruments, and projects. Second, this chapter also explores the political significance of the new institution, by locating those innovations within the prism of the theoretical, normative, and institutional frameworks of the so-called South–South Cooperation (SSC).[2] This approach seeks to understand to what extent the NDB institutional structure, governance, and lending modalities incorporate the principles and practices of SSC, such as national sovereignty, demand-driven cooperation, mutual benefits, self-reliance, and national ownership.[3]

The empirical exam of the Bank's organizational structure, policies and official documents, and the critical analysis of the NDB's mandate vis-à-vis its proclaimed South–South developmental goals are intended to fill a gap in the burgeoning literature about the NDB and the AIIB. So far, this literature has predominantly focused on the potential impacts of these two institutions in the redistribution of power in world politics and in the future of SSC and intra-BRICS cooperation. Some recent contributions have addressed the institutional and operational features of the NDB and the AIIB,[4] but some issues, such as their lending activities and partnerships, are scrutinized only in passing. More importantly, scholarly and policy debates have largely overlooked how the specific institutional features of these two "Southern-led" institutions may create barriers or opportunities for the fulfillment of their respective mandates of providing funds for sustainable development in the Global South.[5] We argue, however, that any consideration about the potential of the NDB to reshape current IDC architecture and challenge well-established ideas and paradigms of development needs to devote proper attention to its institutional design and policy frameworks.

Though the chapter's focus is on the NDB, it also attempts to highlight and address some identified tensions and challenges that are emerging as central aspects of contemporary debates on the role of development finance institutions in delivering sustainable development and in furthering the Sustainable Development Goals (SDGs), also referred to as the Agenda 2030, approved by the United Nations' General Assembly in 2015. They include partnership with the private sector, conditionalities, and use of country systems, among others. Particularly for the NDB, the main question is how it will frame and realize its approach to sustainable development while concentrating its resources in infrastructure investments, which have been contentiously described, on the one hand, as capable of lifting people out of poverty and promoting economic development[6] and, on the other, as bringing about serious adverse impacts to the rights and livelihoods of already marginalized groups—especially traditional and indigenous populations—and environmental degradation.[7]

In this sense, we argue that the NDB, an institution born amidst high expectations, especially among those that are more critical of current world order, is under the challenge of developing innovative mechanisms to mitigate the impacts of infrastructure projects to make them more sustainable, while speeding up the approval and disbursement process—a key proposition of emerging and developing countries within MDBs. The Bank will equally need to reflect on its role in challenging, or subscribing to, mainstream thinking on what the key drivers to sustainable development are.[8] Since better infrastructure is only one in the myriad of components of the extensive list of SDGs (Goal 9), NDB's value proposition—of a niche bank—will likely remain under continuous scrutiny, and as such its overall relevance in the current ecosystem of development finance providers. In this regard, this chapter seeks to demonstrate that, in its current form and structure, the NDB is, at best, displaying only a modest ambition to become an "incubator" of alternative visions and models of development policies. The empirical research that preceded this chapter leads to the conclusion that the first decade of the NDB will probably see an institution consolidating itself as a "project bank," with knowledge possibly playing only a subsidiary role. If this forecast holds true, the NDB will be setting itself an identity markedly different from the World Bank (WB)'s[9] (despite the Bretton Woods institution' recent attempts to revamp its "project financing" facilities). However, as discussed later, by overlooking this knowledge component, the NDB might be, contradictorily, holding back its own mission to foster transformative development in the Global South.

Theoretically, this chapter undertakes a multi-disciplinary approach. It discusses the NDB through the lenses of development finance and SSC, while mobilizing the tools and concepts from two main disciplines: International Relations and Public Administration. A legal perspective is also featured in some parts of our analysis, such as in the discussion about voting rights and accountability (in the third section), and the reflections on the prospects of the NDB making provide policy loans in the future and how this would raise not only political but also legal consequences for its current foundational documents, including its Articles of Agreement (in the fourth section). The dialogue with the literature on SSC is performed in a critical fashion. For that, we draw on Emma Mawdsley's (2014) distinction between "justice between States" and "justice within States" to go beyond "State-centered" accounts of emerging (or alternative) forms of global governance, under the label of SSC, and to perform a critical evaluation of what the "needs of the South" means both to the Bank and to a diverse range of actors in the IDC community.

In the following sections, this chapter will, firstly, explore the state of the debate around the BRICS, the NDB, and their impact on the current international development landscape. Secondly, we present an empirical account of the major innovations the NDB is currently pushing forward, emphasizing where they differ from, or are similar to, current development finance policies, frameworks and practices, and highlighting remaining contentious issues. Finally, we conclude by addressing relevant institutional and political areas that deserve greater attention, connecting them to innovative SSC practices that could strengthen NDB's claims to advance new sustainable development models.

Tracking Down the Innovation Debate: The BRICS, South–South Cooperation, and the NDB

Grappling with any policy and institutional innovations advanced by the BRICS-led NDB requires a short digression to a larger debate on the political emergence of the BRICS, and other so-called rising powers, and on their transformative impact on the international development landscape. The Bank is the first and, insofar, most concrete outcome of the BRICS grouping. NDB's so-called innovations are also deeply embedded in BRICS countries' desire to create for themselves a legitimate space to challenge current established international relations ideas, narratives and practices (Hurrell 2013; Eyben and Savage 2013). In the case of the NDB, the "innovation marketing" is also a useful tool for a new MDB aiming to differentiate itself in an increasingly competing landscape.

The BRICS Effect Under Review

Operating in what Richard Carey and Li Xiaoyun (2016) call the "informal space outside of the post-Second World War global governance framework," the BRICS grouping is a product of an increasingly multipolar world. As such, it has since its inception operated a "challenge function," without necessarily directly confronting the current US-led global order, navigating under a certain degree of strategic and tactic ambiguity. Particularly in the development cooperation field, Mawdsley argues that the ascent of rising powers, such as the BRICS, challenges the system materially, ideationally, and ontologically: in the volume of assistance/cooperation flows, in the recognition of Southern countries as relevant IDC providers, and in the discursive construction and projection of development "norms," such as those concerning modalities, priority sectors, languages of partnership, and so on (Mawdsley 2015).

In spite of the initial consensus on the so-called "challenge function" of the BRICS, scholars' predictions on the concrete impacts (or what some would see as "BRICS-effects") have varied significantly. Taking an *ex ante* approach, a first wave of literature sought to theorize and anticipate the consequences of the rise of the BRICS before its actual impacts. This literature focused on two set of questions. On the one hand, it analyzed the potential *complementarity or antagonism* vis-à-vis existing global institutions, regimes, and norms. Alternative formulations for the same question are seen in Esteves and Zoccal's (2017) use of Pierre Bourdieu's concepts of *competition or differentiation* or, in more in political and institutional terms, in the couple *revisionism-reformism* (Alastair 2003). On the other hand, the second cluster of questions, a rather normative one, investigated whether these anticipated impacts would *strengthen* or *weaken, stabilize* or *destabilize, improve* or *worsen* current institutions, regimes, and norms in a series of sub-fields, including global economic governance, IDC, human security, and climate change, among others.

In the recent years, albeit initially, a second wave of studies on rising powers and on the BRICS attempted to analyze the *ex post* impacts of the rise of the South. This literature is still incipient. It takes a less normative approach and draws on observed convergence and divergence dynamics. Jennifer Constantine and Alex Shankland (2017), for example, assess the recently established Global Partnership for Effective Development Cooperation, drawing on previous studies (e.g., Eyben and Savage 2013; Mawdsley et al. 2014) of how the rising powers, and particularly the BRICS, have influenced the Organization of Economic Co-operation and Development (OECD)-led IDC governance to "recognize and incorporate many elements of SSC in its discourse on development cooperation" (Constantine and Shankland 2017, 112). Similarly, other observers have come to their own conclusions looking at a broad range of other sub-agendas, such as climate change, trade, and peacekeeping.

Multiple Views on the Challenge Function of the NDB

A similar dynamic is observed when it comes to scholarly work on the NDB. Akin the first wave of studies on BRICS, some envisioned the NDB as the "first coordinated challenge to Western supremacy" in the world economy coming from developing countries since the Non-Aligned Movement (Desai 2013). Others took a more nuanced position, referring to the NDB as an institution gradually rewriting the terms, definitions, and assumptions framing the development narrative (O'Riordan 2014). A third group of commentators assume the NDB to be less of an instrument of strong contestation of current world order and more a means to challenge the Western leadership of it (Stuenkel 2015). For Andrew Cooper and Asif Farooq (2015), the NDB sends a "clear message to the international community that [the BRICS] are well capable of advancing alternative resolution unless the existing IFIs do not make progress in accommodating the demands of emerging powers".

Table 7.1 is an attempt to summarize this first body of literature, as well as the different voices and narratives on the NDB and on expected consequences of the Bank's coming into existence.

In line with the second wave of studies on the BRICS, one that seeks to advance empirical knowledge on the outcomes of the rise of the grouping in a range of policy arenas, in what follows this chapter will assess NDB's potential innovations and their initial impact in shaping development finance global norms and practices in areas such as governance, financial instruments, cooperation with other MDBs, and environmental and social risk management.

Table 7.1 Narratives on the NDB and its potential effects on global governance

Narrative	Key propositions
Optimistic revisionism	NBD will break away from standard practices from the World Bank and from other well-established MDBs and set up new sustainable development paradigms (*optimistic competition*)
Pessimistic revisionism	NDB will force other financial institutions to weaken their environmental and human rights safeguards and political conditionalities ("rogue aid"), intensifying a perceived "race to the bottom" in sustainable standards within development finance (*pessimistic competition*)
Optimist reformism	NBD will complement other MDBs' efforts to promote sustainable development and will democratize world economic order without breaking away from its political, economic, and normative pillars (*optimistic complementarity*)
Pessimist reformism	NBD will fund predatory infrastructure geared to exploit natural resources from developing countries, undermining efforts at alleviating indebtedness from countries in the South; or NBD will finance an "old" development model based on large infrastructure projects, which have high social–environmental impacts, are economically inefficient, and corruption-prone (*pessimistic complementarity*)

Source Authors' own compilation

NDB's Key Innovations: Potentialities and Blind Spots

The NDB has constantly presented itself—in all its initial strategic documents and senior leadership discourses[10]—as a "ground-breaking twenty-first century international financial institution (IFI)." In its General Strategy for 2017–2021, this rhetoric finally gained a concrete formulation, with three main innovation clusters: (i) *relationships*, (ii) *projects and instruments*, and (iii) *approaches*. In this section, these innovations are analyzed considering: (a) their background, (b) how they have been institutionalized and the extent of this institutionalization, and (c) how different are those innovations from current practices of other existing MDBs—particularly the World Bank and the recently established AIIB—and what are the remaining institutionalization and implementation blind spots. This assessment not only tries to uncover some of the institutional dynamics playing out at the NDB, but it is also an attempt to capture cross-fertilization dynamics and genuine efforts to generate innovation in MDBs' legal and institutional frameworks.

Relationships

With respect to relationships, the main innovations are found in governance and in relationships with borrowers and other economic agents, including other financial institutions and the private sector. On the governance side, it is a novelty to have an IFI founded by developing countries, governed based on the principle of equality,[11] and whose statutory provisions determine that the Bank will remain in the hands of developing countries' shareholders. For that, NDB is a unique case among the existing MDBs (global, regional, and sub-regional) and reflects the shifts of an increasingly multipolar world.

NDB's Constitutive Agreement provides that founding members will retain, at any given time, a minimum of 55% of the voting rights, and non-borrowing member countries (high-income countries) cannot exceed 20% of the total voting power. Consequently, non-BRICS borrowing countries (medium- and low-income countries) can end up holding between 25 and 45% of the total shares. Despite having limited its membership to the five founding countries during its first three years of operations, the Bank's plans are to expand its membership slowly and gradually, ensuring "geographic diversity and a reasonable mix of advanced, middle- and lower-income countries" (NDB 2017a, 4). A membership policy was approved in 2017, setting the Bank into a potential expansion track from 2018 onward.

The process of inviting new members is being delayed, however, for alleged disagreements between member countries on the expansion strategy. Brazil has become more vocal about the idea by highlighting the potential positive effects of having more countries as members, especially from the developed world, to influence credit rating agencies to assign the NDB a good score. China would also be in favor of expanding the membership to advance its "BRICS plus" strategy, spearheaded before and during the 2017 BRICS Summit in Xiamen. On the opposite side, India and Russia are objectors for distinct reasons. Russia has allegedly been more resistant to the entry of countries that have imposed economic sanctions to it, while India has reportedly decided to oppose any new members, regardless of their ties with the country or level of development, and also to demarcate, at the institutional level, its resistance to any expansion of the political bloc,[12] hence counter-balancing China's political ambitions to instrumentally use BRICS to its own broader foreign policy goals. In contrast to the NDB, the AIIB has approved 97 countries (as of April 2019), of which 70 have completed the steps to become full members. Of these, 44 are regional and 26 are non-regional members. As these figures show, and as suggested by Andrew Cooper (2017, 3), unlike the AIIB, the NDB shows a strong and resilient club culture, favoring the political sovereignty of the five founding members over the unevenness of their current economic performance. This institutional arrangement represents an emerging "distinctive model in the design of global policy." For Cooper (2017), the equality principle among founders is one of the NDB's most important innovations—one that marks a distinctive shift in the application of the tenets of global governance.

The NDB has also rejected the veto rule, opting instead for the simple majority rule for most decisions, combined with the two-thirds majority rule for key strategic decisions, such as amendments to the Agreement or the establishment of special funds, as well as the vote of five founding members. Such governance arrangements can be considered additional tools to strengthening SSC with non-founding members, as it would allow for a "true ownership by EMDCs [emerging and developing countries] of their development strategy – a goal that is facilitated by the fact that all founding members of the Bank are borrowing countries" (NDB 2017a, 11).

It remains to be seen, however, how this initial equality (or "democratically oriented financial institution," in Cooper's words) will evolve and adapt, both with new capital commitments from the individual BRICS countries in the next few years and after subscriptions of shares of new non-BRICS members in the future. Although it would be logic to speculate that China will be tempted to proceed with additional subscriptions to capital, exceeding the contributions of the remaining founding members, existing accounts of how NDB fits China's larger "Going Out" strategy suggest a different picture (Chun 2015; Xu and Carey 2015). Accordingly, there are grounds to believe that NDB will potentially remain the "soft face" of Chinese development finance diplomacy, leaving its hard face to the AIIB. There, China holds a 28% stake, followed by India with 8%, somehow reproducing traditional asymmetries among shareholders, albeit with new players.

Apart from governance issues, the NDB equally claims its partnerships with other financial institutions and with the private sector will be innovative and a major component of its business model.[13] The Bank has signed a series of Memoranda of Understanding (MoU) with other financial institutions, both national and international, such as the Asian Development Bank, the World Bank Group, the Development Bank of Latin America (CAF), the AIIB, the European Investment Bank, the Fund for the Development of the River Plate Basin (FONPLATA), just to name a few. It has also signed MoUs with all the national development banks (or equivalent) in the five BRICS countries. For the first batch of projects, in 2016, the NDB signed two-step loans with some national public financial institutions in the BRICS (such as the Brazilian BNDES) and private banks (such as the Canara Bank in India). But unlike the AIIB, the NDB has yet to start co-financing ventures with multilateral agencies, a major feature of AIIB's initial projects. Partnerships, in the case of AIIB, are understood as a sign of the bank's will to keep the momentum for traditional infrastructure finance in Asia through a new impetus from this, the China-led institution, thus re-engaging traditional MDBs on funding for infrastructure in the region. In the case of the NDB, partnerships are also framed by bank officials as an important source of hands-on know-how for a "lean and start-up-like institution."

In line with one of the major trends in global development landscape (Kharas and Rogerson 2017), namely partnerships with private sector, the statute of the NBD—and also the AIIB—authorizes direct lending to the corporate sector. This illustrates BRICS' alignment with the current SDGs' framework of assigning to the private sector a potentially positive role as development actors, committed to the 2030 Agenda and to the Leave No

One Behind principle. It also echoes the group's adherence to the "Billions to Trillions" agenda[14] that features prominently in the development discourse, by which development finance institutions should serve as mobilizers of private capital for the achievement of the SDGs.[15]

Yet, in the history of multilateral development agencies, lending to the corporate sector is a relatively recent phenomenon, and direct participation of private capital is still a contentious issue within the debate on design and implementation of international development policies.[16] Notwithstanding the differing views, private capital has accounted for over 80% of long-term flows to developing countries since 2000 (Kharas 2014). And it is now one of the major components of external development finance flows, especially for low-income countries. Hence, NDB's commitment to support projects operated by the private sector also reflects a convergence between its vision and that of other key institutions of global governance—such as the OECD, the G-20, and the WB—on MDBs playing a subsidiary role in financing infrastructure projects to concentrate efforts in attracting ("crowd-in") private capital. In fact, a private sector-oriented (or, at least, friendly) approach to economic and social development has featured in virtually all recent global commitments to sustainable development, including the 2030 Agenda. Goal 17 of the SDGs, for instance, states that successful sustainable development agenda requires partnerships between governments, the private sector, and civil society. Furthermore, paragraph 43 of the 2030 Agenda frames international public finance as having the vital role of catalyzing additional resource mobilization from other sources, public and private. The same idea is also present in the Addis Ababa Action Agenda (AAAA), adopted in 2015 at the 3rd International Conference on Financing for Development, which complements and helps contextualize SDGs' means of implementation targets.[17]

Interestingly, the NDB and the AIIB have chosen not to set up an entity exclusively dedicated for private sector financing, but rather to concentrate sovereign and non-sovereign lending into one single entity. In the case of the World Bank Group, the International Finance Corporation (IFC), entity that lends to private sector, was created in 1956. The Inter-American Bank (IADB) consolidated its private sector operations in 2016 into a single institution called the Inter-American Investment Corporation (IIC), recently renamed IDB Invest. The NDB has declared, however, that it will "move cautiously into private sector operations in parallel with its growing capacity to evaluate project risks" (NDB 2017a, 22). According to the 2017–2021 strategy, the NDB intends to maximize arrangements with the private sector and PPPs (public-private partnerships) could become an important instrument for the Bank to leverage resources of the private sector and increase its participation in major infrastructure projects. Recently, the Bank declared that it wants loans to the private sector to eventually take up a 30% share of its project portfolio.[18] However, the first non-sovereign transaction was extended to the Brazilian big oil company, Petrobras, whose shares are traded in São Paulo and New York stocks exchanges, while the company remains under the control of the federal government.[19]

Another dimension of NDB's innovations in relationships is found in the realm of bank–client relations. Echoing a series of key SSC principles such as national sovereignty, demand-driven cooperation, self-reliance, and ownership, the NDB claims its projects to be demand-driven, with the Bank upholding countries' project ownership, respecting borrowers' development priorities and strategies, and "engaging in a dialogue of equals with borrowers." Also resonating with SSC narratives on ownership and effectiveness (BPC et al. 2017), the NDB affirms "projects will be most successful when borrowing countries are in charge of their own development path" (NDB 2017a, 6). Furthermore, NDB's narratives on "success," linking it to "founders' own experiences," do resonate with SSC providers' narratives on the "appropriateness" of SSC (Constantine and Shankland 2017).

Another correlated innovation in NDB's relationships with its clients is the use of borrowers' country systems for procurement and for environmental and social safeguards (NDB 2017a, 15). Country systems have been described as national arrangements and procedures regarding public financial management, public contracts, audit, monitoring and assessment, and social and environmental procedures (OECD 2010). For the NDB, it means working along national institutions and using "nationally-defined laws, regulations and oversight procedures." Favoring this approach is officially described as assisting in achieving two interrelated goals of: (i) protecting against misuse of project resources and negative impacts on the environment and vulnerable groups and (ii) strengthening local frameworks and implementation capacity to the long-term benefit of a country's development path. The rationale behind the second goal is very synergic to SSC principles and narratives around self-reliance and ownership. On that, the NDB sees using national systems "as the best way to strengthen a country's own capacity and achieve better long-term development results" (NDB 2017a, 15–16).

Although the country systems approach is certainly not new, the NDB has mainstreamed it in a way no other MDBs did so far, not even the

AIIB. In fact, the AIIB has adopted a mix of safeguards and country systems approach, combining a more "traditional" Environment and Social Framework (ESF) with an intention to make use of country systems whenever possible (AIIB 2016). Both the AIIB and the NDB also mention the use of corporate systems, in case of direct loans to business enterprises.

World Bank's own experience with country systems began in 2004. At the time, the bank's declared intent was of increasing the impact on development (in terms of efficiency, quality, and punctuality), increasing the ownership by the country on development programs and projects, facilitating the harmonization, and simplifying and reducing costs (Pallas and Wood 2009). In 2005, the WB introduced a two-year pilot use in the area of environmental safeguards in cases where national systems were deemed "equivalent to the Bank's applicable safeguard policy framework" and where relevant country implementation quality was deemed satisfactory according to the World Bank's standards and policies.[20] A few years later, all the other relevant regional MDBs, such as the African Development Bank, the Asian Development Bank, the IADB, and CAF, followed suit in enacting their own frameworks for the use and strengthening of country systems. More than a decade later after the first pilot projects started, MDBs' own internal evaluations of their experiences with country systems point to the conclusion that results have been, at best, mixed. In a 2011 review, the WB's own internal watchdog (the Independent Evaluation Group [IEG]) highlighted the need for the bank to: (i) articulate clear criteria and procedures for determining the acceptability of a country's environmental and social systems and performance, (ii) adopt country and/or sector-level approaches in addition to project-level approaches, and (iii) orient, in country systems' capacity strengthening efforts, more toward internationally agreed principles, outcomes, and benchmarking, rather than equivalence/acceptability/gap-filling (WB 2011). The IADB country systems' use assessment, undertaken on the occasion of its Ninth Capital Increase, listed as a critical point greater coordination between areas responsible for validation and improvement in domestic systems (Schiavo-Campo et al. 2013).

Projects and Instruments

Regarding the second cluster of innovations, on projects and instruments, NDB's main proposed innovation is to be a "niche bank," focusing its investments on a smaller range of sectors, namely sustainable infrastructure, traditional infrastructure, and sustainable development. In terms of sectorial allocation, NDB's key areas of operation include: (i) clean energy; (ii) transport infrastructure; (iii) irrigation, water resource management, and sanitation; (iv) sustainable urban development; and (v) economic cooperation and integration among member countries.

Following what Cooper (2017) calls NDB's "product innovation," the institution aspires to be as green as possible, in both the funding and lending sides (Batista Jr. 2017). Accordingly, NDB's first bonds, a total of U$448 million of yuan-denominated green bonds in the Chinese capital market, were issued in 2016 to raise funds internationally for clean energy projects in member states. The Bank also plans to issue other bonds denominated in other BRICS countries' national currencies, starting with India.

More recently, NDB's strategy announced its intention to allocate two-thirds of all financing commitments during the first five years to sustainable infrastructure. The remaining third will be devoted to the two other sectors: traditional infrastructure and sustainable development. All five projects approved during the first roll, in October 2016, were small-scale clean renewable energy projects. By mid-2018, at least 8 out of 23 approved projects were on renewables (see Table 7.2). The NDB defines sustainable infrastructure in broad terms as "infrastructure projects that incorporate economic, environmental and social criteria in their design and implementation." According to the Bank, this concept of sustainable infrastructure prioritizes "longer-term and broader assessment of economic, environmental and social impacts" going "beyond doing no harm to generate overall positive impacts in these fields" (NDB 2017a, 12).

Another major novelty within this second cluster is related to NDB's lending in local currencies. According to the Bank and financial experts, this can be considered a major step forward since it can "mitigate risks faced by borrowers and supports the deepening of capital markets of member countries" (NDB 2017a, 3). The NBD also aspires to innovate by deploying a smart mix of financial instruments (guarantees, syndicated loans with the private sector, project bonds, co-financing with other MDBs, special funds, etc.). As discussed earlier, the use of a wide range of financing tools for infrastructure financing by MDBs is one of the building blocks of a new "consensus" on the distribution of responsibilities among public and private actors operating in the field of development cooperation (Kharas and Rogerson 2017, 32–35).

Table 7.2 Projects funded by the NDB on renewables[a]

Project name	Loan amount (USD/m)	Borrower	Guarantor	End-user/On-lendee	Lending modality	Target sector
Canara (India)	250	Canara Bank	Government of India	Sub-projects	Sovereign guaranteed: 3 tranches	Renewable energy (wind, solar, etc.)
Lingang (China)	81	PRC Government	–	Shanghai Lingang Hongbo New Energy Development Co. Ltd.	Sovereign project loan	Renewable energy (solar rooftop PV)
BNDES (Brazil)	300	BNDES	–	Sub-projects	National financial intermediary (NFI): two-step loan	Renewable energy (wind, solar, etc.)
ESKOM (South Africa)	180	ESKOM	Government of RSA	ESKOM	Sovereign guaranteed project finance facility	Renewable energy (transmission)
EDB/IIB (Russia)	100	EDB/IIB	–	Nord Hydro-Bely Porog + other subproject(s)	National financial intermediary (NFI): two-step loan	Renewable energy (hydropower) + green energy
Pinghai (China)	298	PRC Government	–	Fujian Investment and Development Group	Project loan	Renewable energy (wind power)

(continued)

Table 7.2 (continued)

Project name	Loan amount (USD/m)	Borrower	Guarantor	End-user/On-lendee	Lending modality	Target sector
Jiangxi (China)	200	PRC Government	–	Government of Jiangxi Province	Sovereign project finance facility	Energy conservation
DBSA[b] (South Africa)	300	DBSA	–	Sub-projects	National financial intermediary (NFI): two-step loan	Renewable energy and energy efficiency
Guangdong Yudean Yangjiang Shapa (China)	297	PRC Government	–	People's Government of Guangdong Province. Implementing agency: Guangdong Yudean Group	Project loan	Renewable energy (offshore wind power)
Putian Pinghai Bay (China)	297	PRC Government	–	Implementing agency: Fujian Investment and Development Group Co., Ltd.	Project loan	Renewable energy (offshore wind power)

Source NDB
[a] As of April 2019; [b] The details of this loan were collected through media releases

Approaches

According to the NDB, one of its main differential approaches is being a "fast, flexible and efficient" bank. In its 2017–2021 strategy, it commits to adopt a cutting-edge private sector management culture—one that is lean, efficient, innovative (NDB 2017a, 6). Informally, NDB's senior management representatives often describe their organization as a start-up.

The lean and flat organization structure is also reflected in NDB's choice to have a non-resident Board. The Bank and the AIIB justify their option as contributing to reduce administrative costs and helping the Board focus "on high-level policy issues and particularly complex projects rather than routine day-to-day operations" (NDB 2017a, 14). In general, scholars have been enthusiastic about it, valuing its cost-effective character. This option is also seen as preventing the Board to become over-politicized, as is often the case in other MDBs (Humphrey 2015). Alternatively, while commenting on the AIIB, observers from civil society watchdog groups have raised concerns over the ability of a non-resident Board to oversee AIIB's operations and to guarantee civil society and affected communities' full representation (Orr 2016).

NDB's rationalized approach also means a streamlined project review and implementation oversight "without unnecessary bureaucracy," according to the strategy. Beyond its intention to conduct *ex ante* risk reviews for complex projects, leaving low-risk projects with *ex post* reviews, it remains unclear how the first projects were categorized and reviewed, since project documents were not made public. As discussed in the next section, observers have voiced concerns that the speed of project approvals and disbursements could come at the expense of project quality (Griffith-Jones et al. 2016).

In fact, the trade-offs and dilemmas involved in speeding up the operations, and how this movement may create negative side effects, such as less attention to the environmental and social sustainability of the projects, emerged as a central element of the debates held, for instance, in the process of review of the World Bank's Environmental & Social (E&S) safeguards policies, ended in 2016 with the approval of a new E&S framework by the WB's Board. While the World Bank views the final product as achieving a stronger balance between meeting clients' demands for faster approval and disbursements, on the one hand, and public participation and accountability, on the other, organizations from civil society have been more skeptical about the capacity of the new framework in furthering these goals, pointing to less clarity on the distribution of roles and responsibilities and the absence of a firm commitment to human rights.[21]

As for the accountability mechanisms, a first observation is that "accountability" as a word is seldom mentioned in NDB's official documents. In the whole strategy, there is only one section where this concept is mobilized, along with two other concepts: transparency and integrity. Considering both this framing and how the concept is treated in NDB's ESF, one can assume the Bank is geared toward an inward-looking concept of accountability and still not so much in line with MDBs' progressive steps in recent decades to enhance their external accountability mechanisms (including "social accountability") such as consultations, ombudsperson offices, grievances mechanisms, and other established accountability procedures. In its ESF, and much in line with a country systems approach, the NDB requires the client to establish and maintain a grievance mechanism, adding that "existing national mechanisms for grievance redressal" may be "deemed appropriate" in complying with this requirement (NDB 2017b). The strategy does mention an evaluation unit to be established within the Bank (NDB 2017a, 32), reporting directly to the Board of Directors, that could serve as a potential "soft accountability mechanism," as it will work to promote learning within the institution.[22] However, the mandate of an internal evaluation department is not the same as that of an independent accountability mechanism like the WB's Inspection Panel, an independent accountability mechanism with jurisdiction to handle complaints brought by private actors (including local communities) alleging the lack of compliance of the bank's operations with its own internal policies. This kind of independent accountability mechanism has since been transplanted—albeit with variations in mandate and institutional design—into every other major MDB. They are widely recognized as an important forum of accountability in spite of their general lack of any powers to make binding decisions.[23]

Taking the most advanced international discussions on MDBs' accountability mechanisms, it is reasonable to say that these bodies need rethinking in their institutional design and rules of procedures. Despite their importance in partially filling an accountability gap caused by the immunity MDBs enjoy in national judiciary systems, these mechanisms have been described as vulnerable to interference from management and are reported not to deliver on their expected role to provide effective remedy to individuals and groups that claim they have been harmed by projects funded by development finance institutions (Caitlin et al. 2016). Considering that the NDB is a SSC venture and will be operating under the country systems framework, there is room for institutional engineering and experimentation for the design of an innovative Southern-crafted accountability mechanism suitable for a lean, twenty-first-century MDB. Innovating in this area, and in contrast to NDB's approach, the AIIB has opened for public consultation a draft of its "complaints handling mechanism" structure.[24]

THE NDB AT THE CROSSROADS: WHERE PRAGMATISM MEETS SUSTAINABILITY

The previous sections of this chapter addressed some of the narratives about the "NDB effect" and offered a contextualized analysis of its advertised innovations in the fields of partnerships, projects and instruments, and approaches. Not aiming to create an absolute meta-narrative or interpretation of a phenomenon as complex as the coming into existence and functioning of the NDB, this section intends to contribute for greater coherence between the various analyses and viewpoints about the NDB coming from practitioners, scholars, and other observers in the development community. It connects the two previous discussions—the narratives and the institutional structure of the NDB—with a reflection on salient, and often sensitive, issues that are relevant not only for the NDB, but also to other development finance institutions, in what relates to sustainable development as it manifests itself (or not) in infrastructure financing in the developing world.

As things currently stand, it has been mainly the NGO community (and other few practitioners) that has captured the importance of assessing NDB's commitment to sustainability as an issue that should be prescribed the same status of other mainstream objects of study and policy debate, such as NDB's innovations in governance and voting power arrangements. These actors have been acting with the intention of raising the profile, so as they can reach public mainstream debate, of issues such as: the absence of clear socio-environmental criteria underpinning the choice of the projects, the low levels of public participation in the design and implementation of policies and projects (in deviation from well-established practices within MDBs), and the need for the NDB to articulate a clear vision and lay down a framework to operationalize its own mission, including by providing more clarity on what are the sustainability benchmarks, the criteria for assessing socio-environmental risk, as well as for measuring performance, and developmental outcomes of its operations (Vazquez et al. 2017).

As a first and fundamental observation, we highlight, based on our empirical analysis, the importance of locating NDB's innovations in a historical perspective. In doing so, it emerges that the innovative practices advertised by the NDB and by other observers might be better understood as part of a "continuum" of institutional learning and experimentation accumulated over the past 70 years, and that has come to shape the current landscape of development finance. Under this broader frame, a series of NDB's so-called innovations are not particularly unique to the BRICS-led bank and have been discussed and/or implemented in other new or traditional MDBs, albeit not systematically or in a less mainstreamed fashion, something the NDB recognizes in its own strategy (NDB 2017a, 10).

Take, for instance, NDB's strong appetite toward a greater use of country and corporate systems. A recent comparative analysis of the NDB, AIIB, and WB environmental and social safeguards has concluded that "regarding both the attribution of responsibilities and the use of country systems, the socio-environmental policies of the three banks are remarkably convergent', in the sense that all of them 'transfer the burden of compliance [...] to the client' and 'depend on the extensive use of country systems to achieve environmental and social protection" (Esteves et al. 2016, 11). The frameworks are also alike, in the same authors' view, in their lack of clear guidance on how country systems will be strengthened and according to which parameters.

Coming a decade later, the NDB's approach to the use of country systems draws on hardly learned lessons that took years to be assimilated by other MDBs. An example is the adoption of the "strengthening" component from the start (NDB 2017a, 16), which only became a concern and a strategic and policy objective at a later stage of other MDBs' experience with country systems. This example is quite interesting to illustrate the usefulness and appropriateness of placing NDB's innovations in a spectrum of institutional experimentations and changes that have been transforming MDBs in the last decades (with a considerable acceleration since the onset of the Global Financial Crisis). The country systems' example seems to also support the perception of authors such as Carey and Xiaoyun, for whom the new MDBs—namely the NDB and the AIIB—precipitate the generation of new impetus, from "outside" the system, creating convergence dynamics (with push and pull forces and reputational incentives) within the enlarged multilateral development financing system. The new financial institution created by the five emerging countries is an attempt to break with the path dependence that makes institutional change in development finance polit-ically costly. Hence, the geopolitical dimension of how the NDB wants to do development finance lies exactly in its instrumental role in pushing harder on practices and trends that are already progressively acquiring more acceptance and universal status within the development community, such as greater use of country systems, the deployment of a wide range of financial instruments to crowd-in private capital, and the need to streamline opera-tions to speed up the approval and disbursement of funds for development projects. The expected effect is that traditional institutions become more responsive to "non-Western" countries, who constantly accuse them of having rigid procedures for the evaluation and monitoring of environmen-tal and social risks and of being selective on the use of fraud, corruption, and economic concerns to impose standards of macroeconomic policy, thus restricting their "autonomy" and undermining their "policy space," with negative spillover effects on how they provide their citizens with social safety nets and welfare-enhancing services (Borges and Waisbich 2014).

Even if geopolitical allegations of this kind have not dissipated and main-tain their capacity to explain today's world, many examples of institutional innovation—and, where applicable, also paradigm changes—are in fact the result of efforts by traditional MDBs to meet the demands coming "from the South." The less bureaucratic environmental and social requirements of more recent lending facilities of the World Bank, such as the Development Policy Loans (DPLs) and the Program for Results (P4R), are a case in point. In comparison with the classic "Investment Project Financing" modality, which is the instrument *par excellence* to fund traditional infrastructure projects, such as hydropower plants and highways, the former two allow for a far greater use of the borrower's domestic country systems, being the P4R the most flexible of the three in granting the client ample autonomy to assess and mitigate the impacts of the loans (Borges 2015).[25]

Following this first initial observation, the issues that have been iden-tified as sensitive and deserving of greater attention by policy and schol-arly analyses on the NDB relate to the specific challenges that arise from the bank's value proposition of being a niche bank, focused on sustain-able development and infrastructure. To a lesser or greater extent, they are derived from the previously discussed "flexibility vs. accountability" dilemma: the competing goals of being fast and efficient while being accountable to taxpayers and to affected communities ("end users") (Sarkar 2009).

To begin with, and as put by Kathryn Hochstetler (2013), NDB's focus on infrastructure can be challenging as sustainable development and infrastructure investments can be at least "partially incompatible priorities." This is for two reasons: firstly, because heavy social and environmental costs of many infrastructure projects will require more attention from the Bank and cannot be offset by a separate set of sustainable development projects; secondly, because even "green infrastructure," such as solar and wind energy, can generate its own impacts absent a robust set of standards for environmental and social impact and risk management, or if monitoring mechanisms are fragile to oversee the impacts throughout the lifecycle of the project, and without a proper territory-sensitive analysis (or in face of competing conceptions of what should constitute the appropriate scale/territory for risk and impact assessment and management).[26]

As for now, considering the projects approved until mid-2018, the majority are on small-scale renewable energy. This demonstrates that the NDB has decided to play safe in its first years, probably with a view of shielding itself from criticisms emanating from its lack of engagement with civil society—and even the private sector (Leal 2016), but also a strategic move considering India and China's ongoing strategy to pursue green agendas nationally. This safe choice also reflects a key feature of BRICS countries' club dynamics, namely the pragmatism in every aspect of their cooperation and the shared desire to first "test the waters."

Leaving aside the practical allocation of NDB funds in the initial years and the underlying debate on the intrinsic sustainability friendliness of specific sectors (such as renewable energy and hydric management or sanitation projects), an inquiry into the NDB's tools and frameworks to ensure a right balance between economic and E&S concerns involved in infrastructure projects yields a picture that, again, is not fully apprehended by many of the existing studies. Unlike the AIIB that held discussions with non-borrower governments and CSOs, official public consultations on the NDB's ESF were inexistent. Furthermore, the first batch of four projects was approved in 2016 even before the policy was out, prompting environmental groups and rights-based organizations in the development community to believe the NBD is ready to trade-off its "sustainability commitments" or, in the best-case scenario, to adopt an uncritical view of renewables as a panacea. Also, alike the AIIB, much will depend on how the policy is operationalized, including unpacking bank–borrower obligations, the exact role and authority of environmental and social experts staff in project development and oversight and transparency mechanisms (Humphrey 2015, 6).

NDB documents, until 2018, were also not clear about the methods by which the Bank was assessing corporate clients' capacity to implement the projects in full observance of its own environmental and social standards, such as through the requirement that private sector borrowers adhere to universal standards of responsible business conduct (for instance, Global Compact, ISO 26000, and the United Nations Guiding Principles on Business and Human Rights). Furthermore, the ESF is unclear about whether and how the national grievances mechanisms will be accessible at a project level. Finally, the ESF is also silent about compliance requirements and timelines, and potential remedy funds to ensure redress.

From a sustainability perspective, further challenges might arise when it comes to defining the "appropriate scale" (Lotta and Favareto 2016) of infrastructure projects and when it comes to sectors such as "clean coal," on which the development community is highly divided. While some environmental experts assume it could hinder NDB's adherence to the highest climate change commitments (Vasudha Foundation 2017), clean coal technology is a sector the government of India is particularly interested in (*Times of India* 2017). It has been recommended that the NDB should adopt a "sliding scale" of sustainability, based on a pragmatic approach, to help countries transition to a green economy, including by a progressive tightening of sustainability criteria (Vazquez et al. 2017). For the time being, this is a sector the NDB has yet to openly rule in or out. Although clean coal is not explicitly mentioned in the strategy,[27] it has been featuring in the descriptive part of a series of NDB's job announcements, making it clear that NDB is seeking technical expertise on that realm.[28]

In light of the undeniable E&S impacts caused by infrastructure projects, a pressing conceptual and technical challenge is how to move forward with NDB's aimed sustainable developmental outcomes both by measuring them through indicators attesting the success of project-level outputs and through the deployment of innovative methodologies that can assess the positive impacts of credit lines, instruments, or even managerial techniques on a territory and/or national-wide scale. Even more challenging is how to ensure the broader "transformative" impact of NDB's target approach can be accomplished in highly unequal settings, such as those found in several of emerging and developing economies. A recent study with a review of thousands of infrastructure megaprojects around the world concluded that such projects are governed by an "iron law": "over budget, over time, under benefits, over and over again" (Flyvbjerg 2014). The study also found that biases from the main actors of the governance of large infrastructure projects tend to result in the overestimation of their positive outcomes, while simultaneously downplaying their social and environmental impacts. Another recent review of more than two hundred projects financed by the Inter-American Development Bank in the Latin America and Caribbean region has equally concluded that the benefits of infrastructure are not evenly distributed among the different groups, and that the main conflicts arise from the lack of consultations with local communities (Watkins et al. 2017).

The NDB has moved on to invest in the development of methodologies to assess the sustainability of its projects, even labeling those that are, in their view, considered "sustainable" or "traditional" infrastructure." According to informal accounts, by the end of 2018, the bank had 42% of its investments assessed as sustainable infrastructure.[29] Although it can be considered an expressive figure, it falls short of their target to invest two-thirds (approximately 66%) in this area in the first five years. Moreover, the framework upon which the NDB assessed the sustainability of the projects is not yet of public domain.

A proposition that was made at the earlier stages of the MDBs' adoption of country systems, but that still resonates today in the discourse of proponents of this approach, is that the short-term risks of the provider in having a smaller role in assessing the potential E&S risks and impacts of the projects would be countered by long-term improvements to the legal, regulatory, and policy frameworks of the borrower. But as discussed in a recent study, the assessment of long-lasting solutions to weaknesses of national frameworks is made hard by the shortcomings of the methodologies devised so far by the MDBs to perform such evaluation (Conectas Human Rights 2018). In this sense, analysts have pointed to the vagueness of NDB's ESF when it comes to operationalizing its technical assistance in cases where "a country's systems are not deemed acceptable" (Kweitel et al. 2017). The five-year strategy provided a little more clarity on the matter. Based on an analysis of this document, it is possible to affirm that NDB's language on country systems reveals NDB's "intention" to "verify *ex-ante* the quality of borrowing-country environmental, social, fiduciary, and procurement systems, and use them whenever they meet NDB's requirements." According to the document, "in cases where a country's systems are not deemed acceptable, NDB will fill gaps with additional requirements tailored to the specific needs of the project at hand" (NDB 2017a, 15). The Bank is progressively building its own criteria and procedures for filling the gaps in country systems. The exact type of intervention the NDB has adopted to act on the identified failures of laws, policies, and implementing agencies is yet to become clearer in the Bank's publicly available information.

The challenges to tackle gaps in laws, regulations, and enforcement mechanisms at the national level become particularly acute in a context where countries—developing and developed alike—are considering, or have already enacted, several changes in their legal and regulatory frameworks and reducing the levels of social and environmental protection. Brazil is a case in point, with the ongoing disputes spurred by draft legislative bills that would cause what social groups and United Nations' (UN) human rights experts label as "setbacks." One proposed bill currently being discussed in Brazilian congress fast-tracks the licensing process—from three steps to one step—to make it simpler and quicker to obtain a license for infrastructure projects considered to be of national interest and to exempt some activities from the licensing process (ISA 2016). The measure is seen as potentially harmful to indigenous peoples and environmental rights (UN 2017). In a report submitted to the UN Human Rights Council after an official mission to Brazil in December 2015, the UN Working Group on Business and Human Rights regretted that, instead of strengthening the legal and regulatory framework after the massive disaster caused by the collapse of the iron waste dam of the mining company Samarco (owned by the Brazilian Vale and the BHP Billiton) in November 2015, there were developments that seemed to be going in the opposite direction, such as the mentioned draft legislations on the reform of the environmental licensing process and bills that seek to dilute the concept of "slave labor" in the country (UN 2016).

Against this background, the question that arises is to what extent is it realistic that an infrastructure project might perform well under the three pillars of sustainability—economic, social and environmental—when it is enmeshed in a political and legal environment that presents dysfunctionalities in terms of governance, participation mechanisms, and prevention of rights violations. This challenge calls for a stronger debate over the need for the NDB, as a partner in development, to build up innovative horizontal methodologies and instruments to allow the assessment of clients' capacities to uphold their own national and international standards and commitments, beyond correction measures taken under the safeguards, "do no harm," approach.

This is a challenging proposition, because it might seem like suggesting the development of services and products that would resemble the WB's DPLs (Development Policy Loans) or other types of programmatic lending and advisory services on public policy reform. Any change in that direction would surely be met with certain resistance from both the NDB and the AIIB. As rightly noted by Wang (2016), both institutions "reject the use of development financing as leverage to promote social and political change in borrowing countries."[30] For these banks, not prescribing policies is a matter of upholding the primacy of sovereignty and ensuring the relationship with borrowers is built over the principles of equality, mutual respect, and trust (NDB 2017a, 3). Furthermore, studies have shown that "top-down" approaches to development were ultimately proved counterproductive for their simplistic assumptions of what are the bottlenecks and correspondent solutions to economic and social development (Trubek and Santos 2006).

Whether the NDB will be able to support national transformative initiatives without working on policy-based lending and whether there is room for designing a sort of South–South policy lending, this is a new frontier to be explored. Here, SSC practices can also provide the Bank with learnings on more comprehensive, while non-interfering, cooperation frameworks, such as the Indian development compact (Chakrabarti 2016) and the Brazilian structuring cooperation (Ferreira and Fonseca 2017; Leite et al. 2014).

The contours of a "South-South policy-based lending program" are, hence, still largely undefined. Drawing upon the core principles of SSC and in the strategic positioning of the NDB and the AIIB, some preliminary guidelines can be, nonetheless, asserted. For instance, cooperation for the strengthening of policy and legal frameworks could be limited only to those policy domains and sectors that can reasonably be regarded as having material relevance to help the Bank in the fulfillment of its mandate. While legal argumentation can easily stretch the boundaries of an IFI mandate—as it historically occurred with the WB and the IMF, which expanded their mandate to issues which were questionably not under their purview[31]—NDB's target approach seemed to exclude (absent a major reform of its Articles of Agreement) its involvement on every imaginable policy domain, such as reform of judicial systems or financial regulation frameworks.[32]

In this area, the NDB might rely on existing SSC, particularly South—South Technical Cooperation (SSTC), reflections, on, for instance, *capacity development*,[33] one of the key approaches enshrined in the 1978 Buenos Aires Plan of Action on SSTC, and more recently in the 2009 Nairobi Outcome document (UN 2009). In its 2017–2021 strategy, the Bank states its "technical support will focus on practical solutions derived from on-the-ground experiences" (NDB 2017a, 9). Going forward, NDB's own

SSC approach could rely and build on existing knowledge on the conditions under which SSC technical exchanges have been contributing to the endogenous processes of developing national capacities (in several dimensions such as individual, organizational, and inter-institutional). For those countries engaging in SSC capacity development initiatives, including most of the BRICS countries, a key learning has been on the role played by horizontal and multi-stakeholder diagnosis exercises to identify the full range of capacities to be strengthened or developed (BPC et al. 2017).

Based on those reflections, and to move forward the discussions on, for instance, the use and strengthening of country systems for social and environmental safeguards, the Bank could include in its strategic discussions with countries joint diagnosis exercises aiming at underscoring areas for Bank's cooperation—in a horizontal and conditions-free manner—with its clients as to strengthen existing norms, procedures, and policies relevant to its mandate. In any case, the "push for infrastructure," which has emerging powers as great champions, should not hinder the continuous development of a critical Southern-based perspective to identifying and acting upon obstacles to development, erected by issues such as poor governance and market failures (Rodrik 2013).

CONCLUSIONS

This chapter aimed to explore how the recently created BRICS-led NDB is incrementally changing the architecture of global development. It offered a contextual analysis and explored institutionalization gaps in the three areas identified by the NDB as innovation clusters: relationships, projects and instruments, and approaches.

The heralded innovative practices assemble a range of competing views on what the Bank describes as its own vision for the future transformative development finance, together with a broad range of stakeholders and development experts' recommendations on what could better serve the needs of the people and states of the South. Against this background, it was highlighted how the NDB is building its institutional body as to balance between its own vision of what is different and innovative in management, products and services, and financing for development, while playing out on strategic ambiguity and vagueness to grant itself a certain room for maneuver. The NDB is much aware of the reputational factors weighing on its policies and operations and it understands the odds of being "new" in a world where its soundness is measured against indicators of "traditional" actors, such as credit rating agencies. Hence, it has carefully crafted the language of its strategic documents and it has chosen safe sectors and sovereign financial intermediaries for its first round of funded projects.

This chapter further claimed that NDB's novelty rhetoric can be located and analyzed through the lenses of SSC. For instance, when the Bank claims to be upholding horizontal relationships with its shareholders or to be following a demand-driven approach, it is also echoing core SSC and SSTC principles' most of its founding members, except perhaps for Russia, have been vocal about for the past decades.

As NDB's operations put up on scale, it might require additional institutional reflection efforts in addressing some of the institutional blind spots of how to operationalize its "sustainable infrastructure" focus, what sustainability benchmarks it will be referring to under a fully operating country systems approach, and the criteria for assessing socio-environmental risk, as well as for measuring performance, and developmental outcomes of its operations (Roychoudhury and Vazquez 2016). Overall, the NDB will have to adjust the balance between its non-interference imperatives and those of having a transformative impact, as a development partner of its borrowers-members (Jain 2017). Current transparency and accountability deficits, particularly in regard to local communities negatively affected by projects on the ground, can eventually compromise NDB's ability to deliver on its sustainability promises. Achieving this balance is a challenge SSC providers, including most of the BRICS countries, have been reflecting on and dealing with, for some years now.

As the Bank progressively recognizes the need for carving to itself a knowledge-based space on sustainable infrastructure, it will certainly have to prioritize more systematically investing in internal expertise, strengthening of institutional capacities of governments, and civil society and in solid partnerships to be able to deal with the complex challenges this sector will bring to a lean structure. Considering how capacity development and knowledge sharing having been shaping SSC in the past decades, the NDB should make more concrete efforts to implement SSC practices within its daily operations. If the NDB succeeds on that, it will be collaborating not only to lead MDBs toward the so-needed development finance "next practices," but also will provide SSC with concrete examples of how mutual learning can work, in practice. As Southern providers' debates on monitoring and evaluation evolve and gain more evidence-based mature contours, some of its learnings could also inform the ongoing institutionalization of the NDB.

Acknowledgements This chapter is based on a paper presenter presented by the authors first in September 2017, in the 2nd BRICS Governance Forum (Fudan University, Shanghai) and then in a graduate and scholars' forum meeting at the Center of International Politics and Economics (NEPEI-USP) at the University of Sao Paulo (Brazil). We thank all those who have commented on the previous versions during this process. The authors are also grateful to Conectas Human Rights for the support provided to the elaboration of this chapter. All remaining errors and omissions remain ours.

Notes

1. As of July 2018. Based on media releases and the NDB database. NDB's projects available in: https://www.ndb.int/projects/list-of-all-projects/.
2. For an inter-governmentally agreed definition of SSC, see the United Nations Nairobi Outcome Document, from 2009, available in: http://southsouthconference.org/wp-content/uploads/2010/01/GA-resolution-endorsed-Nairobi-Outcome-21-Dec-09.pdf.
3. On a previous effort to connect the NDB to SSC debates, see Abdenur (2014) and Schablitzki (2014).
4. See Ong (2017), Serrano (2017), Cooper (2017), Xi (2016), and Kasahara (2017).
5. For a discussion on the concept of "sustainable infrastructure" and a framework for operationalizing NDB's mandate on this area, see Vazquez et al. (2017).
6. According to Bhattacharya et al. (2015), "Infrastructure is an essential component of growth, development, poverty reduction, and environmental sustainability."
7. For a discussion on the environmental and social conflicts arising from the implementation of infrastructure projects, see IADB (2017) and Alexander (2015).
8. Literature on development cooperation has emphasized that the mainstream discourse on the pre-conditions and necessary steps to achieve development has changed significantly over time. It goes beyond the scope of this chapter to depict in detail the practical and discursive features of the current "consensus" around the "best" policies for economic and social development. But some of what we see as indisputable elements, such as partnerships with private sector and sustainability, are dealt with in more or less detail in further sections. For a legal perspective on discourses of development theory, see Kennedy (2006) and Sarkar (2009).
9. For a historical and critical perspective on the construction of the "Knowledge Bank Paradigm" within the World Bank, see Bazbauers (2018). See, for example, Leal-Arcas (2013) and Abdenur (2016).

10. See, for example, an interview by Paulo Nogueira Batista Jr., Brazilian NDB Vice President until 2017, for the Russian paper Sputnik at: https://br.sputniknews.com/mundo/201706208691871-brasil-russia-brics-entrevista-paulo-nogueira/.

11. As stated in NDB's Articles of Agreement (Art. 2): "The New Development Bank shall have an initial subscribed capital of US$ 50 billion and an initial authorized capital of US$ 100 billion. The initial subscribed capital shall be equally distributed amongst the founding members. The voting power of each member shall equal its subscribed shares in the capital stock of the Bank."

12. See Moreira (2018) and Dasgupta (2017).

13. The trategy emphasizes that "projects will be undertaken whenever possible in collaboration with local, national and international institutions to maximize NDB's impact" (NDB 2017a, 6).

14. For a critical view on the "Billion to Trillions" discourse, see the foreword by Paulo Esteves, "Country Systems at the center of transformations of international development finance," at Conectas Human Rights (2018).

15. Lee, Nancy. 2018. *Billions to Trillions? Issues on the Role of Development Banks in Mobilizing Private Finance.* Washington, DC: Center for Global Development.

16. For a favorable view of private sector in development, see Adriaenssens (2015) where the author argues that "development initiatives should be implemented 'with the private sector, by the private sector and for the private sector." For a compilation of criticisms, see Beghin, N. 2015. *Parcerias e pobreza no Brasil: As contradições dos arranjos realizados entre entidades governamentais e empresas privadas para combater a pobreza.* Saarbrücken: Novas Edições Acadêmicas.

17. The final text of the outcome document adopted at the Third International Conference on Financing for Development (Addis Ababa, Ethiopia, 13–16 July 2015) and endorsed by the General Assembly in its resolution 69/313 of 27 July 2015. Available in http://www.un.org/esa/ffd/wp-content/uploads/2015/08/AAAA_Outcome.pdf.

18. See Reuters (2018).

19. According to Brazilian constitutional and administrative law, Petrobras is a "joint economic venture," a kind of a state-owned business that is controlled by the federal government, but open to private shareholders.

20. See a fact-sheet on how the WB was justifying, in 2004, its country systems pilots and what were the duties and procedures, including staff guidelines in http://www1.worldbank.org/publicsector/pe/befa05/usecountrysystems.pdf.

21. The revised E&S framework is available at: https://www.worldbank.org/en/projects-operations/environmental-and-social-framework. The Web

site of the Bank Information Center (BIC) provides a compilation of comments and submissions sent by governments and civil society organizations to the World Bank (available at: http://www.bankinformationcenter.org/our-work/safeguards/). For a critique of the World Bank's inconsistencies on human rights, see Alston (2017).

22. For a discussion on "soft accountability" for SSC, see Kim and Lim (2017).
23. On the significance of the creation of the Inspection Panel ("far-reaching even revolutionary in a sense"), see Sarkar (2009). See also Bradlow and Schlemmer-Schulte (1994).
24. See AIIB (2017).
25. This interpretation is not blind, however, to complementary explanations of how new lending modalities and practices by the WB fit the interests of the dominating powers. Sarah Babb (2009), for instance, assertively explains how the creation of the policy-based lending by the WB and other MDBs was part of a strategy to promote economic policy reforms in the then "Third World" in exchange for the support of the US Treasury and Congress when they needed additional funds and political legitimacy to continue their operations.
26. For a discussion on those complex discussions on the case of Brazil, see Lotta and Favareto (2016).
27. The sectors explicitly mentioned in the recently launched 2017–2021 General Strategy are renewable energy, energy efficiency, clean transportation, and water and waste management.
28. For instance, for a job opening of Senior Professional and Principal Professional in Project Finance, from August 2016, the Bank has invited applicants with technical training in the following sectors: energy generation (solar, wind, hydro, waste-to-energy, geothermal, clean coal power generation), transmission, and distribution; water, waste, and sanitation (water supply, distribution, wastewater treatment, solid waste management/incineration); transport (airports, seaports, roads, rail, and transport services); telecommunications and environment and efficiency improvement (solid waste incineration).
29. This information was shared during the 2nd NDB-Civil Society Meeting, held on 28–29 November 2018, at NDB's headquarters, in Shanghai.
30. Policy loans (also referred to as "budgetary support") support policy and institutional reforms. They do not support physical investments—e.g. roads, hydropower plants, etc.—and are not earmarked for specific projects (Moll et al. 2015). However, the IEG assessment of a Development Policy Loan the WB extended to Brazil in 2010 contained a criticism that the resources were channelled to specific projects under the "Accelerated Growth Program" (IEG 2015). For an account of how policy lending became relevant in the practice of MDBs through the lenses of the domestic political economy of the major shareholder (the USA), see Babb (2009).

31. For a review of the mandate of the IMF throughout history, from support to crises of balance of payments to microeconomic surveillance, see Shaffer and Waibel (2016).
32. However, NDB's demand-driven approach could lead to the Bank progressively stretching its operational definition of sustainability, as seen in the recently approved judicial support project in Russia, aimed at increasing "judicial transparency and efficiency, and enhanced protection of judicial rights of citizens of the country." Under the tag of "social infrastructure," the NDB has recently extended a loan for the development of infrastructure and implementation of information technology systems of the judicial system in Russia. According to the Bank, the loan should lead to "increased judicial transparency and efficiency, and enhanced protection of judicial rights of citizens of the country." See NDB Board of Directors Approves 4 Projects in China, Russia and India with Loans Aggregating Over USD 1.4 bln. Available in: http://www.ndb.int/press_release/ndb-board-directors-approves-4-projects-china-russia-india-loans-aggregating-usd-1-4-bln/. NDB. Project: Judicial Support (Russia). Available in: https://www.ndb.int/project/judicial-support-russia/.
33. On the most common approaches to capacity development within IDC, see Pearson (2011). On monitoring and evaluation IDC initiatives on capacity development, see World Bank (2012), Simister and Smith (2010), and United Nations Development Programme (2010).

Bibliography

Abdenur, Adriana Erthal. 2014. "China and the BRICS Development Bank: Legitimacy and Multilateralism in South–South Cooperation." *IDS Bulletin* 45 (4): 85–101.

Abdenur, Adriana Erthal. 2016. "Rising Powers and International Security: The BRICS and the Syrian Conflict." *Rising Powers Quarterly* 1 (1): 109–33.

Adriaenssens, Philippe. 2015. "How to Involve the Private Sector in Development Cooperation." *GREAT Insights Magazine* 4 (5): 13–15. (August/September).

Alastair, Iain Johnston. 2003. "Is China a Status Quo Power?" *International Security* 27 (4): 5–56.

Alexander, Nancy. 2015. "The Age of Megaprojects: Project Syndicate." *Project Syndicate*, July 10. https://www.project-syndicate.org/commentary/g20-infrastructure-investment-by-nancy-alexander-2015-07.

Alston, Philip. 2017. "The World Bank Is a Human Rights Free Zone." NYU School of Law, Public Law Research Paper No. 17-50. https://papers.ssrn.com/sol3/papers.cfm?abstract_id=3079899.

Asian Infrastructure Investment Bank. 2016. *Environment and Social Framework*. https://www.aiib.org/en/policies-strategies/_download/environment-framework/20160226043633542.pdf/.

Asian Infrastructure Investment Bank. 2017. *Call for Public Consultation for the Proposed: Complaints Handling Mechanism*. Beijing: AIIB. https://www.aiib.org/en/policies-strategies/_download/consultation/consultation_aiib.pdf/.

Babb, Sarah. 2009. *Behind the Development Banks: Washington Politics, World Poverty, and the Wealth of Nations*. Chicago: University of Chicago.

Batista Jr., Paulo Nogueira. 2017. "Estratégia do NBD." *O Globo*, July 7. https://oglobo.globo.com/opiniao/estrategia-do-nbd-21562434.

Bazbauers, Adrian Robert. 2018. *The World Bank and Transferring Development: Policy Movements Through Technical Assistance*. Cham: Palgrave Macmillan.

Beghin, Nathalie. 2015. *Parcerias e pobreza no Brasil: As contradições dos arranjos realizados entre entidades governamentais e empresas privadas para combater a pobreza*. Saarbrücken: Novas Edições Acadêmicas.

Bhattacharya, Amar, Jeremy Oppenheim, and Nicholas Stern. 2015. "Driving Sustainable Development Through Better Infrastructure: Key Elements of a Transformation Program." Brookings Global Working Paper Series. https://www.brookings.edu/research/driving-sustainable-development-through-better-infrastructure-key-elements-of-a-transformation-program/.

Bond, Patrick, and Ana Garcia, eds. 2015. *BRICS: An Anti-capitalist Critique*. London: Pluto Press.

Borges, Caio. 2015. "A proteção dos direitos humanos e do meio ambiente no financiamento do desenvolvimento: tendências globais, visões emergentes e desafios para o fortalecimento da Política Socioambiental do BNDES." In *Política Socioambiental do BNDES: Presente e Futuro*, 23–54. Brasília. Instituto de Estudos Socioeconômicos.

Borges, Caio, and Laura Trajber Waisbich. 2014. *The BRICS' New Development Bank and the Integration of Human Rights into Development Cooperation: A New Era or More of the Same?* Washington, DC: Heinrich Böll Stiftung North America.

Bradlow, Daniel, and Sabine Schlemmer-Schulte. 1994. "The World Bank's New Inspection Panel: A Constructive Step in the Reform of the International Legal Order." *Zeitschrift für Ausländisches Öffentliches Recht und Völkerrecht* 54: 392.

BRICS Policy Center, South–South Cooperation Research, and Policy Centre, Brazilian Agency of Cooperation. 2017. *Paths for Developing South–South Cooperation Monitoring and Evaluation Systems*. Brasília: Ministry of Foreign Affairs.

Caitlin, Daniel, Kristen Genovese, Mariëtte van Huijstee, and Sarah Singh. 2016. "Glass Half Full? The State of Accountability in Development Finance." *Centre for Research on Multinational Corporations (SOMO)*, January 1. www.glass-half-full.org.

Carey, Richard, and Li Xiaoyun. 2016. "Understanding the BRICS Evolving Influence and Role in Global Governance and Development." *IDS Policy Briefing Issue* 119.

Chakrabarti, Milindo. 2016. "Development Compact—The Cornerstone of India's Development Cooperation: An 'Externalities' Perspective." *International Studies* 53 (1): 2–14. https://doi.org/10.1177/0020881717717524.

Chun, Zhang. 2015. "China's New Blueprint for an 'Ecological Civilization'", *The Diplomat*, September 30. http://thediplomat.com/2015/09/chinas-new-blueprint-for-an-ecological-civilization/.

Conectas Human Rights. 2018. "Country Systems and Environmental and Social Safeguards in Development Finance Institutions: Assessment of the Brazilian System and Ways Forward for the New Development Bank." *Conectas*, May 30. http://www.conectas.org/en/news/country-system-trend-multilateral-financing.

Constantine, Jennifer, and Alex Shankland. 2017. "From Policy Transfer to Mutual Learning? Political Recognition, Power and Process in the Emerging Landscape of International Development Cooperation." *Novos Estudos* 36 (1): 99–122.

Cooper, Andrew. 2017. "The BRICS' New Development Bank: Shifting from Material Leverage to Innovative Capacity." *Global Policy* 8: 275–284. https://doi.org/10.1111/1758-5899.12458.

Cooper, Andrew, and Asif Farooq. 2015. "Testing the Club Dynamics of the BRICS: The New Development Bank from Conception to Establishment." *International Organisations Research Journal* 10 (2): 1–15.

Dasgupta, Saibal. 2017. "China Wants 'BRICS Plus' to Include 'Friendly' Countries, Plan Might Hurt India's Interests." *Times of India*, March 9. https://timesofindia.indiatimes.com/world/china/china-wants-brics-plus-to-include-friendly-countries-plan-might-hurt-indias-interests/articleshow/57542116.cms/.

Desai, Radikha. 2013. "The BRICS are Building a Challenge to Western Economic Supremacy." *The Guardian*, April 2. https://www.theguardian.com/commentisfree/2013/apr/02/brics-challenge-western-supremacy.

Esteves, Paulo. 2017. "Agora somos todos países em desenvolvimento? A Cooperação Sul-Sul e os ODS." *Pontes* 13 (2): 8–12.

Esteves, Paulo, and Giovana Zoccal. 2017. "The BRICS Effect: The Impact of South–South Cooperation in the Social Field of International Development Cooperation." Centre for Rising Powers and Global Development (CRPD) Seminar, June 21. http://www.ids.ac.uk/events/the-brics-effect-the-impact-of-south-south-cooperation-in-the-social-field-of-international-development-cooperation.

Esteves, Paulo, Geovana Zoccal Gomes, and Gabriel Torres. 2016. "Os Novos Bancos Mutilaterais de Desenvolvimento e as Salvaguardas Socioambientais." *BPC Policy Brief* 6 (3): 1–14.

Eyben, Rosalind, and Laura Savage. 2013. "Emerging and Submerging Powers: Imagined Geographies in the New Development Partnership at the Busan Fourth High Level Forum." *The Journal of Development Studies* 49 (4): 457–69. https://doi.org/10.1080/00220388.2012.733372.

Ferreira, José Roberto, and Luiz Eduardo Fonseca. 2017. "Structural Cooperation, the Fiocruz Experience." *Ciência & Saúde Coletiva* 22 (7): 2129–33. https://doi.org/10.1590/1413-81232017227.04412017.

Flyvbjerg, Bent. 2014. "What You Should Know About Megaprojects and Why: An Overview." *Project Management Journal* 45 (2): 6–19.

Griffith-Jones, Stephany, Li Xiaoyun, Jing Gu, and Stephan Spratt. 2016. "What Can the Asian Infrastructure Investment Bank Learn from Other Development Banks?" *IDS Policy Briefing* 113. Brighton: IDS. https://opendocs.ids.ac.uk/opendocs/bitstream/handle/123456789/11170/PB113_AGID545_AIIB_Online.pdf?sequence=1.

Hochstetler, Kathryn. 2013. "South–South Trade and the Environment: A Brazilian Case Study." *Global Environmental Politics* 13 (1): 30–48.

Humphrey, Chris. 2015. "Will the Asian Infrastructure Investment Bank's Development Effectiveness Be a Victim of China's Diplomatic Success?" Multilateral Development Banks in the 21st Century, ODI Discussion Paper, November.

Hurrell, Andrew. 2013. "Narratives of Emergence: Rising Powers and the End of the Third World?" *Brazilian Journal of Political Economy* 33 (2): 203–21.

Independent Evaluation Group (IEG). 2015. "First Programmatic Reform Loan for Environmental Sustainability." Project Performance Assessment Report, February 19. http://lnweb90.worldbank.org/OED/OEDDocLib.nsf/DocUNIDViewForJavaSearch/4DB64B1DFCD69B4085257DF2007BAD7F/$file/brazil-env-prl-ppar.pdf.

Instituto Socioambiental (ISA). 2016. "Nova legislação do licenciamento ambiental vai instaurar guerra fiscal', diz advogado do ISA." *Instituto Socioambiental*, December 16. https://www.socioambiental.org/pt-br/noticias-socioambientais/novo-legislacao-do-licenciamento-ambiental-vai-instaurar-guerra-fiscal-diz-advogado-do-isa.

Jain, Pooja. 2017. "The BRICS Agenda: Functional Co-operation Between Competing Logics." *Global Dialogue* 15 (2) (March 8): 77–94.

Kasahara, Shigehisa. 2017. "The New Development Bank (NDB) vs The Asian Infrastructure Investment Bank (AIIB): An Analytical Comparison from a Critical Perspective." The 5th International Conference of the BRICS Initiative for Critical Agrarian Studies, Conference Paper No. 19.

Kennedy, Duncan. 2006. "Three Globalizations of Law and Legal Thought: 1850–2000." In *The New Law and Economic Development: A Critical Appraisal*, edited by Alvaro Santos and David Trubek. New York: Cambridge University Press.

Kharas, Homi. 2014. *Financing for Development: International Financial Flows After 2015*. Washington, DC: Brookings Institute.

Kharas, Homi, and Andrew Rogerson. 2017. *Global Development Trends and Challenges Horizon 2025 Revisited*. London: Overseas Development Institute.

Kim, Taekyoon, and Sojin Lim. 2017. "Forging 'Soft' Accountability in Unlikely Settings: A Conceptual Analysis of Mutual Accountability in the Context of South-South Cooperation." *Global Governance* 23 (2): 183–203.

Kweitel, Juana, and Srinivas Krishnaswamy. 2016. "O Banco dos BRICS está apto a impulsionar o desenvolvimento sustentável?" *Dialogo Chino*, October 14. http://dialogochino.net/o-banco-dos-brics-esta-apto-a-impulsionar-o-desenvolvimento-sustentavel/?lang=pt-pt.

Kweitel, Juana, Ana Toni, and Gretchen Gordon. 2017. "The BRICS Bank Needs a Bold and Participatory Strategy for Sustainable Development." *Open Democracy*, April 19.

Leal, Milton. 2016. "Does Anyone Know Anything About the New BRICS Bank?" *Chinadialogue*, January 28. https://www.chinadialogue.net/article/show/single/en/8568-Does-anyone-know-anything-about-the-new-BRICS-bank.

Leal-Arcas, Rafael. 2013. "The BRICS and Climate Change." *International Affairs Forum* 4 (1): 22–26.

Leite, Iara Costa, Bianca Suyama, L. Trajber Waisbich, Melissa Pomeroy, Jennifer Constantine, Lizbeth Navas-Alemán, Alex Shankland, and Musab Younis. 2014. *Brazil's Engagement in International Development Cooperation: The State of the Debate*. Brighton: Institute of Development Studies.

Lotta, Gabriela, and Arilson Favareto. 2016. "Desafios da integração nos novos arranjos institucionais de políticas públicas no Brasil." *Revista de Sociologia e Política* 24 (57): 49–65.

Mawdsley, Emma. 2014. "Human Rights and South–South Development Cooperation: Reflections on the 'Rising Powers' as International Development Actors." *Human Rights Quarterly* 36: 630–52.

Mawdsley, Emma. 2015. "Development Geography 1: Cooperation, Competition and Convergence Between 'North' and 'South'." *Progress in Human Geography* 41 (1): 108–17.

Mawdsley, Emma, Laura Savage, and Kim Sung-Mi. 2014. "A 'Post-aid World'? Paradigm Shift in Foreign Aid and Development Cooperation at the 2011 Busan High Level Forum." *The Geographical Journal* 180 (1): 27–38. https://doi.org/10.1111/j.1475-4959.2012.00490.x.

Moll, Peter, Patricia Geli, and Pablo Saavedra. 2015. "Correlates of Success in World Bank Development Policy Lending." Policy Research Working Paper No. 7181. https://elibrary.worldbank.org/doi/abs/10.1596/1813-9450-7181.

Moreira, Assis. 2018. "China e Brasil querem mais países no Banco dos BRICS." *Valor Econômico*, May 30. http://www.valor.com.br/financas/5558911/china-e-brasil-querem-mais-paises-no-banco-dos-brics/.

New Development Bank. 2017a. *Environment and Social Framework*. Shanghai: New Development Bank.

New Development Bank. 2017b. *NDB's General Strategy 2017–2021*. Shanghai: New Development Bank.

Ong, David. M. 2017. "The Asian Infrastructure Investment Bank: Bringing 'Asian Values' to Global Economic Governance?" *Journal of International Economic Law* 20 (3): 535–60.

Organization for Economic Cooperation and Development. 2010. *Country Systems, and Why We Need to Use Them*. Paris: OECD.

O'Riordan, Alexander. 2014. "South Africa: The Gentle but Subversive Power of South–South Cooperation." *Allafrica*, October 2. http://allafrica.com/stories/201410021328.html.

Orr, Robert M. 2016. "Why the Asian Infrastructure Investment Bank Needs Resident Directors." *ChinaDialogue*, August 23. https://www.chinadialogue.net/article/show/single/en/9206-Why-the-Asian-Infrastructure-Investment-Bank-needs-resident-directors.

Oxfam. 2014. "The BRICS Development Bank—Why the world's Newest Global Bank Must Adopt a Pro-Poor Agenda." Oxfam Policy Brief. https://www.oxfam.org/sites/www.oxfam.org/files/bp-brics-development-bank-110714-en_0.pdf/.

Pallas, Christopher L., and Jonathan Wood. 2009. "The World Bank's Use of Country Systems for Procurement: A Good Idea Gone Bad?" *Development Policy Review* 27 (2): 215–30.

Pearson, Jenny. 2011. *LenCD Learning Package on Capacity Development: Part 1: The Core Concept*. Learning Network on Capacity Development.

Reuters. 2018. "BRICS Development Bank to Expand Lending to Private Sector." *Reuters*, May 29. https://www.reuters.com/article/us-china-brics-bank/brics-development-bank-to-expand-lending-to-private-sector-idUSKCN1IU0P2/.

Rodrik, Dani. 2013. "What the World Needs from the BRICS." *Project Syndicate*, April 10. https://www.project-syndicate.org/commentary/the-brics-and-global-economic-leadership-by-dani-rodrik/.

Roychoudhury, Supriya, and Karin Vasquez. 2016. "What Is New About the BRICS-Led New Development Bank?" *Devex*, May 9. https://www.devex.com/news/what-is-new-about-the-brics-led-new-development-bank-88126/.

Sarkar, Rumu. 2009. *International Development Law: Rule of Law, Human Rights, and Global Finance*. Oxford: Oxford University Press.

Schablitzki, Jan. 2014. "The BRICS Development Bank: A New Tool for South-South Cooperation?" *BPC Policy Brief* 5 (1) (December 2014–January 2015). Rio de Janeiro: PUC. BRICS Policy Center, pp. 1–15.

Schiavo-Campo, Salvatore, Laura Atuesta, Agustina Schijman, and Monika Huppi. 2013. Mid-term Evaluation of IDB-9 Commitments – Country Systems. *Background Paper*. https://publications.iadb.org/en/idb-9-country-systems.

Serrano, Omar. 2017. "New Multilateral Lenders and the Purported Challenge to Existing MDBs: Institutional Design, Staffing and Lending Practices at the NDB and the AIIB." Paper presented at the Second International Symposium on Development and Governance in the BRICS, Fudan University, Shanghai, China on 23–24 September.

Shaffer, Gregory, and Michael Waibel. 2016. "The Rise and Fall of Trade and Monetary Legal Orders: From the Interwar Period to Today's Global Imbalances." In *Contractual Knowledge: One Hundred Years of Legal Experimentation*, edited by Gregoire Mallard and Jerome Sgard, 289–323. New York, NY: Cambridge University Press.

Simister, Nigel, and Rachel Smith. 2010. "Monitoring and Evaluating Capacity Building: Is It really That Difficult." Praxis Paper 23. Oxford: International NGO Training and Research Centre.

Stuenkel, Oliver. 2015. "The BRICS Bank Isn't Challenging the System, Only Western Leadership of It." *The Wire*, September 3. http://thewire.in/9853/the-brics-bank-isnt-challenging-the-system-only-western-leadership-of-it/.

Times of India. 2017. "India Pushes for $2 Billion Infrastructure Loan from New Development Bank." *Times of India*, April 2. http://timesofindia.indiatimes.com/india/india-pushes-for-2-billion-infrastructure-loan-from-new-development-bank/articleshow/57968661.cms/.

Trubek, David, and Alvaro Santos, eds. 2006. *The New Law and Economic Development: A Critical Appraisal*. New York: Cambridge University Press.

United Nations. 2009. *Nairobi Outcome Document of the High-Level United Nations Conference on South–South Cooperation*. New York: United Nations.

United Nations. 2016. "Brazil Must Move Forward on Business and Human Rights—UN Expert Group." *United Nations High Commissioner for Human Rights (OHCHR)*, June 17. http://www.ohchr.org/EN/NewsEvents/Pages/DisplayNews.aspx?NewsID=20125&LangID=E.

United Nations. 2017. "Indigenous and Environmental Rights Under Attack in Brazil, UN Rights Experts Warn." *United Nations Sustainable Development Blog*, June 8. http://www.un.org/sustainabledevelopment/blog/2017/06/indigenous-and-environmental-rights-under-attack-in-brazil-un-rights-experts-warn/.

United Nations Development Programme. 2010. *Measuring Capacity*. New York: UNDP.

Vasudha Foundation. 2017. *Policy Wayforward for the New Development Bank: A Compendium of Policies and Practices of Some of the Multilateral and Southern Banks*. New Delhi: Vasudha Foundation.

Vazquez, Karin Costa, Supriya Roychoudhury, and Caio Borges. 2017. *Building Infrastructure for 21st Century Sustainable Development: Lessons and Opportunities for the BRICS-Led New Development Bank*. Delhi and Sao Paulo: Center for African, Latin American and Caribbean Studies—O.P. Jindal Global University.

Wang, Hongying. 2016. "New Multilateral Development Banks Opportunities and Challenges for Global Governance." Discussion Paper Series on Global and Regional Governance. Washington, DC: Council on Foreign Relations. https://www.cfr.org/content/publications/attachments/Discussion_Paper_Wang_MDBs_OR.pdf.

Watkins, Graham George, Sven-Uwe Mueller, Hendrik Meller, Maria Cecilia Ramirez, Tomás Serebrisky, and Andreas Georgoulias. 2017. *Lessons from Four Decades of Infrastructure Project Related Conflicts in Latin America and the Caribbean*. Washington, DC: Inter-American Development Bank. https://publications.iadb.org/handle/11319/8502.

World Bank. 2011. *2010 Environment Strategy: The Use of Country Systems for Environmental Safeguards*. Washington, DC: World Bank. http://siteresources.worldbank.org/EXTENVSTRATEGY/Resources/6975692-1289855310673/20110222-Use-of-Country-Systems.pdf.

World Bank. 2012. *Guide to Evaluating Capacity Development Results*. Washington, DC: World Bank.

Xi, Chao. 2016. "Financial Infrastructure of B&R: The Asian Infrastructure Investment Bank—Governance Issues." In *Legal Dimensions of China's One Belt One Road Initiative, Wolters Kluwer*, edited by Lutz-Christian Wolff and Chao Xi, 341–54. Wan Chai: Wolters Kluwer.

Xu, Jiajun, and Richard Carey. 2015. "The Economic and Political Geography Behind China's Emergence as an Architect of the International Development System." In *Multilateral Development Banks in the 21st Century: Three Perspectives on China and the Asian Infrastructure Investment Bank*. London, UK: Overseas Development Institute (ODI Discussion Paper, November 11–14).

CHAPTER 8

BRICS Banking and the Demise of Alternatives to the IMF and World Bank

Patrick Bond

INTRODUCTION: WILL BRICS AND THE WEST STRUGGLE, OR SNUGGLE?

The Brazil-Russia-India-China-South Africa (BRICS) bloc has raised expectations since 2014—starting with its formal announcement at the Fortaleza summit with hosting by the Brazilian Workers Party—about the potential for an "alternative" institution, working in a manner completely different to the World Bank and other multilateral development banks. By the time of the Fortaleza summit, there was also the potential for a "New Developmentalism" identified by former Brazilian Finance Minister Luiz Carlos Bresser-Pereira and advanced at the Getulio Vargas Foundation. This philosophy, entailing more active management of international economic relations, including financial and monetary matters, was drawn

P. Bond (✉)
University of the Witwatersrand School of Governance, Johannesburg, South Africa
e-mail: pbond@mail.ngo.za

© The Author(s) 2020
J. A. Puppim de Oliveira and Y. Jing (eds.), *International Development Assistance and the BRICS*, Governing China in the 21st Century,
https://doi.org/10.1007/978-981-32-9644-2_8

in part from Brazil's successful strategy during the late 1990s and 2000s, leading up to the 2011 peak of the commodity super-cycle.

One additional aspect was the sense of not only BRICS' ascendance, but the decline of Western power and legitimacy, which in turn reflected how the Bretton Woods Institutions imposed conditionality-heavy credits and reproduced leadership unfairly: always a US citizen leading the Bank, and a European heading the International Monetary Fund (IMF). As Bresser-Pereira (2018) explained, the World Bank fell "into an identity crisis when, in the early 1980s, the American government constrained it to change from a developmental multilateral bank whose policies were oriented by development economics to be the agency charged with making the neoliberal reforms to advance in the developing countries – to change their economic policy regimes from developmental to liberal." The BRICS' prospects for global financial reform had, even earlier, been identified in part based on a gap in the sustainability financing marketplace, with two former World Bank chief economists—Joseph Stiglitz and Nicolas Stern—writing the original concept paper in 2011.

This dual narrative—drawing attention to the West's neoliberalism, illegitimacy and decay on the one hand, and the rise of the BRICS as an alternative power bloc on the other hand—is worth considering in detail, using as a case study global financial governance. As Tapscott et al. (2017, 1) argue, "relatively little comparative research has been undertaken on the respective state-building and governance regimes of its member states and on how these might influence the closer integration of their activities in the future." The same is true internationally, in a context of a division-prone BRICS where different agendas now proliferate. When driving the BRICS agenda forward, China's capacity to serve its own national interests may be dominant in the long term, but the governments of Donald J. Trump and Jair Bolsonaro have already caused problems for Beijing's global strategy, as shown below. In 2019, both have the power to choose the presiding officer of the World Bank and BRICS New Development Bank (NDB), respectively.

Prior to whatever orientation Bolsonaro chooses as host of the BRICS in 2019, what is the nature of the challenge to the World Bank and IMF posed by the BRICS' most advanced institutional innovations—the NDB and Contingent Reserve Arrangement (CRA)—as well as by the BRICS' foreign economic policy-makers? The ideas of New Developmentalism and "sustainable development financing" have been rhetorically important.

But service to BRICS borrowers—national states and State Owned Enterprises—appears to be of overarching importance, regardless of ideology and sustainability. Reflecting power relations within the BRICS, both new institutions have vital Chinese influences, not least in Shanghai's headquarters role for the former, and Beijing's outsized 41% financial contribution to the latter.[1] If the analytical dilemma discussed below is whether the new BRICS financial institutions are operating against, or within, existing global financial governance, the ability of China to guide the BRICS reflects its leaders' "pragmatism and incremental adaptation," as Yijia Jing (2016, 37) shows in relation to domestic governance.

Yet seen from South Africa, such incrementalism is not satisfying, at a time the West's self-interested financial agenda parallels its chaotic roles in global climate governance, geopolitics and macroeconomic management (Garcia and Bond 2018). These will only intensify with Donald Trump's uncontested appointment of David Malpass as Bank president in 2019, reflecting the West's durable power to not only manage multilateral finance and its institutions (including leadership), but also set the agenda for an era of increased West-BRICS conflict, given Malpass' hostility to China. On the other hand, according to the Bank's former China director Yukon Huang, "China is doing the World Bank a favor by borrowing, because people realize it's not going to default on those loans." He does not expect Malpass to make major changes in relation to China during an era of economic turmoil, because "America always goes for a solution which strengthens the global financial system, because that's America's strength. The global financial system is essentially America's financial system" (Igoe 2019).

The power and arrogance of the Malpass appointment are not surprising. As another example of Western malevolence within global financial management, former World Bank chief economist Nicolas Stern (2013) bragged to a 2013 London conference that *he* was the co-instigator of the very idea of a BRICS Bank, for reasons that had nothing to do with alleged sustainability and climate financing (as claimed by Stern and Stiglitz 2011). Instead, he desired an institutional lock-in between business deal-makers and a dependable cohort of national officials who would respect their states' contracts with such corporations. He specifically sought ways to avoid policies that adversely affected those corporations:

If you have a development bank that is part of a [major business] deal then it makes it more difficult for governments to be unreliable... What you had was the presence of the European Bank for Reconstruction and Development (EBRD) reducing the potential for government-induced policy risk, and the presence of the EBRD in the deal making the government of the host country more confident about accepting that investment. *And that is why Meles Zenawi, Joe Stiglitz and myself, nearly three years ago now, started the idea. And is there any press here, by the way? Ok, so this bit's off the record. We started to move the idea of a BRICS-led development bank* for those two reasons (emphasis added). (Stern 2013)

In a "world turned upside down" (Panitch and Albo 2018) where nothing is as it seems, the critical approach adopted below includes political-economic observations about power within multilateral financial politics. This is achieved partly through an assessment of the Pretoria government's own contributions during the two relevant regimes: Zuma from mid-2009 through early 2018 and Ramaphosa since. During the former's reign, the NDB prepared work on several loans, gaining cabinet approval in late 2015 (Malcolmsen 2016).

One loan was advanced in 2016, but then was not activated by the borrower, the state national electricity firm Eskom. The $180 million was earmarked for renewable energy transmission lines, which the new chief executive (Brian Molefe) did not want to implement, given the utility's financial crisis and his desire to instead contract for Russian-supplied nuclear energy. After Molefe's departure in 2017, a sudden threat of a default on Eskom's $3.75 billion loan to the World Bank in early 2018—which was resolved at an emergency Davos World Economic Forum meeting (Paton 2018)—and Ramaphosa's ascendance, the renewable energy program was reinstated and was one of three loans codified to South Africa's parastatal agencies in 2018. The other two were to the shipping parastatal Transnet ($200 million for Durban port expansion) and the Development Bank of Southern Africa ($300 million for unspecified municipal infrastructure).

In 2019, two additional loans were anticipated: $480 million to Eskom to enhance the largest coal-fired power plant under construction on earth, Medupi (specifically for desulphurization) and $220 million (in local Rand currency) for another dam within the Lesotho Highlands Water Project, which provides cross-catchment water supply to Johannesburg. Both projects have been so bribery-riddled in past phases that the World Bank debarred several international construction companies due to Lesotho corruption (Bond 2002), and the Securities and Exchange Commission fined the main Eskom power-plant builder, Hitachi, $19 million due to its relationship with a fronting company (with no related experience) which also served as the South African ruling party's main fund-raising arm (Bond 2014a, b). These loans contrast the BRICS NDB rhetoric of sustainability with the realities of corrupt, carbon-centric, crony-based accumulation, with no intention of community consultation (i.e., a bank indistinguishable from the World Bank). From 2016 to 2018, the three South African loans were authorized from the NDB Shanghai headquarters, but the Africa Regional Centre in Johannesburg deserves most blame for shortcomings, such as non-existent governance safeguards and a refusal to engage in stakeholder participation.[2]

As for the $100 billion CRA fund, it may one day become relevant in the event of financial meltdowns and contagion similar to 1998 and 2008, especially in South Africa. But at that stage, the IMF is likely to be even more important, if repayment of the country's now-unprecedented $180 billion foreign debt is in question. Seen from South Africa, the institutional connections between the Bretton Woods Institutions and the BRICS, not to mention the NDB staff's own backgrounds in Western-oriented banking (whether global banks or Pretoria's Treasury and Reserve Bank) (Bond 2014b, 2016), together suggest a relationship nowhere near as hostile to the Washington Consensus as some leftist politicians and analysts hope for.[3]

The BRICS have retained a certain credibility as "middle power" accompaniments to multilateralism, to be sure. But in 2019, with Brazilian President Jair Bolsonaro's new right-wing agenda coming into focus (including his appointment of the next BRICS NDB president), the situation remains fluid. His neoliberal Finance Minister Paulo Guedes was named chair of NDB at the April 2019 Annual General Meeting. But macroeconomic trends will likely be decisive, and here—just as in the institutional arena that Stern (2013) explained—it again appears that the BRICS are no *alternative*, but instead an *amplifier*, of contradictions created within Western-centric capitalism (Bond and Garcia 2015). It is in that context that we begin the discussion of the BRICS and global financial governance, given that New Developmentalism has been suggested as an antidote to these trends and has failed to materialize.

A DIFFICULT NEW DEVELOPMENTALISM

Hopes that BRICS countries will offer new strategies and ideas about development and governance are fading, especially in relation to financial markets. The 2014 Fortaleza founding of the NDB raised expectations that the BRICS could generate an exciting new potential: to break the grip on multilateral financial governance by the neoliberal Bretton Woods Institutions, whose conditionality-riddled credit control grew after the 2008 financial crisis. The Western-backed banks came to rule not just impoverished but also emerging economies (e.g., Argentina recently)—just as in the 1980s— and even a few wealthier countries (Portugal, Ireland, Greece and Spain) that recently fell into crisis.

Brazil's New Developmentalism, in contrast, consisted of rising levels of social inclusion and lower inequality, coinciding with successful export orientation. The New Developmentalism's promotion of manufactured exports is closely associated with four macroeconomic, monetary and fiscal policy factors. First is falling exchange rates, given the bias is to undervalue the local currency and thus keep relative wage rates low. Second is a shrinking state deficit on current (not capital) spending so as to avoid crowding out financing for private sector investment. Third is a commitment to establishing new infrastructure. Fourth is a relatively low real interest rate.

Brazil has many lessons; in the second Lula administration, as Bresser-Pereira (2011) explained, "God was Brazilian," because thanks to the commodity super-cycle and his New-Developmentalist *Programa de Aceleração do Crescimento*, Lula "did not bring inflation nor adversely affect growth." The PT "did not fear to displease the rich," but nevertheless "was fiscally responsible" and "reacted well to the 2008 global financial crisis," in part by "lowering the real interest rate by nearly half" and imposing "controls over capital inflow." Lula, said Bresser-Pereira, "remembered that there is such a thing as the entrepreneur and the national enterprise, or, in other words, that there is a nation, whose strength and ability to compete with the other nations will depend on the clarity and cohesiveness of the political coalition between entrepreneurs, public bureaucracy and workers" (Bresser-Pereira 2011).

In South Africa and a few other emerging-market countries, these ideals motivated debates over needed policy shifts, especially where the early 2000s boom provided sufficient macroeconomic space to attempt aspects of New Developmentalism. In Johannesburg phraseology, during the height of Worker Party power, the desire for a "Lula Moment" was expressed by leading center-left policy academics and trade unionists from South Africa and Brazil alike (Netshitenzhe 2013; Braga 2014; Coleman 2014; Schutte 2014), led by the Communist Party's Chris Hani Institute (Webster and Hurt 2014). Of South Africans, however, it was only Neil Coleman (2014) from the main trade union federation who took the trouble to sketch out concrete comparisons.

To be sure, Lula Moment advocacy also attracted criticism, especially insofar as it was a strategy encumbered by unsustainable "corporatist" philosophical underpinnings (Morais and Saad-Filho 2013). Comparing with South Africa's potential, Ben Fogel (2015) complained, Lula "failed to build a new political culture through constitutional and political reforms or by tackling an institutionally hostile media" and instead made "alliances with corrupt and reactionary regional power brokers, embracing Brazil's traditional patronage political culture to gain institutional power at the expense of trade union and social movement allies."

The South African debate coincided with the expulsion of the largest trade union—the 350,000-member National Union of Metalworkers of South Africa (Numsa)—from the country's main union federation because it was too leftwing. So the contrast was with a potential "Numsa moment" that would have much more radically changed ownership of the economy's commanding heights.[4] However, regardless of whether South Africa *should* have pursued this approach, especially in macroeconomic terms, by the mid-2010s there was little left to hope for, in either country. South Africa suffered a kleptocracy from 2009 to 2018 under Zuma's leadership, combining talk-left populist-developmentalist rhetoric with walk-right neoliberalism and extreme corruption.

In Brazil, the 2013 turn to neoliberalism by Lula's successor, Dilma Rousseff, meant the domestic bourgeoisie's support for the PT evaporated after widespread 2013–2016 protests. These were originally catalyzed by leftists dissatisfied by public transport price rises, but were soon taken over by wealthy right-wing elements which by 2016 resulted in a parliamentary coup against Rousseff. So while in the 1998–2004 period, mostly under Fernando Henrique Cardoso's centrist rule, Brazil drove its trade/GDP ratio from 15 up to 30%, this measure of integration subsequently fell to 24% by 2017 (Fig. 8.1). Indeed, the rest of the BRICS trade/GDP ratios also dropped markedly after peaking during the 2000–2008 period, even further than the world's drop, from 61 to 56%. Matters are now deteriorating further what with Donald Trump's US protectionism, for the World Trade Organization (2019) recorded dramatic declines in the

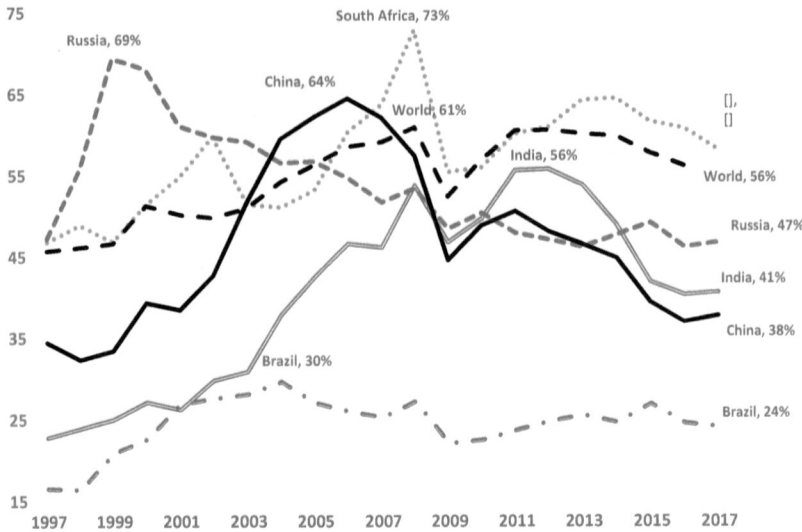

Fig. 8.1 Trade/GDP ratios decline at world scale, driven by the BRICS (*Source* World Bank database)

2018 WTO Index of trade, including a fall in that index of 6.3% (year-on-year from December 2017), as well as −7.9% on export orders, and double-digit crashes in demand for automobiles (−10.3%) and electronics (−12.9%).

The era of Workers Party rule, resulting in Brazil's relatively more inclusive growth and (briefly) rising export-led growth route, followed Bresser-Pereira's framing. But this was not the only Latin American country offering lessons for development. In addition, there were successful—and far more radical—approaches to global-national-local interfaces especially in relation to finance. These included default on Odious Debts (e.g., by Ecuador in 2009) and tighter exchange controls to halt illicit financial flows (e.g., Venezuela in 2003), as well as (stillborn) proposals for a Bank of the South by Hugo Chavez that would have injected a strong developmental and environmental agenda into South–South cooperation.

All these radical strategies emerged with one overarching concern: Acute consciousness of how foreign indebtedness would derail developmental ambitions, as Latin Americans and all other Third World countries recalled from the 1980s to 1990s era. Bresser-Pereira in 2018 remarked on one of the most crucial features of new, alternative financing strategies, which is to match assets to liabilities when it comes to the currency in which lending occurs.

> The NDB, the bank governed by BRICS countries, spelt out the proposal to follow this line of action. Some multilateral banks, particularly the Asian Development Bank, the International Finance Corporation and even the World Bank are already lending in local currency. Why? Would it be the new concern with currency mismatches and the development of local capital markets?... the Multilateral Banks are turning to domestic currencies because their customers are most of the time private companies that resist to take loans in hard currency to avoid foreign exchange risks. Second, because after the Asian 1997 financial crisis, many countries, particularly the Asian countries, realized the financial crisis risk involved in getting indebted into foreign money and began to accumulate large international reserves. Third, because, after the disastrous attempt to grow with foreign indebtedness ("foreign savings") that the Washington Consensus proposed from the early 1990s (just after the major 1980 s' foreign debt crisis was overcome), the governments of the developing countries went back to the policy of keeping the current account balanced or with a surplus, as China has been doing for long. (Bresser-Pereira 2018, 3)

Unfortunately, again in South Africa, the New Developmentalism's valid insights were not followed by policy-makers. First, they allowed the NDB to issue the loans discussed below in US dollars, not South African rands; only in March 2019 was the first announcement of a proposed rand bond issued by the NDB. Second, they ran up consistently large current account deficits, for reasons worth remarking upon. The main international economic imbalance in South Africa is not—as is commonly assumed—the trade deficit with China (although that remains large). Indeed, mainly because of the export of raw materials (minerals and cash crops), semi-processed metals (steel, aluminum and manganese) and (highly subsidized) automobiles to mainly Western markets, the trade account often reached mild surpluses in the 2010s, including in 2016–2018.

Instead, the cause of the current account deficit was the outflow of profits, dividends and interest (the current account's "balance on income"), mainly to London and other overseas financial headquarters (Table 8.1).[5] Although the current account deficit was 7% of GDP in 2009, it recovered thanks to the commodity crash of 2015, which temporarily lessened the pressure on profit repatriation. Indeed, the currency dropped to as low as

Table 8.1 The South African current account in deficit due to "income payments," 2013–2023

	2013	2014	2015	2016	2017 Est.	2018	2019	2020	2021 Proj.	2022	2023
					(In billions of US dollars)						
Balance on current account	−21.2	−17.8	−14.6	−8.2	−8.6	−11.0	−12.7	−13.4	−14.0	−14.8	−15.6
Balance on goods and services	−8.4	−5.3	−4.1	1.8	4.8	1.9	−0.1	−0.7	−0.7	−0.8	−1.0
Exports of goods and services	113.6	110.4	95.8	90.8	104.0	112.5	116.3	120.7	126.4	132.0	137.8
Imports of goods and services	−122.0	−115.7	−99.9	−89.0	−99.2	−110.6	−116.4	−121.4	−127.0	−132.7	−138.9
Balance on income	−9.6	−9.4	−7.9	−8.2	−10.5	−10.1	−10.2	−10.4	−11.0	−11.5	−12.0
Income receipts	6.7	7.6	7.7	6.0	6.1	14.3	16.7	18.4	16.3	14.6	14.5
Income payments	−16.3	−16.9	−15.6	−14.2	−16.6	−24.5	−27.0	−28.8	−27.2	−26.1	−26.5
Balance on transfers	−3.2	−3.2	−2.6	−1.9	−2.9	−2.7	−2.3	−2.3	−2.4	−2.5	−2.6

R17.9/$ in January 2016, which compelled cuts in imports and assisted South Africa's export recovery. But the current account deficit has still been negative, even in years of trade surplus, in the range of 2–5% of GDP from 2016 to 2018. In those years, trading surpluses of $8.5 billion were registered, yet South Africa suffered $28.8 billion in net profit and transfer outflow.[6]

Profit inflows should actually be much higher than outflows, because the net foreign investment position of South African capital has been positive since 2015 (Fig. 8.2), largely because of one major investment made by the largest firm on the Johannesburg Stock Exchange—Naspers—in Chinese firm tech company Tencent. That stake, of nearly a third ownership in what soon became the highest-capitalized firm in Asia, grew from $32 million to $150 billion in value from 2001–2018. It increased the country's net international investment by 40% of GDP from 2010 to 2015 (although income receipts suggest Tencent's dividends are not flowing back into Naspers at anywhere near the rate profits are flowing out of South Africa). Given the extreme volatility of the currency caused in part by this income vulnerability, daily Over-the-Counter Foreign Exchange (OTC FX) market activity is far greater in South Africa than elsewhere, rising to 17% of GDP by 2017 (IMF 2018).

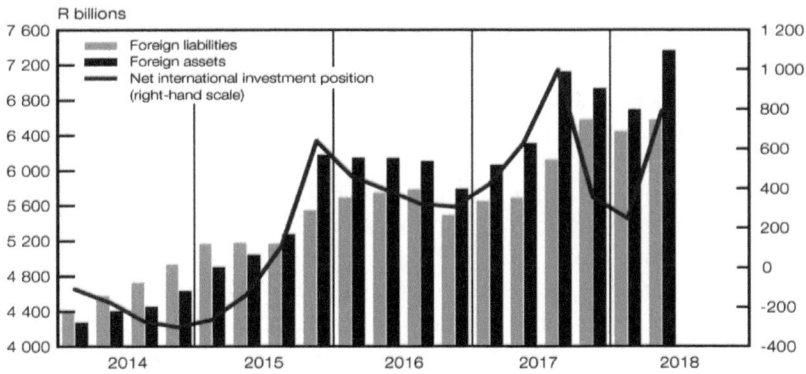

Fig. 8.2 South Africa's international investment position, 2014–2018 (billions of SA Rands) (*Source* South African Reserve Bank, *Quarterly Bulletin*, December 2018)

In addition to egregious mistakes in international financial relations, South African policy-makers made other errors. Their early 2000s "developmental state" debate in South Africa did not stress crucial New Developmentalism features, so compared to Brazil, there was far less economic sovereignty. One reason was South Africa's massive deindustrialization during the 1990s, as East Asian imports decisively outcompeted local clothing, textiles, appliances, electronics and other local manufactured goods once South Africa liberalized trade. Thus in the early 2000s, the developmental debate largely revolved around how to best link up the so-called two economies (the advanced capitalist sector and informal sector) and how to advance minerals beneficiation (Mbeki 2004; Masondo 2007). The country's $2.5 trillion natural resource base was seen as the basis for downstream investment, at least prior to the commodity super-cycle fizzling out in 2011. But the crash in world commodity prices (including metals), and in South Africa, electricity black-outs and soaring electricity prices starting in 2008, together hampered further investment in smelting.

As institutional economists have pointed out, South Africa's structural bias remains located within the "Minerals Energy Complex," which combines large multinational-corporate mining houses, the state electricity firm Eskom, and associated downstream industries including petrochemicals, metals processing and other sectors that comprise about 20% of GDP (Fine and Rustomjee 1996; Padayachee 2010). The bias within the state transport firm, Transnet, is, likewise, to emphasize export of raw ores—especially coal—through expanded port capacity (while closing down or neglecting maintenance for both long-distance and intra-urban passenger services). The fossil intensity of these energy-generation and transport biases has become even worse within Eskom and Transnet.

The inability of Eskom to reduce its reliance on coal-fired power plants and replace generation capacity with renewable sources and the intensity of Transnet's reliance upon coal exports are together reflected in the two largest mega-project investments in the 2012–2030 National Development Plan (NDP). First, the state—led by Transnet and major mining houses—made a $60 billion commitment to the export of 18 billion tons of coal (mostly to China and India) along new rail lines, using imported locomotives that can carry 3-kilometer-long ore-carrying trains. Eskom relies on coal from the same areas (Limpopo and Mpumalanga provinces) for 90% of its generation capacity, so the expansion of high-volume coal transport benefits its two massive new coal-fired plants (Medupi and Kusile). The second largest mega-project is a $20 billion expansion of the port-petrochemical complex in Durban, again led by Transnet. These two are the first two priority projects within the Presidential Infrastructure Coordinating Commission's Strategic Integrated Projects (PICC SIPs), developed as part of the National Infrastructure Plan (Bond 2014a).

It is therefore no surprise that the first two BRICS New Development Bank loans to South Africa also reflect these biases. The 2016 and 2018 credits of $180 million to Eskom and $200 million to Transnet quickly fell into controversy, and in both cases, projects went into immediate hibernation in part due to the borrowers' systemic corruption and in part to the failure of both to properly make their projects sustainable. In short, New Developmentalism was stillborn, missing a critical mass of patriotic business elites committed to the four components usually considered crucial ingredients.

The vision of Bresser-Pereira (2011) was never realized through the NDB. One leading Asian advocate of the developmental state, Jomo Kwame Sundaram (2019), was wistful when asked about the NDB: "I wish the new multilateral development banks would be bolder, but thus far, they have largely chosen to work within the dominant framework shaped by the Washington Consensus, probably to secure market confidence." To help understand this failure of nerve in South Africa, we next contemplate how the NDB handled macroeconomic context, currency exposure, corruption and climate change within its first three loans.

NDB RISKS: MACROECONOMIC CONTEXT, CURRENCY EXPOSURE, CORRUPTION AND CLIMATE CHANGE

The problem, we observe next, is not just BRICS elites' impotence at the scale of global institutional reform, even at peak when Lula's accomplishments were well recognized. Other risks within the BRICS development finance agenda come from the deteriorating macroeconomic environment since the early 2010s, a point at which "deglobalization" tendencies (Garcia and Bond 2018) and structural fragility associated with financialization (e.g., $250 trillion in outstanding world debt) were amplified by US dollar exposure and rampant corruption within BRICS banking. The core economic problem facing three of the BRICS was the collapse of commodity prices after the 2002–2011 super-cycle upturn and 2011–2015 plateau. This led to junk credit ratings suffered by three borrower countries: Russia from 2015, Brazil from 2015 and South Africa from 2017, as the commodity super-cycle's demise was accompanied by political problems in each. Russia was punished with sanctions due its 2014 invasion (or some say "liberation") of Ukraine's Crimea. Corruption delegitimized key functions of the state in Brazil and South Africa. And indeed those were the three countries which had defaulted on foreign debt within the bankers' living memory: Russia in 1998, Brazil in 1987 and South Africa in 1985. So the exchange rates of their three currencies crashed in 2015, to levels between 32 and 38% lower than in 2000 (whereas India had by then risen by 20% and China by 30%) (Fig. 8.3).

On the one hand, this adverse macroeconomic situation would logically suggest that poorer countries should no longer attempt to seek a piece of a vanishing pie, namely the prior expanding rate of world trade, which since 2017 went into reverse. Instead, they should seek more balanced, inward-oriented growth, such as was recommended by *dependencia* scholars since the 1950s, including Raúl Prebisch (1950) in Latin America and Samir Amin (1990) in Africa. As a concrete reflection of such a shift, the BRICS cities should no longer be re-arranged to support export-platform economies, of which Durban and Rio de Janeiro were perhaps most infamous (Bond et al. 2016); instead, they should have a greater share of infrastructural funds dedicated to meeting basic needs. Since the mid-1980s, such basic needs have been underserved thanks to the method of arranging neoliberal investments in electricity, water and wastewater, roads,

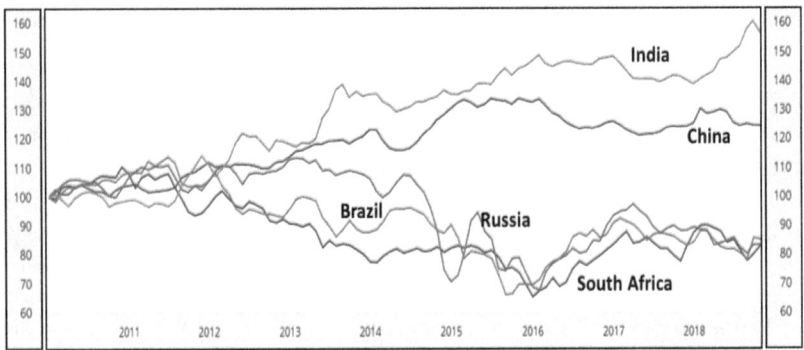

Fig. 8.3 Relative currency values of the BRICS against the US dollar, 2010–2019 (*Source* https://data.worldbank.org/indicator/PX.REX.REER?end=2017&locations=BR-ZA-CN-RU&start=2000)

ports and other economic infrastructure enhancements. The objective was to attract and serve multinational corporations, for the sake of increasing revenues from world trade, as advocated initially in the World Bank's mid-1980s Urban Management Program (Bond 2000). But the ability of poor residents to afford corporatized or privatized services was minimal in most user-pay systems.

On the other hand, even as the Baltic Dry Index—world shipping's main indicator of container transport prices—fell from a level of 12,000 in 2008 to less than 1000 over the subsequent decade, there appears to have been increasing not decreasing pressures from the mercantile circuit of capital to expand port investments. This is especially evident in the BRICS where Beijing's Belt and Road Initiative and the Delhi-Tokyo Asia-Africa Growth Corridor both encourage new harbors or existing port expansion. At the BRICS 2017 Xiamen summit, reporters observed a failed merger strategy between the two projects, with South Africa squeezed in between (Singupta 2017; Woody 2018). This confirms that instead of collaboration, the current era may instead witness a form of ultra-competitive economic cannibalism, a point vividly illustrated in debates surrounding South Africa's BRICS NDB-financed port expansion (Bond 2014a).

In this context, macroeconomic stabilization has been in China's self-interest, what with Beijing's ongoing financing of Washington's massive trade deficit (typically the Chinese state holds more than $1.3 trillion of US Treasury Bills). A trade war with Donald Trump may change this, if it transpires after a brief truce in 2019. But what is ultimately required, to assure durable world economic stability, is a new currency that could be more democratically managed, in contrast to the US Federal Reserve Board's current bias to serving the interests of the West's largest banks. Indeed, in 2013, the Fed's revised monetary policy signaling—known as the "tapering of Quantitative Easing"—adversely affected four of the BRICS' currencies (all except the still-rising yuan), as it drew liquid funding back to the US dollar (Fig. 8.3). Notwithstanding rhetoric about increasing use of BRICS currencies or barter trade, not much more is being done to end the destructive system in which the US dollar has world "seignorage": i.e., it is the world's reserve currency, no matter how badly Washington officials abuse that power. If China really wants its currency to one day take the place of the dollar, and if Russia wants to find routes out of the current squeeze caused by financial sanctions, the pace at which this is happening is agonizingly slow. (A 2019 "BRICS Pay" strategy of clearing funds on retail purchases without recourse to the dollar is one encouraging sign.)

Can the NDB and CRA contribute to constructive change away from dollar dependency? According to the SA foreign ministry's Dave Malcolmson, there is strong political will to engage in non-dollar lending. Malcolmsen (2016) reported to Parliament about a 2015 presentation by K. V. Kamath, the NDB President. Among the innovative features of the NDB, "The actual challenge in respect of loan payments for developing countries pertain moreover to that of the currency fluctuation which increases the loan repayment terms (usually in USD) rather than agreed interest rates for such loans. He emphasized the importance of raising loans in local currencies to lessen such a burden."[7]

Yet in its first five years, the vast majority of the $8 billion in NDB loans were dollar denominated, even though these were mainly projects characterized by local-currency expenditures. There were minimal import requirements in loans for transportation (29%), energy (26%), water/sanitation/irrigation (22%), social infrastructure (15%) and cleaner production (8%). The main borrowers were India (40%) and China (25%), both of which could produce project inputs locally. In South Africa, it was only in the second half of 2019 that the NDB would raise funds in the local currency, on the most liquid and over-capitalized market in world history, the Johannesburg Stock Exchange, a market whose Buffett Indicator ratio (share capitalization over GDP) by then had peaked at over 350%, three times the world average.

Another major factor that will create additional risk to all parties is systematic corporate and state corruption. It pervades all the BRICS, at a level just as high as can be found in the USA, Europe or Africa. The top four countries in which economic crime occurs, according to PricewaterhouseCoopers (2018), are South Africa, Kenya, France and Russia, with China ranked eighth. *Financial Times* commentator Gideon Rachman (2018) expressed concern that "In all five countries, popular rage about graft is at the very heart of politics." Moreover, the BRICS "may be spreading corrupt practices more widely. The USA, EU and UK pride themselves on their sound institutions. But western bankers, lawyers, real estate agents, PR firms (and perhaps even presidents) are often all too willing to share in the proceeds of corruption." (In South Africa, such firms included Bell Pottinger—which as a result of South African corruption went into bankruptcy—and consultancy and law firms KPMG, McKinsey, Hogan Lovells, Bain, Deloitte, PwC, SAP and others.)

A degree of corruption-denialism exists within the NDB. Asked about the corruption associated with its loan to Transnet in mid-2018, the institution's Compliance Officer Srinivas Yanamandra (2018) claimed,

> At the time of loan appraisal, NDB gives consideration to corruption risks in accordance with internal policies and guidelines, which articulate a zero-tolerance policy against corruption. These policies and guidelines stipulate adequate mechanisms to ensure compliance with highest standards of ethics, accountability and integrity. The Bank further reckons adverse media news, if any about the prospective borrower, taking into account the country system of law enforcement for handling corruption issues. The Bank supplements internal assessment with a co-operative relationship externally with law enforcement as well as other responsible agencies that deal with matters relating to anti-corruption at national / international level. (Yanamamdra 2018)

Such "zero-tolerance" policy claims cannot be taken seriously given the widespread media and law-enforcement attention to Transnet at the time the loan was granted, in May 2018. Recognizing the contradiction, Yanamandra (2018) further explained,

> The appraisal of loan to Transnet went through the above-mentioned procedures of the Bank. While approving the loan in May 2018, the Bank recognized the ongoing efforts by the South African Government to address corruption issues both at the national level and at the level of Transnet as a particular entity (including through the new Special Investigative Unit set up by the President of South Africa). The Bank further took note of internal developments at the Company (viz., forensic investigations under the oversight of Board Audit Committee and ongoing review of procurement processes). The Bank has also noted the ongoing improvements in oversight of the Company by the Ministry of Public Enterprises, including through leadership changes that were implemented in recent times. (Yanamamdra 2018)

Such improvements were not adequate to halt a major episode of corruption in late 2018, one so serious as to halt the Durban port's expansion. Although the notorious Transnet Chief Executive Officer Siyabonga Gama's contract was by October 2018 finally terminated due to corruption, a $500 million component of the Durban port deepening project, commissioned in July 2018, became the source of a controversy over the procurement process. It involved not only the Italian-South African CMI

Emtateni Joint Venture, but in particular, Durban's best-known procurement fraudster, Shauwn Mpisane (Cowan 2018). Without disclosing details about the malfeasance, which included a lawsuit by a competitor who raised substantive complaints about the process, Transnet stated, "In the interest of good corporate governance, Transnet has decided to issue a stop work instruction on the Main Marine Construction Works contract pending the outcome of the investigation" (Mkentane 2018). (By May 2019, there was no word on the investigation and the NDB project remained stalled.)

In 2019, a leading BRICS official admitted that the 2016 loan to Eskom—which had been put on hold allegedly by Brian Molefe due to his opposition to solar energy—was actually "saddled with corruption allegations and governance challenges. So that loan was put on ice and never formally concluded" (although it was reaffirmed in mid-2018) (Wright 2019). The character of this particular case of corruption was not revealed. However, like other BRICS countries, South Africa remains bedeviled by procurement fraud, which has been estimated by a leading Treasury official as costing 35–40% more on each outsourced contract than is reasonable, on $50 billion in annual corporate procurements (Mkokeli 2016).

In Brazil, Operation Car Wash revealed *mensalão* bribery in Congress and widespread Petrobras patrimonialism. Russian elites, including several close to Putin, were fingered as having multi-billion dollar offshore accounts in tax havens, in the leaked lawyers' emails known as the Paradise and Panama Papers. In India, the extent of citizens' experience with petty bribery has been measured by Transparency International at more than 60% of respondents. And China's highest-profile corruption case—the prosecution of former Chongqing mayor (and Xi competitor) Bo Xilai—was seen as a political hatchet job, although to Beijing's credit, many thousands of corrupt officials have been jailed (Zhao 2012).

A final risk is faced by all financiers in the current period: Fossil-intensive investments considered to be "stranded assets," resulting in devaluation of their portfolios. This is not merely an institutional risk, but—due to ongoing species-extinguishing climate change—one that extends deep into the future of global civilization. Ironically, NDB rhetoric leaves the impression that the 2013–2014 leaders of the BRICS, prompted by the institution's illustrious designers Nicolas Stern and Joseph Stiglitz (2011), had a strong commitment to earth stewardship. In reality, all five BRICS are among the world's most unsustainable countries in terms of pollution loads, and naturally this will affect the availability of infrastructure investments (e.g., a high emphasis on ports, railroads and roads, such as in the case of Transnet).

Indeed, the BRICS are amplifying the inherited Western corporate traditions of externalizing environmental costs onto nature and onto the societies surrounding their main industrial districts. Although the NDB's commitment to the vaguely defined promise of "sustainability" is a noble sentiment, it has little hope of ever being realized given the broader BRICS project of high-carbon extractive infrastructure.

South Africa alone is engaged in massive new fracking investments, offshore oil and gas exploration (in early 2019 Total discovered a billion oil-equivalent barrels); 18 billion tons of coal exports (mainly to India); and coal-fired power generation including two 4800 MW plants now under construction and a 4600 MW plant promised in a Chinese metallurgical complex, as well as several others in the 1000 MW range.[8] South Africa's lack of commitment to cut its historically extremely high-carbon addiction was matched by not only USA and Canadian failures to cut back emissions, and even Germany's late 2030s' commitment to cut back on coal (which activists and scientists say is far too late). The other BRICS also adopted ecologically catastrophic policies: Bolsonaro's commitment to unleashing cattle ranchers, soy farmers, mining corporations and timber interests on the Amazon; Putin's unlimited extraction of Siberian fossil fuels; Modi's massive construction of new coal-fired power plants; and Xi's carbon-intensive Belt and Road Initiative.

In this context, it was reasonable to ask whether the BRICS leaders were really serious about challenging the United Nations Framework Convention on Climate Change, Bretton Woods Institutions and other structures of global power. After all, if revolutionizing development finance was the objective, there was an alternative already in place they could have supported: the Bank of the South. Founded by the late Venezuelan President Hugo Chavez in 2007 and supported by Argentina, Bolivia, Brazil, Ecuador, Paraguay and Uruguay, Banco del Sur had acquired $7 billion in capital by 2013. It offered a more profound challenge to the Washington Consensus, especially after Ecuadoran radical economists led by Pedro Paez (2016) improved the design. Instead, the BRICS appear to favor the stabilization of the world financial *status quo*, rather than radically changing the most unfair and intrinsically destabilizing components.

Conclusion

In all the respects discussed above, the NDB is a high-risk institution. However, this view is not widely shared among establishment observers, as witnessed in the Standard & Poors Global Ratings review of the bank in mid-2018:

> We assess NDB's risk management policies as sound and similar to its highly rated peers'. The bank has established prudent risk management policies, especially in terms of liquidity and capital adequacy, and has set various limits for single obligor, country, and sector concentration... we expect the institution to instill sound governance and risk management principles across its operations... we expect NDB to abide by the same high standard as leading peers in terms of governance, procurement, and social responsibility... we estimate that NDB currently, as well as in the foreseeable future, could survive an extremely stressed scenario without market access for 12 months and without withdrawing any principal resources from borrowing members...

In other words, although macroeconomic stress is mentioned in passing, Phua and Ekbom (2018) see no dangers in the conditions that might lead to borrower default, rampant corruption and the BRICS infrastructure contributions to climate change discussed above. Instead, Phua and Ekbom (2018) advocate that the NDB expand to include other potential members:

> We would raise the rating if NDB is able to increase its public policy profile and importance. In this scenario, we envisage a substantial geographical expansion of NDB's operations through an increase in the number of shareholders with more than token stakes. Also, we expect the loan portfolio to be more evenly balanced, away from the current heavier concentration in loans to India and China.

Perhaps already aware of then-candidate Bolsonaro's antipathy to China, Phua and Ekbom (2018) subtly warned that in the event of "any of the founding members withdrawing their membership, [s]uch a scenario will cast serious doubts on NDB's ability to fulfil its mandate." But in only one other respect was Phua and Ekbom (2018) slightly cautious:

> The shareholder structure, with borrowing-eligible members holding all the voting shares, could present a certain degree of agency risk, in our view. This potential conflict of interest and the fact that the shareholders do not rank very high in terms of governance constrains our assessment of NDB's governance and management expertise.[9]

The S&P analysts' neglect of the other major structural risks identified above parallel the failure of credit rating agencies in relation to Enron,

Lehman Brothers, AIG insurance and other calamitous episodes of myopia. The general risks should be obvious, but examination of the three project borrowers from South Africa funded by the NDB in 2016–2018 reveals systematic concrete deficiencies. The NDB's renewable energy and sustainability rhetoric appear designed to beguile. Consultation with affected parties is non-existent. Privatized supply of services is common. Hard currency loans—all three of South Africa's—will be extremely expensive to repay as the rand continues its long-term decline. Corruption among borrowers—including the two leaders at Eskom and Transnet who signed NDB loans and were subsequently fired for graft—is treated flippantly by a Compliance Officer whose due diligence defense at Transnet was subsequently shown to be extremely weak.

In short, the NDB is not an alternative to a system of development finance that, based in Washington, is rife with problems and that apparently cannot be reformed. Instead, it appears from the South African case that the ingredients exist for the NDB to *amplify* uneven development through financing some of the country's most notoriously corrupt institutions, for projects which are themselves highly dubious. For these reasons, the NDB was the subject of a protest of more than 100 environmental activists led by four African Goldman Prize winners in July 2018, just at the start of the BRICS Johannesburg summit. This was the first of what will be many more protests against the NDB, it is safe to say, unless it shifts away from the projects and policies that are doing so much harm to people and planet.

None of these conflicts would have surprised seasoned observers of the divergence between BRICS elites and the needs of their societies and environment. As Indian political economist, Prabhat Patnaik predicted so presciently in 2014,

> The question of the BRICS Bank cannot be analyzed without reference to the big bourgeoisie of the BRICS countries, as the commentators have almost universally done. In other words, the class nature of these regimes has a crucial bearing on the direction that the BRICS Bank will take: whether the BRICS Bank and the CRA will become mere replicas of the World Bank and the IMF with some delegation of authority from the "top" to the BRICS powers, or whether they will expand the elbow room of the countries of the South...
>
> Several BRICS countries in short had connived with the US-led imperialist bloc to sabotage a proposal to bring countries of the South to the forefront of "global economic governance", and had even resuscitated a near-defunct IMF for this purpose. To imagine that the same countries are now going

to stand with the South, through the BRICS Bank, to loosen the hold of imperialism, is utterly fanciful. (Patnaik 2014)

Assuming the BRICS and global elites can one day be dislodged, is a different philosophical approach possible? John Maynard Keynes (1933) offered one of the most generous of formulas: "I sympathize with those who would minimize, rather than with those who would maximize, economic entanglement among nations. Ideas, knowledge, science, hospitality, travel – these are the things which should of their nature be international. But let goods be homespun whenever it is reasonably and conveniently possible and, above all, let finance be primarily national." That approach implies an older form of developmentalism, one that applies tight exchange controls, that balances an economy's various sectors through import-substitution industrialization, that therefore has a great chance to meet society's basic needs in an environmentally conscious way and that welcomes skilled and unskilled labor to its shores.

None of the BRICS are following this strategy at present, but at some stage in future, their countries' progressive politicians will recognize the need to move in a genuinely developmentalist direction. The reactionary, failing characteristics of the BRICS global financial governance reform agenda and institutions will then fade into history, where they belong.

NOTES

1. The NDB has a notional capitalization of $50 billion, but only $10 billion is, by 2021, required from BRICS taxpayers as paid-in capital, equally divided among the five members. In addition the NDB issues bonds occasionally, such as a 2016 "green bond" in Chinese yuan for the equivalent of $450 million. The CRA's capitalization is $100 billion, consisting of countries' foreign currency reserves which are dedicated to on-lending in the case of a member's balance-of-payments emergency. In addition to China at 41%, Brazil, Russia and India have 18% shares each, and South Africa 10%.

2. In August 2017, the BRICS Bank's Johannesburg African Regional Centre branch was hurriedly opened just ahead of the September 2017 BRICS summit in China. In December 2015, the Centre's new director general was suddenly announced: Nhlanhla Nene. But the job was a hot potato, and Nene's appointment was a fig-leaf excuse Zuma gave for firing the pro-business finance minister who then spurned the supposed (but non-existent) offer. There is little doubt that instead of "deploying" him to this important

job, Zuma simply wanted Nene out of the way, because of repeated Treasury opposition to a $100 billion nuclear energy deal. It was a project that Zuma, Molefe and others in Eskom were intent on concluding with Rosatom, especially following a July 2015 BRICS summit in Ufa where the deal was confirmed. Nene refused on grounds of state poverty, and so for one weekend, was briefly replaced by an ally of Zuma's most corrupt patronage network, run by the Gupta brothers (three immigrants from India). After pressure was exerted on Zuma especially by the Chinese minority shareholders owners of South Africa's largest bank, Standard (Bruce 2016), Gordhan was then installed as Finance Minister (until he was fired in 2017, also for opposing the Zuma-Gupta agenda). Nene was never offered the job and, under the influence of the Gupta brothers, Zuma became a laughing stock for trying this gambit. The Africa Regional Centre in Sandton was slated by Auditor General Kimi Makwetu on grounds of "fruitless and wasteful expenditure" worth millions of dollars—mainly due to empty office space—in November 2017.

3. The South African chosen as NDB Vice President, Leslie Maasdorp, previously worked at Goldman Sachs, Barclays and Bank of America—as well as leading Pretoria's internal privatization office. One mega-dam project discussed by Maasdorp as a potential NDB financing target is the Lesotho Highlands Water Project. Dating back two decades, the Project may be the world's most infamous case of construction company bribery in World Bank lending history. More than $2 million flowed from a dozen multinational corporations to the Swiss accounts of the leading dam official, Masupha Sole, who served 9 years in jail but was then, to everyone's astonishment, reinstated thanks to his political influence. Lesotho's dam water flows to South Africa, even in times (such as 2016) when the country faces ruinous drought. Although the World Bank debarred some of the most corrupt companies (in the process catalyzing the bankruptcy of Canada's once formidable civil engineering firm Acres International), nothing was done to punish the firms by Pretoria officials. Maasdorp discussed his own role at the helm of the institution responsible: "I served for example as chairman of TransCaledon Tunnel Authority, which is a state-owned enterprise with a mandate to finance and implement bulk raw water infrastructure projects in South Africa, and played an oversight role from a governance perspective for seven years of large infrastructure projects" (Mnyandu 2015). Several of the same construction firms that were implicated in Lesotho reappeared in notorious collusion cases involving white-elephant World Cup 2010 stadiums and other mega-projects in which billions of dollars were stolen from South African taxpayers. *South African firms are obviously not alone*; in 2014, the World Bank debarred the China Three Gorges Corporation's subsidiary building dams in Africa after extreme corruption was identified in another African project.

From July 2015 through August 2017, the South African non-executive director serving the NDB was Tito Mboweni of Goldman Sachs, a former Reserve Bank governor (and from October 2018 South Africa's finance minister) best remembered for maintaining extremely high interest rates during his 1999–2009 tenure (Bond 2014c). As soon as he was appointed to the NDB board, Mboweni—then at the BRICS summit in Ufa, Russia—was interviewed by Bloomberg (2015) and argued that a proposed $100 billion South African nuclear deal with Rosatom, already signed on a preliminary basis by Zuma in 2014, "falls squarely within the mandate of the NDB." This was in spite of enormous local controversy surrounding Zuma's corruption-prone deal-making regarding not only Rosatom but the Gupta family, whose firm Oakbay would have been the main uranium supplier. But then, in his own words, he was "Fired, you might say!!" (*Citizen* 2017). Instead of a customary roll-over, Mboweni was replaced by the South African Treasury director general, Dondo Mogajane. He had served as a World Bank board member during the institution's controversy over a corrupt $3.75 billion loan—its largest ever—to South Africa for the world's largest new coal-fired power plant, one opposed by everyone from community and climate activists to *Business Day* newspaper and the center-right opposition party, in part because of extreme corruption that witnessed Hitachi paying a $19 million fine under the US Foreign Corrupt Practices Act in 2015, for bribing the African National Congress.

4. In 2014, Alfredo Saad-Filho argued that contextual differences between the two countries require more nuance in analysis: "The attempt to build a 'Numsa moment' in South Africa will face much greater difficulties than those that confronted the Workers Party (PT) and trade unions (CUT) in Brazil, back in the early 1980s. South Africa has *already* gone through the transitions to democracy and to neoliberalism, while the PT and CUT emerged before these two transitions. Political democracy and neoliberalism have had very adverse implications for the composition, organic unity and capacity of mobilization of the working class almost everywhere. So the challenge is now greater, but the working class movement and the left in South Africa are also much stronger than they ever were in Brazil. The point, then, is to build a political left with working class hegemony, rather than under the intellectual leadership of sections of the middle class, or the economic hegemony of the domestic bourgeoisie, as was the case in the 'Lula Moment' in Brazil" (personal communication, February 21, 2014).

5. South Africa's debt repayments are becoming increasingly expensive. A major fear expressed periodically is South Africa's potential inability to service foreign loans, especially those borrowed by the main State Owned Enterprises. As reported in 2018 by *Business Day's* Carol Paton (2018), "If the World Bank issues a default letter… it will trigger a 14-day recall on its $3.75 billion

loan, which could trigger a recall on Eskom's $26 billion debt mountain." Eskom has by far the largest component worth of state-backed loans, representing a dangerously high contingent liability whose costs are carried by the general citizenry. Eskom is also repaying the World Bank's largest-ever loan, for the Medupi power plant (the Bank's last such coal-related lending, due to a belated climate-change policy). Medupi's $5 billion worth of boilers were supplied by Hitachi, which in 2015 was fined $19 million by the US government for violating the Foreign Corrupt Practices Act: bribing the ANC's investment arm through a 25% ownership in a local affiliate. Medupi cost triples its original estimates, at $15 billion, and was delayed nine years due to numerous design and implementation flaws (including 7000 welding mistakes on the Hitachi boilers). The high costs—exacerbated by a crashing currency—were passed to poor consumers, whose electricity bills rose far faster than inflation from 2008 to 2017. In mid-2018, Eskom received another $2.5 billion in loans from the China Development Bank to build the $15 billion Kusile power plant, also with Hitachi/ANC boilers. That bank's prior major loan to South Africa was to Transnet ($5 billion), for corruption-riddled locomotive and Durban crane procurement from China South Rail and Shanghai Zhenhua Heavy Industries (via the Gupta family empire) (D'Sa and Bond 2018). Such mega-projects mainly benefit well-connected elites, at the cost of the poorest.

6. The central reason for South Africa's vulnerability to high levels of net income payment outflows and currency speculation against the rand is Pretoria's regular relaxation of exchange controls. As one example, in 2018 Treasury granted permission for an additional $38 billion worth of pension and insurance funds to move abroad. As another example, whereas in 2015 the maximum annual externalization of funds by wealthy South Africans was $300,000, it was raised that year to $750,000. Such loosening weakens the Reserve Bank's ability to defend against currency crashes and financial outflows, given that Pretoria's $50 billion in currency reserves have not increased over the past decade. As the IMF (2018, 35) warned, "Foreign exchange reserves are assessed to be below adequacy... 70% of the assessing reserve adequacy metric adjusted for capital flow measures."

7. The real interest rate on the dollar-denominated loans depends upon currency devaluation: South Africa's crashed from R6.3/$ in 2011 to R17.9/$ in early 2016 before stabilizing around R14/$ in 2017–2018. Kamath (cited in Bond 2017) once conceded to *Russia Today*, "The effective costs of borrowing in hard currencies, for any of us developing countries, appears low. It appears to be 2 to 2.5%. But when you add the exchange loss, the weakening of the currency over time, you end up paying 12, 13, 14%. So that' s your true cost." Kamath has committed to future lending in Chinese renminbi, Indian rupees, Brazilian reals and Russian rubles and considered including South

African rands as a potential currency. The NDB's Eskom lending would have financed locally sourced materials such as steel and cables (and local labor) for the electricity grid extension. Any such further NDB dollar loan offers make no sense.

8. To illustrate the dangers, recall that the Development Bank of Southern Africa (DBSA) was granted a $300 million loan by the NDB in 2018 for municipal on-lending. However, that institution also is committed to financing a portion of two proposed coal-fired power plants costing $2.9 billion (producing 863 MW of power), for Japanese, Korean and Saudi Arabian owners. Requested by anti-coal campaigners to halt and reverse these commitments in 2018, the DBSA declined—although its CEO, Patrick Dlamini, later expressed his personal opposition to coal financing.

9. S&P (2018) continued, "However, we note that no member holds veto power. A special majority (four out of five members) is required for milestone decisions, including earnings distributions and increases in capital subscriptions… Although NDB's shareholder structure could present agency risks, we believe the institution will manage potential conflicts through governance best practices and prudent risk management."

References

Amin, Samir. 1990. *Delinking*. London: Zed Books.

Bloomberg. 2015. "$100 Billion BRICS Lender More Keen on Risk Than World Bank." July 10. http://www.bloomberg.com/news/articles/2015-07-10/brics-100-billion-lender-seeks-riskier-projects-than-world-bank.

Bond, Patrick. 2000. *Cities of Gold, Townships of Coal*. Trenton: Africa World Press.

Bond, Patrick. 2002. *Unsustainable South Africa*. London: Merlin Press.

Bond, Patrick. 2014a. "Theory and Practice in Challenging Extractive-Oriented Infrastructure in South Africa." *Research in Political Economy* 29: 97–132.

Bond, Patrick. 2014b. "Global Financial Governance and the Opening to BRICS Banking." In *South Africa: State of the Nation 2013–14*, edited by Thenjiwe Meyiwa, Muxe Nkondo, Margaret Chitiga-Mabugu, Moses Sithole, and Francis Nyamnjoh, 442–63. Pretoria: Human Sciences Research Council.

Bond, Patrick. 2014c. *Elite Transition*. London: Pluto Press.

Bond, Patrick. 2016. "BRICS Banking and the Debate over Subimperialism." *Third World Quarterly* 37 (4): 611–29.

Bond, Patrick. 2017. "Falling BRICS Endanger Their Citizens' Health, Starting with South Africa's Jacob Zuma." *CounterPunch*, August 18. https://www.counterpunch.org/2017/08/18/falling-brics-endanger-their-citizens-health-starting-with-south-africas-jacob-zuma/.

Bond, Patrick, and Ana Garcia, eds. 2015. *BRICS: An Anti-capitalist Critique*. London: Pluto Press.

Bond, Patrick, Ana Garcia, Mariana Moreira, and Ruixue Bai. 2016. *Take the Ports!* New York: Rosa Luxemburg Foundation. http://www.rosalux-nyc.org/wp-content/files_mf/citiesasexporthubs_bondet.al..pdf.

Braga, Ruy. 2014. "Limits of a Precarious Development Model." In *A Lula Moment for South Africa: Lessons from Brazil*, edited by Edward Webster and Karen Hurt, 33–38. Johannesburg: Chris Hani Institute.

Bresser-Pereira, Luiz Carlos. 2011. "God was Brazilian during the Lula Administration." *Folha de Sao Paulo*. http://www.bresserpereira.org.br/articles/2011/139.Deus_foi_brasileiro-i.pdf.

Bresser-Pereira, Luiz Carlos. 2018. "From Classical Developmentalism and Post-Keynesian Macroeconomics to New Developmentalism". *Brazilian Journal of Political Economy* 39 (2): 187–210. https://doi.org/10.1590/0101-35172019-2966.

Bruce, Peter. 2016. Oops! Zuma, on Slope, Slips in Snow. *Business Day*, 22 January. https://www.businesslive.co.za/bd/opinion/columnists/2016-01-22-thick-end-of-the-wedge-oops-zuma-on-slope-slips-in-snow/.

Citizen. 2017. "Tito Mboweni Fired as Director at BRICS Bank." August 10. https://citizen.co.za/business/1606254/tito-mboweni-fired-as-director-at-brics-bank/.

Coleman, Neil. 2014. "What Can South Africa Learn from Lula's Brazil? A Cosatu Perspective." In *A Lula Moment for South Africa: Lessons from Brazil*, edited by Edward Webster and Karen Hurt, 81–102. Johannesburg: Chris Hani Institute.

Cowan, Kyle. 2018. "The Italian Job." *CityPress*, December 9. https://www.news24.com/SouthAfrica/News/the-italian-job-transnets-r7bn-durban-port-project-flounders-amid-alleged-corruption-20181209.

D'Sa, Desmond, and Patrick Bond. 2018. "BRICS Bank Should Have Consulted Before Lending to Corrupt Transnet." *Pambazuka*, June 22. https://www.pambazuka.org/emerging-powers/brics-bank-should-have-consulted-lending-corrupt-transnet.

Fine, Ben, and Zav Rustomjee. 1996. *The Political Economy of South Africa*. Johannesburg: Wits University Press.

Fogel, Ben. 2015. "South Africa Doesn't Need a 'Lula Moment'." *Jacobin*, December 17. https://www.jacobinmag.com/2015/12/south-africa-zuma-anc-mandela-sacp-cosatu-numsa/.

Garcia, Ana, and Patrick Bond. 2018. "Amplifying the Contradictions." In *The World Turned Upside Down: Socialist Register 2019*, edited by Leo Panitch and Greg Albo. London: Merlin Press.

Igoe, Michael. 2019. "Q&A: Former World Bank China Director on David Malpass." *Inside Development*, Washington, February 14. https://www.devex.com/news/q-a-former-world-bank-china-director-on-david-malpass-94306.

International Monetary Fund. 2018. *South Africa—Article IV Consultation*. Washington, DC: International Monetary Fund, July 30. https://www.imf.

org/en/News/Articles/2018/07/27/pr18319-south-africa-imf-executive-board-concludes-2018-article-iv-consultation.

Jing, Yijia. 2016. "The Transformation of Chinese Governance: Pragmatism and Incremental Adaption." *Governance* 30 (1): 37–43. https://doi.org/10.1111/gove.12231.

Keynes, John Maynard. 1933. "National Self-Sufficiency." *The Yale Review* 22 (4): 755–69.

Malcolmsen, Dave. 2016. *How South Africa's Participation in BRICS Addresses Domestic Challenges.* Briefing to the Parliamentary Portfolio Committee, Cape Town, February 24. https://pmg.org.za/files/160224BRICS.ppt.

Masondo, David. 2007. "Capitalism and Racist forms of Political Domination." *Africanus* 37 (2): 66–80.

Mbeki, Thabo. 2004. "Two Worlds: Two Economies." *South African Labour Bulletin* 28 (2): 10–11.

Mkentane, Luyolo. 2018. "Transnet Clean-Up Costs Port of Durban Multibillion-Rand Contract." *The Mercury*, November 25. https://www.iol.co.za/business-report/economy/transnet-clean-up-costs-port-of-durban-multibillion-rand-contract-18255893.

Mkokeli, S. 2016. "Overpricing Is Where the Real Leakage Is, Treasury's Kenneth Brown Says." *Business Day*, October 6. https://www.businesslive.co.za/bd/economy/2016-10-06-overpricing-is-where-the-real-leakage-is-treasurys-kenneth-brown-says/.

Mnyando, Ellis. 2015. "An Institution that BRICS can Bank on Takes Off." *Business Report*, July 7. https://www.iol.co.za/business-report/markets/an-instititution-that-brics-can-bank-on-takes-off-1881423.

Morais, Lecio, and Alfredo Saad-Filho. 2013. "Da Economia Política à Política Econômica." *Brazilian Journal of Political Economy* 31 (4): 507–27.

Netshitenzhe, Joel. 2013. "Will South Africa Have a Lula Moment?" *Sunday Independent*, February 10. https://www.iol.co.za/sundayindependent/will-south-africa-have-a-lula-moment-1467399.

Padayachee, Vishnu. 2010. "Reintroducing the Minerals-Energy Complex." *Transformation* 71: 1–2. https://muse.jhu.edu/article/378409?casa_token=2Z6WCzdIdSwAAAAA:f4Om74yero3qzWuV_SbVs0x7ENhepdSrYfNgN-HdKq1UWCj5sNBVz1Qjaz4QmcEDPvKFUNDrtuw.

Paez, Pedro. 2016. "Banco de Sur (Bank of the South): A History of the Project." Speech at the Global University for Sustainability, Hong Kong, July 28. https://commons.ln.edu.hk/southsouthforum/2016/day6/2/.

Panitch, Leo, and Greg Albo (eds.). 2018. *The World Turned Upside Down: Socialist Register 2019.* London: Merlin Press.

Patnaik, Prabhat. 2014. "The BRICS Bank." *People's Democracy* XXXVIII (30). https://www.networkideas.org/news-analysis/2014/07/the-brics-bank-2/.

Paton, Carol. 2018. "Treasury to Approach Banks in Bid to Avert Eskom Default." *Business Day*, January 22. https://www.businesslive.co.za/bd/companies/energy/2018-01-22-treasury-to-approach-banks-in-bid-avert-eskom-default/.

Phua, YeeFarn, and Alexander Ekbom. 2018. "New Development Bank Assigned 'AA +/A-1+' Ratings: Outlook Stable." *S&P Global Ratings*, August 29. https://www.ndb.int/wp-content/uploads/2018/08/RatingsDirect_ResearchUpdateNewDevelopmentBankAssignedAAA1RatingsOutlookStable_39685193_Aug-29-2018.pdf.

Prebisch, Raul. 1950. *The Economic Development of Latin America and Its Principal Problems*. New York: United Nations Economic Committee for Latin America, April 27. https://repositorio.cepal.org/bitstream/handle/11362/30088/S4900192_en.pdf?sequence=1&isAllowed=y.

PricewaterhouseCoopers. 2018. "Global Economic Crime Survey." Johannesburg. https://www.pwc.co.za/en/publications/global-economic-crime-survey.html.

Rachman, Gideon. 2018. "Graft Thrives in a Globalised World." *Financial Times*, June 19. https://www.ft.com/content/0c178666-731a-11e8-aa31-31da4279a601.

Schutte, Giorgio. 2014. "Brazil: 10 Years of a Workers' Party Government." In *A Lula Moment for South Africa: Lessons from Brazil*, edited by Edward Webster and Karen Hurt, 15–32. Johannesburg: Chris Hani Institute.

Singupta, Jayshree. 2017. *BRICS 2017 Summit: Agenda for Action*. New Delhi: Observer Research Foundation. https://www.orfonline.org/expert-speak/brics-2017-summit-agenda-action/.

Stern, Nicolas. 2013. "Emerging Powers as Emerging Economies." London: Statement at the British Academy's Emerging Powers Going Global Conference, October 8–9. YouTube. Accessed June 10, 2014. https://www.youtube.com/watch?v=4ZKQ6wQ-29w.

Stern, Nicolas, and Joseph Stiglitz. 2011. "An International Development Bank for Fostering South-South Investment." Unpublished paper, London and New York.

Sundaram, Jomo Kwame. 2019. "Belt and Road Initiative vs Washington Consensus." *IDEAs Blogs*, March 20. http://www.networkideas.org/news-analysis/2019/03/belt-and-road-initiative-vs-washington-consensus/.

Tapscott, Christopher, Jose Puppim de Oliveira, Yijia Jing, Alexey Barabashev, and Navdeep Mathur. 2017. "Introduction: BRICS in Search of Governance Models." *Chinese Political Science Review* 2 (1): 1–6.

Webster, Edward, and Karen Hurt (eds.). 2014. *A Lula Moment for South Africa: Lessons from Brazil*. Johannesburg: Chris Hani Institute.

Woody, Christopher. 2018. "Japan Is Quietly Gaining an Edge on China, and SA is Getting Caught in the Middle." *Business Insider*, June 1. https://www.

businessinsider.co.za/japan-developing-projects-in-indian-ocean-amid-china-india-rivalry-2018-5.

World Trade Organisation. 2019. "World Trade Outlook Indicator." Geneva, February 19. https://www.wto.org/english/news_e/news19_e/wtoi_19feb19_e.pdf.

Wright, Chris. 2019. "NDB: The Brics Bank Takes Shape." *Euromoney*, May 9. https://www.euromoney.com/article/b1f9vf7w1cf3d8/ndb-the-brics-bank-takes-shape?copyrightInfo=true.

Yanamandra, Srinivas. 2018. "Correspondence with Patrick Bond." July 7. Available from author.

Zhao, Yuezhi. 2012. "The Struggle for Socialism in China: The Bo Xilai Saga and Beyond." *Monthly Review* 64 (5): 1–17. https://monthlyreview.org/2012/10/01/the-struggle-for-socialism-in-china/.